THE ILLUSTRATED BRIDGE ENCYCLOPEDIA

Gillian Rosario

Copyright © 2025 Gillian Rosario

All rights reserved

No part of this book may be reproduced, or stored in a retrieval system, or transmitted in any form or by any means, electronic, mechanical, photocopying, recording, or otherwise, without express written permission of the publisher.

CONTENTS

Title Page
Copyright
Ancient and Historic Bridges — 2
Pont du Gard (France) — 3
Ponte Vecchio (Florence, Italy) — 8
Charles Bridge (Prague, Czech Republic) — 13
Old Bridge Mostar (Mostar, Bosnia and Herzegovina) — 18
Si-o-se Pol (Isfahan, Iran) — 23
Khaju Bridge (Isfahan, Iran) — 27
Széchenyi Chain Bridge (Budapest, Hungary) — 31
London Bridge (UK) — 36
Ponte Santa Trinita (Florence, Italy) — 40
Kintaikyo Bridge (Japan) — 45
Industrial-Era Marvels — 50
Brooklyn Bridge (New York City, USA) — 51
John A. Roebling Suspension Bridge (USA) — 56
Tower Bridge (London, UK) — 61
Forth Bridge (Scotland) — 66
Royal Albert Bridge (UK) — 70
Golden Gate Bridge (San Francisco, USA) — 74

Akashi Kaikyō Bridge (Japan)	79
Quebec Bridge (Canada)	83
Bridge of the Americas (Panama)	88
Erasmusbrug (Rotterdam, Netherlands)	93
Modern and Innovative Designs	97
Helix Bridge (Singapore)	98
Viaduc de Millau (France)	103
Langkawi Sky Bridge (Malaysia)	108
Zhangjiajie Glass Bridge (China)	112
Banpo Bridge (Seoul, South Korea)	116
The Rolling Bridge (London, UK)	121
Puente de la Mujer (Buenos Aires, Argentina)	126
Juscelino Kubitschek Bridge (Brasília, Brazil)	131
Zhivopisny Bridge (Moscow, Russia)	136
Pont de Normandie (France)	141
Engineering Feats	146
Charilaos Trikoupis Rio-Antirrio Bridge (Greece)	147
Danyang–Kunshan Grand Bridge (China)	151
Øresund Bridge (Denmark-Sweden)	156
Tsing Ma Bridge (Hong Kong)	161
Henderson Waves Bridge (Singapore)	166
Eshima Ohashi Bridge (Japan)	170
Confederation Bridge (Canada)	175
Seven Mile Bridge (Florida Keys, USA)	179
Suez Canal Bridge (Egypt)	184
25 April Bridge (Lisbon, Portugal)	189
Cultural and Natural Wonders	194
Living Root Bridges (Meghalaya, India)	195

Lucky Knot Bridge (China)	200
Chengyang Bridge (China)	205
Da Vinci-broen (Norway)	209
New High Line Bridge (New York City, USA)	214
Peace Bridge (Buffalo, USA/Canada)	220
Sunshine Skyway Bridge (Florida, USA)	225
Nanpu Bridge (Shanghai, China)	229
Harbour Bridge (Sydney, Australia)	233
Lupu Bridge (Shanghai, China)	238
Future and Experimental Bridges	243
Salginatobel Bridge (Switzerland)	244
Gateshead Millennium Bridge (UK)	250
Jacques Cartier Bridge (Canada)	255
Alamillo Bridge (Seville, Spain)	260
Zubizuri (Bilbao, Spain)	265
Golden Horn Metro Bridge (Istanbul, Turkey)	269
Ponte Rio-Niterói (Rio de Janeiro, Brazil)	273
Luzhniki Metro Bridge (Moscow, Russia)	277
Dragon Bridge (Da Nang, Vietnam)	281
Kurilpa Bridge (Brisbane, Australia)	285

Bridge Builders:
Stories Behind the World's Most Innovative Bridges and Their Engineers

Bridges are symbols of human ingenuity, overcoming geographical challenges, and transforming societies. From the ancient stone constructions that date back thousands of years to modern architectural feats powered by cutting-edge technology, bridges have played a pivotal role in shaping civilizations. This collection of sixty bridges, categorized into six distinct groups, takes you on a journey through time, showcasing the engineers and their visionary designs that turned seemingly impossible tasks into reality. Whether it's the simple yet enduring design of early bridges or the futuristic approaches seen today, each story highlights the evolution of engineering and the continual push towards more sustainable, innovative, and aesthetic bridge construction.

ANCIENT AND HISTORIC BRIDGES

The earliest bridges were simple affairs, often built from wood or stone, designed to span rivers, ravines, and other natural obstacles. These bridges, built by ancient civilizations, not only served practical purposes but were often works of art and engineering that laid the foundation for more complex designs in later centuries. The ingenuity and resourcefulness of ancient builders are evident in iconic structures like the Roman aqueduct bridges or the stone bridges of the Middle Ages. The stories behind these ancient bridges are intertwined with the history of their time, reflecting the cultural values and technological capabilities of early societies. These bridges are testament to the fact that, even in their simplest forms, they provided the connections needed for trade, communication, and expansion. Their enduring presence speaks to the foundational role of bridges in the development of human infrastructure.

PONT DU GARD (FRANCE)

The Pont du Gard, an awe-inspiring ancient structure, stands as one of the finest examples of Roman engineering and a testament to their remarkable ingenuity. Located in southern France near the town of Vers-Pont-du-Gard in the Gard department, this aqueduct bridge was constructed during the first century AD to address a vital need: transporting water to the Roman colony of Nemausus, now modern-day Nîmes. The aqueduct system stretched over 50 kilometers (31 miles) and supplied the city with around 40,000 cubic meters (8.8 million gallons) of water daily. This vast volume of water was essential for sustaining public baths, fountains, and even private residences, underscoring the Romans' sophisticated infrastructure and their emphasis on hygiene and luxury.

History
The construction of the Pont du Gard was a monumental achievement. Thousands of workers, including skilled engineers, laborers, and slaves, collaborated on this ambitious project. Heavy limestone blocks, some weighing up to six tons, were transported from nearby quarries using rollers, sledges, and pulleys, often with the help of oxen. Wooden scaffolding and frameworks supported the construction of the arches until the keystones were set in place, ensuring the structure's stability. Additionally, the Romans employed surveying tools like the groma and chorobates to measure angles with precision and maintain the aqueduct's gradient.

For nearly 300 years, the Pont du Gard served as a vital part of the aqueduct system, delivering water to Nemausus and symbolizing the prosperity of the Roman Empire. However, after the fall of Rome, the aqueduct fell into disrepair, and water no longer flowed to the city. Despite this, the bridge itself was repurposed during the medieval period as a toll road, which contributed to its preservation. Unlike many Roman structures dismantled for their materials, the Pont du Gard remained largely intact and has been the focus of several restoration efforts, including significant work ordered by Napoleon III in the 19th century.

Design
To carry water over the Gardon River, the Pont du Gard was built with an extraordinary design that balanced functionality with aesthetic appeal. This bridge-aqueduct is an architectural masterpiece, standing 49 meters (160 feet) tall and stretching 275 meters (902 feet) long, making it the tallest Roman aqueduct bridge still standing today. Constructed from locally sourced yellow limestone, called Pierre de Vers, the stones were meticulously cut to fit together seamlessly without mortar. This precise interlocking method, known as opus quadratum,

contributed to the bridge's impressive longevity.

The Pont du Gard's design is marked by its three tiers of arches, with each level serving both structural and visual purposes. The bottom tier consists of six massive arches, while the second tier features eleven slightly smaller ones, and the topmost level boasts thirty-five delicate arches that carry the aqueduct itself. This tiered system not only provided stability but also distributed the structure's weight evenly, enabling it to withstand centuries of weathering and use. Moreover, the Romans applied their advanced understanding of hydraulics by giving the aqueduct a slight gradient of 1 in 3,000, allowing water to flow smoothly across the entire distance.

Cultural Significance
Today, the Pont du Gard is celebrated as a UNESCO World Heritage Site, inscribed in 1985 for its historical and architectural significance. Its enduring beauty and ingenuity have made it a popular tourist destination, drawing over one million visitors annually. Its cultural importance is evident in its depiction on French euro coins and postage stamps, further cementing its status as a national treasure.

Beyond its functional and historical value, the Pont du Gard is a source of fascination for engineers and historians alike. Its massive size, precise construction, and elegant design offer insights into the technical skills and aesthetic sensibilities of the Roman Empire. The inscriptions and markings left by ancient stonecutters on the bridge provide a glimpse into the lives of the workers who built it, adding a human dimension to this monumental structure.

Functionality
The Pont du Gard was built to carry water over the Gardon River to the Roman colony of Nemausus. The Romans applied their advanced understanding of hydraulics to ensure a steady and smooth flow of water, which was vital for the city's public baths,

fountains, and residences. The aqueduct's design incorporated a slight gradient, about 1 in 3,000, to maintain the water's momentum. This precision in the gradient ensured that the water flowed smoothly over the entire distance, a remarkable feat of engineering. The structure itself was not just functional in transporting water but also visually pleasing, symbolizing Roman architectural mastery.

Renovations and Maintenance
Throughout the centuries, the Pont du Gard has undergone several renovations and restoration efforts. After the fall of the Roman Empire, the bridge was neglected, but its solid construction allowed it to endure. During the medieval period, it was repurposed as a toll road, which helped preserve its structure. Restoration work was carried out during the 19th century under Napoleon III, contributing to its current state. The French government and various heritage organizations have continually worked to preserve and protect this iconic structure, ensuring it remains a symbol of Roman engineering for future generations.

Notable Events
Over the centuries, the Pont du Gard has witnessed numerous iconic moments in history. During its peak, the aqueduct system supported the luxurious lifestyle of Nemausus, including its famous baths and gardens. In modern times, it has been a site of celebration, hosting events like the spectacular millennium light show in 2000. The bridge has also made appearances in films and documentaries, further cementing its place in popular culture. The grandeur and preservation of the Pont du Gard have allowed it to remain a part of contemporary life, constantly reminding visitors of its long-lasting cultural and historical impact.

Tourism
The Pont du Gard is one of the most visited historical sites in

France, attracting over one million visitors annually. Its status as a UNESCO World Heritage Site has significantly boosted its tourism, with people from around the world coming to admire its engineering, history, and beauty. Visitors can walk along the bridge, explore the surrounding park, and learn about its history in the on-site museum. The site offers educational tours, exhibitions, and events that engage visitors with the structure's past and its place in Roman engineering.

Legacy
The Pont du Gard's legacy extends beyond its architectural and engineering achievements. As a symbol of Roman innovation and ingenuity, it continues to inspire engineers, architects, and historians. The structure's preservation and global recognition as a UNESCO World Heritage Site ensure that it remains a lasting legacy of the Roman Empire. The Pont du Gard serves not only as a physical reminder of the past but also as a cultural symbol of the power and reach of ancient Rome.

Future Plans and Developments
As a UNESCO World Heritage Site, the Pont du Gard is carefully preserved for future generations. Current efforts focus on maintaining the integrity of the structure while enhancing its accessibility for tourists. This includes improving visitor facilities, educational programs, and digital interpretations of the site's history. Future developments aim to ensure the preservation of this ancient marvel while making it accessible to a broader audience, allowing the Pont du Gard to continue to captivate and inspire visitors for centuries to come.

PONTE VECCHIO (FLORENCE, ITALY)

The Ponte Vecchio, a historic jewel of Florence, Italy, is one of the most iconic and enduring bridges in the world. Spanning the Arno River at its narrowest point, the bridge is as much a symbol of the city as it is an extraordinary feat of medieval engineering and artistry. Its name, which translates to "Old Bridge," reflects its longevity, as it has stood in various forms since Roman times, with the current structure dating back to 1345. Renowned for its unique architecture, fascinating history, and cultural significance, the Ponte Vecchio remains a celebrated landmark, drawing millions of visitors annually.

History
The primary purpose of the Ponte Vecchio was practical: to

connect the two sides of Florence and facilitate the movement of goods and people. Its location, strategically placed near the Uffizi Gallery and the Pitti Palace, made it a central artery for trade in medieval Florence. Originally, the bridge was built to house butchers and tanners, who took advantage of the proximity to the river to dispose of waste. Over time, the Ponte Vecchio transitioned from a utilitarian structure to one of Florence's most prestigious and picturesque spots.

Design
The Ponte Vecchio, as it stands today, is a masterpiece of medieval craftsmanship. Its design is characterized by three wide arches, with the central arch being the largest to allow for the passage of boats during high water levels. Made from stone, the bridge features fortified piers that provide stability and protect against the force of the river's currents, particularly during seasonal floods. The current version of the bridge was constructed in 1345 under the supervision of Taddeo Gaddi, though some sources attribute its design to Neri di Fioravante. Its architectural style blends functionality with beauty, demonstrating the ingenuity of Florentine builders.

A distinctive feature of the Ponte Vecchio is the row of shops that line its edges, a rare characteristic for a bridge. These shops, originally occupied by butchers, were gradually replaced by jewelers, goldsmiths, and art dealers in the 16th century at the decree of Cosimo I de' Medici, the Grand Duke of Tuscany. This transformation not only elevated the bridge's status but also minimized the offensive smells associated with the butchers' trade. Today, the Ponte Vecchio is synonymous with luxury, as it remains home to high-end jewelry boutiques and artisans.

Cultural Significance
Culturally, the Ponte Vecchio has played a central role in Florence's identity. It has been the inspiration for countless artists, writers, and poets, including Dante Alighieri and Vasari. The bridge's iconic appearance, with its irregularly shaped

shops and warm golden tones, has made it a favorite subject for painters and photographers alike. The Vasari Corridor, an enclosed walkway commissioned by Cosimo I de' Medici in 1565, runs above the bridge, linking the Palazzo Vecchio to the Pitti Palace. This architectural addition allowed the Medici family to cross the city privately and safely while enjoying sweeping views of the river and the city.

Fun facts abound when it comes to the Ponte Vecchio. The term "bankruptcy" is believed to have originated here. When a merchant could not pay their debts, the tables (banco) on which they conducted their business were physically broken (rotto) by soldiers, leading to the term "banco rotto," or broken bank. Over the centuries, the bridge has also been a setting for romantic proposals, musical performances, and even small festivals, reinforcing its status as a place of cultural vibrancy.

Functionality
In addition to its role in commerce and culture, the Ponte Vecchio has been a backdrop for several iconic moments in history. For centuries, it has been a place where Florentines and visitors alike gathered to experience the city's bustling life. The bridge's open design offers sweeping views of the Arno River and the surrounding cityscape, making it a prime spot for reflection and inspiration. Its unique charm has also made it a favorite location for filmmakers, appearing in movies like *A Room with a View* and *The Portrait of a Lady*.

Renovations and Maintenance
The Ponte Vecchio has faced numerous challenges throughout its history. Flooding has been a persistent threat to the bridge, with significant damage occurring in 1333, when an earlier wooden version of the bridge was swept away. The current stone structure, built to withstand the river's fury, has endured centuries of floods, including the devastating flood of 1966, when the Arno River overflowed and wreaked havoc across Florence. Remarkably, the bridge survived, though it required

extensive restoration.

Notable Events
The Ponte Vecchio also holds a unique place in modern history. During World War II, it was the only bridge in Florence spared from destruction by retreating German forces in 1944. According to local legend, this was due to an explicit order from Adolf Hitler, who admired the bridge's beauty. Instead of destroying the Ponte Vecchio, German troops demolished the buildings on either side to block access, leaving the bridge itself intact. This decision preserved a vital piece of Florence's cultural heritage.

Tourism
Today, the Ponte Vecchio continues to thrive as a hub of activity and a testament to Florence's enduring spirit. It stands not only as a bridge between the two sides of the Arno but also as a bridge between the past and the present, connecting modern visitors with centuries of history and culture. Whether admired for its architectural brilliance, its storied history, or its vibrant atmosphere, the Ponte Vecchio remains one of the most beloved and recognizable landmarks in the world.

Legacy
The Ponte Vecchio has long been a symbol of Florence's cultural and artistic legacy. Over the centuries, it has endured as both a functional bridge and a key point of pride for the city, representing the resilience of Florence's heritage. The bridge has influenced generations of architects, engineers, and artists, ensuring its place in both historical and modern contexts. As a center of trade, art, and history, the Ponte Vecchio continues to shape the identity of Florence.

Future Plans and Developments
As a UNESCO World Heritage Site, the Ponte Vecchio remains protected, with efforts focused on preserving its architectural integrity and ensuring that future generations can enjoy its

beauty. Ongoing restoration projects aim to address concerns related to its aging structure, while efforts to maintain the cultural significance of the bridge continue.

CHARLES BRIDGE (PRAGUE, CZECH REPUBLIC)

The Charles Bridge in Prague, Czech Republic, is one of Europe's most celebrated and historically significant landmarks. Spanning the Vltava River, the bridge connects Prague's Old Town (Staré Město) with the Lesser Quarter (Malá Strana) and has stood as a testament to medieval engineering and artistry for centuries. Rich in history, adorned with stunning sculptures, and steeped in local legends, the Charles Bridge serves as both a practical connection and a cultural treasure that attracts millions of visitors every year.

History

Construction of the Charles Bridge began in 1357 under the orders of King Charles IV, after the previous Judith Bridge, built in the 12th century, was destroyed by a flood in 1342. King Charles IV, a forward-thinking and devout ruler, envisioned the new bridge as a monumental symbol of Prague's growing power and prestige. The foundation stone of the bridge was laid on July 9, 1357, at precisely 5:31 a.m. This timing was not random; it was chosen for its alignment with astrological principles and numerological symbolism, forming the palindrome 1-3-5-7-9-7-5-3-1, believed to bring good fortune to the construction.

The bridge was designed by Peter Parler, a master architect also responsible for St. Vitus Cathedral and other Gothic masterpieces in Prague. Built entirely of sandstone, the Charles Bridge is 516 meters long and nearly 10 meters wide, supported by 16 massive arches. The bridge's piers were reinforced with protective ice guards to withstand the powerful currents of the Vltava River, as well as seasonal flooding, which was a recurring threat. It took nearly 50 years to complete, with construction finishing in 1402. Originally known simply as the Stone Bridge or Prague Bridge, it wasn't until the 19th century that it was renamed Charles Bridge in honor of its royal patron.

Design

One of the most remarkable features of the Charles Bridge is its gallery of 30 Baroque-style statues and sculptures, which line the bridge's balustrades. These statues, added between the late 17th and early 18th centuries, depict saints, religious figures, and allegorical themes, transforming the bridge into an open-air museum. Among the most famous is the statue of St. John of Nepomuk, a Czech martyr who was thrown from the bridge into the Vltava in 1393. Touching the plaque at the base of this statue is said to bring good luck and ensure a return to Prague, making it a beloved tradition for visitors.

Despite its enduring beauty, the Charles Bridge has faced numerous challenges throughout its long history. The Vltava River has repeatedly tested the bridge's resilience, with floods in 1432, 1784, 1890, and more recently in 2002, causing significant damage. The 1890 flood was particularly destructive, dislodging two of the bridge's arches and several statues. Restoration efforts over the years have carefully preserved the bridge's historical integrity while reinforcing its structural stability.

Cultural Significance
The Charles Bridge has witnessed pivotal moments in Czech history. In 1648, during the final stages of the Thirty Years' War, Swedish forces attempted to invade Prague and were stopped at the bridge, making it a site of fierce battles. In the centuries that followed, the bridge remained a symbol of Czech resilience and identity, playing a prominent role in both celebrations and protests.

Functionality
The Charles Bridge was a vital piece of infrastructure in medieval Prague. For centuries, it was the only bridge crossing the Vltava, serving as a critical trade route between Eastern and Western Europe. It also played an important role in ceremonial and military activities, acting as a procession route for kings and an entryway for armies. The bridge's durability and strategic location helped solidify Prague as a central hub in Europe.

Renovations and Maintenance
Over the years, the Charles Bridge has undergone numerous restorations to preserve its integrity and combat the effects of natural wear and tear. The most significant of these restoration projects took place in the 20th century, including the repair work following the devastating 2002 flood. Today, modern techniques are employed to ensure the longevity of the bridge, and while some statues have been replaced with replicas, much

of the original structure remains intact, allowing visitors to experience the bridge's historic charm.

Notable Events
The Charles Bridge has been the backdrop for numerous historic moments. In 1648, during the Thirty Years' War, Swedish forces were halted at the bridge, marking a turning point in Prague's defense. Additionally, the bridge has witnessed the coronation processions of Bohemian kings and other important royal ceremonies. Its association with Czech history, national pride, and resilience continues to be celebrated in public events and parades to this day.

Tourism
Today, the Charles Bridge is a pedestrian-only zone and one of Prague's most popular attractions. By day, the bridge is bustling with activity, from street performers and artists to vendors selling handmade goods and souvenirs. By night, the bridge takes on a more serene and romantic atmosphere, offering breathtaking views of the Prague Castle, the Old Town, and the river illuminated by city lights.

Fun facts about the Charles Bridge add to its charm. For instance, its construction coincided with Prague's rise as a major European center of trade, and it played a role in the city's designation as the "Heart of Europe." The bridge has also been the site of several film shoots, including scenes from the 1996 movie *Mission: Impossible*. Furthermore, the bridge's towers, located at either end, serve as gateways and provide panoramic views of the city for those who climb them.

Legacy
The Charles Bridge has endured wars, floods, and centuries of change, yet it stands as a timeless testament to the skill and vision of its creators. Its enduring appeal lies not just in its architectural and artistic brilliance, but in its role as a living connection to the stories and legends of Prague's past.

The bridge continues to inspire both locals and visitors with its beauty, its history, and its ability to connect people from different eras.

Future Plans and Developments
In the future, efforts will continue to maintain the bridge's structural integrity while ensuring its accessibility for visitors. There are ongoing discussions regarding the preservation of the Charles Bridge in light of increasing tourism. Sustainable tourism practices are a priority, as the Czech authorities aim to balance the influx of visitors with the preservation of the bridge's historical and cultural significance. Furthermore, future developments may include the installation of additional lighting to enhance the evening views of the bridge and surrounding areas, ensuring that it remains a vibrant and cherished landmark for years to come.

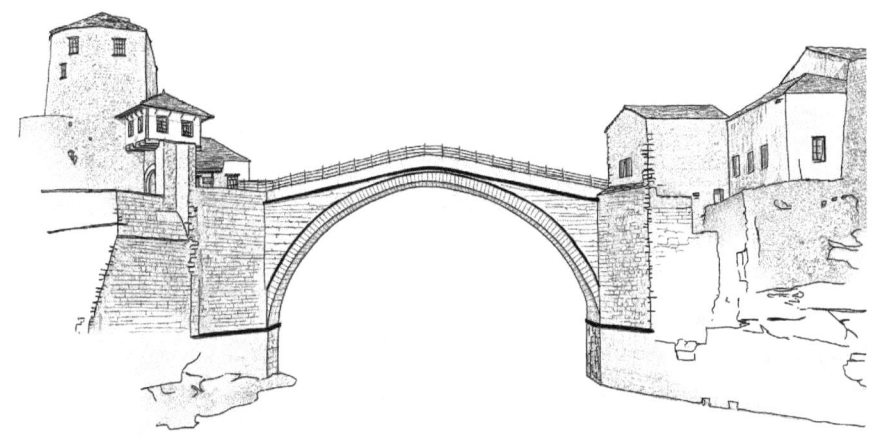

OLD BRIDGE MOSTAR (MOSTAR, BOSNIA AND HERZEGOVINA)

The Stari Most, or "Old Bridge," is a magnificent architectural jewel located in Mostar, a city in Bosnia and Herzegovina. Spanning the emerald-green waters of the Neretva River, the bridge is a powerful symbol of resilience, unity, and cultural diversity. It is not only an iconic piece of Ottoman engineering but also a living testament to the region's turbulent history and the enduring strength of its people. Built in the 16th century during the height of the Ottoman Empire, the bridge continues to captivate visitors with its elegance, historical significance, and enduring legacy.

History

The origins of Stari Most date back to 1557 when Sultan Suleiman the Magnificent commissioned its construction. The project aimed to replace a precarious wooden suspension bridge that had served the local population for years. The new bridge was envisioned as a monumental structure that would reflect the grandeur of the Ottoman Empire while providing a durable and practical crossing for the city's residents. The task of designing and building the bridge was entrusted to Mimar Hayruddin, a student of the famous Ottoman architect Mimar Sinan, who was renowned for designing mosques and public works across the empire.

According to local legend, Hayruddin faced extraordinary pressure to succeed. It is said that he was threatened with execution should the bridge collapse. As a result, he prepared for his own funeral before the project was completed. Despite the immense stress, Hayruddin rose to the challenge, employing innovative engineering techniques to create a structure that defied expectations. Construction took nine painstaking years, with the bridge finally completed in 1566. When finished, it was celebrated as a marvel of its time, featuring a single, soaring stone arch spanning 29 meters (94 feet) and rising 20 meters (66 feet) above the Neretva River. The use of locally quarried tenelija limestone gave the bridge its pale, ethereal appearance, which shimmered beautifully against the surrounding natural landscape.

Design

Stari Most quickly became a defining feature of Mostar. The city, whose name derives from the word "mostari," meaning "bridge keepers," had always revolved around its central crossing. The bridge's graceful design not only provided a vital connection between the two sides of the city but also came to symbolize unity in a region characterized by cultural diversity. Mostar was home to a blend of Bosniaks, Croats, and Serbs, and Stari Most stood as a shared space, bridging not just the physical gap but also the cultural and social divides between communities.

Cultural Significance
For centuries, Stari Most remained a symbol of stability in a region that often experienced political and social upheaval. However, its resilience was tragically tested during the Bosnian War in the 1990s. As Yugoslavia disintegrated into a series of ethnic conflicts, Mostar became a focal point of intense fighting. On November 9, 1993, during the height of the war, the bridge was deliberately targeted and destroyed by Croatian forces. Its collapse into the Neretva River marked one of the most heartbreaking moments of the conflict, as the destruction of the bridge symbolized the deep divisions tearing the region apart.

Functionality
Efforts to reconstruct the bridge began shortly after the war ended. Recognizing its historical and cultural importance, UNESCO, the World Bank, and other international organizations joined forces with local experts to undertake a meticulous reconstruction project. The goal was not merely to rebuild Stari Most but to restore it as authentically as possible, using the same materials and techniques employed in the 16th century. Divers retrieved original stones from the riverbed, while new tenelija limestone was quarried from the same local sources used centuries earlier. Ottoman engineering methods were carefully replicated, ensuring that the reconstructed bridge would be faithful to its predecessor in every detail.

After seven years of painstaking work, the reconstructed Stari Most was unveiled on July 23, 2004, in a grand ceremony attended by dignitaries and representatives from around the world. The reopening of the bridge was more than just a celebration of its physical restoration; it was a powerful act of healing and reconciliation. Once a casualty of war, Stari Most now stood as a symbol of resilience and unity, a testament to the ability of communities to rebuild and move forward.

Renovations and Maintenance
The restoration of Stari Most was an extraordinary feat, but maintaining the bridge has remained a priority for local authorities and cultural preservationists. Given its age and the environmental conditions, ongoing maintenance and restoration efforts are necessary to preserve its integrity. This includes regular inspections and cleaning, as well as preserving the local limestone used in the bridge's construction, which can wear down over time due to exposure to the elements. The combination of local and international efforts has ensured that Stari Most continues to stand as it did centuries ago, not only as a bridge but as a cultural monument.

Notable Events
Stari Most has been the backdrop for many significant cultural and historical events. Beyond its use as a transportation hub, the bridge has played an essential role in local ceremonies and events. The Mostar Diving Competition, held annually, draws people from all over the world to witness the brave divers plunging into the Neretva River. Additionally, the bridge serves as a symbol of reconciliation during cultural and political celebrations. Its destruction and restoration have cemented its place in the collective memory of the people of Bosnia and Herzegovina, making it a source of pride and reflection.

Tourism
Today, Stari Most is a UNESCO World Heritage Site and one of Bosnia and Herzegovina's most popular tourist destinations. Visitors from across the globe are drawn to its timeless beauty, its rich history, and its role as a cultural and social hub. Walking across the bridge, one can feel the weight of its history, from its Ottoman roots to its destruction and rebirth. The surrounding Old Town of Mostar, with its cobblestone streets, Ottoman-

era architecture, and bustling bazaars, offers a vibrant and immersive cultural experience.

Legacy

The story of Stari Most is one of triumph and tragedy, destruction and renewal. It is a bridge that has seen centuries of history, borne witness to both the best and worst of humanity, and emerged as a beacon of hope and resilience. For the people of Mostar, it is a deeply personal symbol of their shared heritage and identity. For the world, it is a reminder of the power of unity and the enduring spirit of cultural preservation. Standing on Stari Most today, gazing down at the Neretva River, one cannot help but feel a profound sense of connection to the past and hope for the future.

Future Plans and Developments

The future of Stari Most remains intertwined with the preservation of its cultural and historical importance. While ongoing maintenance efforts will continue to ensure its structural integrity, there are also plans to enhance the surrounding area to make the bridge more accessible to tourists and locals alike. This includes improvements to the infrastructure around the Old Town and initiatives aimed at increasing awareness of the bridge's significance on a global scale. With its continued importance as a symbol of unity, resilience, and cultural heritage, Stari Most will likely remain a cornerstone of Mostar's identity for generations to come.

SI-O-SE POL (ISFAHAN, IRAN)

Si-o-se Pol, also known as "The Bridge of Thirty-Three Arches," is one of Iran's most celebrated historical landmarks, located in Isfahan. Renowned for its architectural beauty and historical significance, the bridge spans the Zayanderud River and stands as a symbol of Persian ingenuity. With its graceful arches, Si-o-se Pol not only connects two parts of Isfahan but also embodies the rich cultural and artistic heritage of the region.

History

The story of Si-o-se Pol begins during the Safavid era, particularly under the reign of Shah Abbas I (1588-1629). During this period, Isfahan flourished as the capital of the

Safavid Empire, becoming a vibrant center of trade, culture, and innovation. Shah Abbas was committed to improving the city's infrastructure, and one of his most ambitious projects was the construction of bridges over the Zayanderud. These bridges served practical purposes but also created public spaces for people to gather, relax, and socialize. Among these, Si-o-se Pol stood out as the most magnificent, embodying the grandeur of Safavid architecture.

Built between 1602 and 1609, Si-o-se Pol was designed by architect Ali Akbar Isfahani. At 295 meters long and 14 meters wide, the bridge was an extraordinary feat of engineering. The structure consists of 33 arches, which were not only an aesthetic choice but also a symbolic one. In Persian culture, the number 33 represents completeness and unity, reflecting Shah Abbas's vision for a strong, unified empire.

Design
The design of Si-o-se Pol was not only practical but also artistic. The 33 arches are made from brick and stone, with a slight curve, providing a graceful and visually appealing structure. The arches were designed in such a way that they could allow the Zayanderud River to flow smoothly beneath the bridge while maintaining the integrity of the bridge's structure. The bridge is supported by large stone piers that anchor the structure firmly into the riverbank, allowing it to withstand floods and the shifting nature of the river.

In addition to the arches, the design also incorporated niches beneath them, originally intended as seating areas for those wishing to rest by the river. These niches evolved into small pavilions, adding charm and functionality to the bridge. The bridge's graceful form, combined with its strategic location, makes it not just an essential crossing but a visual masterpiece.

Cultural Significance
Si-o-se Pol holds deep cultural and symbolic meaning in Persian

life. Beyond its physical function as a bridge, it has been viewed as a metaphor for the soul's journey, with the flowing water beneath symbolizing the passage of time and the connection between the earthly realm and the divine. This interpretation adds a spiritual layer to the bridge's significance, enhancing its cultural value. The bridge is often seen as a space where the community gathers, shares stories, and bonds.

Functionality

In its early years, Si-o-se Pol served a practical purpose, facilitating the movement of people and goods across the Zayanderud River. The river was vital for agriculture, industry, and daily life, and the bridge became a crucial link between Isfahan's two main sections. Merchants traveling to the city's grand bazaar would cross the bridge, making it an important artery for commerce. Its practical design ensured that it could withstand the challenges posed by the river, such as seasonal floods, ensuring that it remained a reliable crossing for centuries.

Renovations and Maintenance

Si-o-se Pol has faced challenges throughout its history, including natural disasters and political upheavals. The Zayanderud River's seasonal floods have at times put the bridge at risk, but its robust design has allowed it to withstand such pressures. In the 20th century, political tensions escalated, and there were concerns about the bridge's destruction or repurposing. Recognizing its cultural and historical importance, the Iranian government, along with UNESCO, listed the bridge as a World Heritage Site in 1979. This designation helped ensure its preservation.

Notable Events

Si-o-se Pol has been the site of many notable events throughout its history. As one of the primary gathering places in Isfahan, it has witnessed numerous social, political, and cultural gatherings. The bridge has also been the backdrop for many important moments in Isfahan's rich cultural life. In modern times, it has become a hub for artistic expression, with traditional Persian musicians often performing beneath its arches.

Tourism

Today, Si-o-se Pol is a popular destination for both locals and tourists. Its stunning arches and historical significance make it a must-see landmark in Isfahan. The bridge is especially picturesque at sunset when its elegant arches are reflected in the Zayanderud River, creating a breathtaking scene. Visitors come to marvel at the bridge's beauty, learn about its history, and experience the rich culture of Isfahan.

Legacy

Si-o-se Pol has left a lasting legacy as one of Iran's most cherished landmarks. It symbolizes the brilliance of Persian engineering and architecture, the strength of the Safavid Empire, and the enduring spirit of Isfahan's people. The bridge's resilience in the face of natural disasters and political turmoil underscores its enduring legacy as a symbol of strength, unity, and cultural preservation.

Future Plans and Developments

Looking to the future, Si-o-se Pol will continue to play an important role in Isfahan's cultural and architectural heritage. Restoration efforts are ongoing to ensure that the bridge remains a functional and aesthetic part of the city for generations to come. There are plans to further develop the surrounding area, improving access and facilities for visitors while preserving the historical integrity of the site.

KHAJU BRIDGE (ISFAHAN, IRAN)

The Khaju Bridge, located in Isfahan, Iran, is a stunning example of Persian architecture and engineering. Built during the Safavid period, it has long been admired for its design and practical purpose. As both a vital link over the Zayanderud River and a symbol of the city's rich historical and cultural legacy, the Khaju Bridge blends functionality with grandeur. Serving as an integral part of Isfahan's identity, this architectural masterpiece is a testament to the city's cultural and historical significance.

History

Construction of the Khaju Bridge began in 1650 under the reign of Shah Abbas II, the seventh king of the Safavid dynasty, and was completed in 1653. At the time, Isfahan was emerging as the political and cultural center of the Safavid Empire. Shah Abbas II sought to beautify and modernize the city, and Khaju Bridge became part of his broader vision. The bridge was designed not only to serve as a crossing for travelers but also to regulate the flow of the Zayanderud River, which was essential for the region's agriculture and economy. The strategic location and practical function of the bridge reflect the empire's sophisticated approach to infrastructure.

Design
The Khaju Bridge is 133 meters long and 12 meters wide, with a dual-level structure that combines both functional and aesthetic elements. The upper level features 23 arches, while the lower level includes several smaller openings. This design accommodates both pedestrian traffic and water flow, showcasing the advanced engineering capabilities of the Safavid architects. The bridge integrates elements of Persian and Islamic architecture, featuring intricate tile work, grand arches, and a seamless incorporation into the surrounding landscape. Its central pavilion, or "chahar suq," is one of the most distinctive features, serving as a cultural hub as well as a functional water regulator.

Cultural Significance
Khaju Bridge is more than just an infrastructure project; it is a cultural landmark. The bridge served as a social space where people could gather, relax, and enjoy the views of the river. Isfahan's elite often congregated here, enjoying leisurely activities such as listening to music and conversing. The tile work, with floral patterns and geometric shapes, reflects the artistic traditions of the Safavid Empire and gives the bridge a timeless beauty. Over the centuries, the bridge has been immortalized in Persian literature, music, and art, solidifying its status as an iconic symbol of Isfahan's cultural identity.

Functionality

Functionally, Khaju Bridge served multiple purposes. It was an essential transportation link for travelers and merchants crossing the Zayanderud River. The bridge's central pavilion featured sluice gates that regulated the flow of water, directing it into the city's canals for irrigation. These engineering feats showcase the Safavids' advanced understanding of water management. Beyond its utilitarian functions, the bridge became a place of recreation and social gathering, contributing to the city's vibrant public life.

Renovations and Maintenance
Khaju Bridge has endured several challenges throughout its history, including significant damage from floods in the 18th century. Parts of the original structure were repaired or replaced, but the bridge continued to serve as a vital transportation route while retaining its beauty and function. In the 19th and 20th centuries, restoration efforts focused on preserving the bridge's structural integrity. The Iranian government recognized the cultural importance of the bridge, officially designating it as a national monument in 1979. These ongoing efforts have ensured that the bridge remains a cherished landmark, protecting its historical significance for future generations.

Notable Events
Over the centuries, Khaju Bridge has witnessed numerous historical events. As one of Isfahan's most iconic structures, it has been a backdrop for many social and cultural gatherings. It has also played a role in the history of the Safavid Empire, serving as a symbol of the dynasty's grandeur. The bridge has been featured in countless works of art, literature, and music, cementing its status as a beloved cultural treasure. Its unique blend of functionality and beauty continues to inspire artists and visitors from around the world.

Tourism
Today, Khaju Bridge is a popular destination for both locals and

tourists. The upper level of the bridge provides panoramic views of the Zayanderud River and the surrounding landscape, making it an ideal spot for sightseeing and photography. Particularly at sunset, when the golden light illuminates the arches, the bridge becomes a magical setting that attracts artists, photographers, and visitors from across the globe. The bridge also serves as a cultural hub, hosting events such as traditional music performances, which further enrich its appeal. As a result, Khaju Bridge remains a vital part of Isfahan's tourism industry.

Legacy
Khaju Bridge's legacy is far-reaching. It is not just a bridge, but a symbol of Isfahan's artistic and architectural achievements. The bridge has become an enduring symbol of Persian culture and an important part of Iran's national identity. Its image appears in various forms of art, from paintings and photographs to modern media, ensuring its presence in both historical and contemporary contexts. The bridge's legacy is also evident in the resilience it has shown throughout centuries of wear, tear, and natural disasters, a testament to the enduring power of Persian craftsmanship.

Future Plans and Developments
Looking ahead, there are ongoing efforts to ensure the preservation and enhancement of Khaju Bridge. Restoration work is expected to continue, with a focus on maintaining its structural integrity and ensuring that it remains a safe and accessible public space. The Iranian government, in collaboration with local cultural organizations, is also looking to increase the bridge's role in cultural and tourism activities. Future plans include organizing more cultural events, such as music and art festivals, to celebrate the bridge's historical and cultural significance. These developments aim to secure the bridge's place in Isfahan's urban landscape and ensure that it remains a living symbol of the city's rich heritage.

SZÉCHENYI CHAIN BRIDGE (BUDAPEST, HUNGARY)

The Széchenyi Chain Bridge, one of Budapest's most iconic landmarks, spans the mighty Danube River, connecting the historic Buda and Pest sides of the Hungarian capital. Completed in 1849, it was the first permanent bridge to span the Danube in Budapest and became a symbol of the nation's modernization. The bridge's construction was a pivotal moment in Hungarian history, representing a shift toward economic development and political autonomy in the mid-19th century.

History

The idea for the bridge originated with Count István Széchenyi, a prominent Hungarian statesman and reformer. He believed that building a bridge across the Danube would be crucial for the development of Budapest. Before the bridge, crossing the river between Buda and Pest was slow and dangerous, relying on ferries or makeshift wooden bridges. Széchenyi envisioned a permanent and reliable connection that would boost trade, communication, and transportation between the two cities, contributing to Budapest's emergence as a major European center.

Construction began in 1842, led by Scottish engineer William Tierney Clark, who had previously designed London's Hammersmith Bridge. Clark's innovative use of chain suspension was revolutionary at the time. The bridge featured massive stone towers and an intricate network of chains to support the roadway, enabling it to span a wide and turbulent section of the Danube. Despite numerous obstacles—including unpredictable weather, difficult terrain, and a lack of modern technology—the bridge was completed in 1849, hailed as a monumental achievement in Hungarian engineering.

Design

The Széchenyi Chain Bridge's design was groundbreaking in its use of chain suspension. The bridge is supported by two large stone towers, with suspension chains running across to form the bridge's unique structure. This technique allowed for a wider span, making the bridge resilient to the Danube's strong currents and harsh conditions. The design was not only practical but also aesthetically striking. The bridge's massive stone towers were adorned with lion statues designed by Hungarian sculptor János Fadrusz. The lions, with their fierce expressions, have become one of the bridge's most recognizable features. Local legend claims that Fadrusz threw himself into the Danube in frustration after realizing he had forgotten to carve tongues on the lions, a story that, though likely a myth, remains part of the bridge's lore.

Cultural Significance

The Széchenyi Chain Bridge is more than just a piece of infrastructure; it is a symbol of Budapest's modernization and Hungary's growing industrialization in the 19th century. The bridge's completion was seen as a milestone in the country's progress and its aspirations to become a major European power. It not only facilitated the movement of goods and people between Buda and Pest but also became an emblem of national pride.

Functionality

When the Széchenyi Chain Bridge opened in 1849, it immediately became a crucial link in Budapest's infrastructure. It facilitated trade and communication, providing a more efficient route for the flow of goods between the two cities. The bridge was essential in fostering Budapest's expansion and urbanization during the late 19th and early 20th centuries. While it still serves as an important transportation link, the Széchenyi Chain Bridge is now also a key tourist attraction, drawing visitors from all over the world.

Renovations and Maintenance

The Széchenyi Chain Bridge has undergone significant renovations over the years to ensure its preservation. Notably, during and after World War II, the bridge was severely damaged by German forces. In 1945, as they retreated from the city, the central section of the bridge was destroyed. Restoration work began in 1947 and was completed by 1949, just in time for the bridge's centenary celebration. More recently, extensive maintenance efforts have focused on preserving the bridge's structural integrity while maintaining its historical and aesthetic value. These restoration projects ensure that the bridge remains a functional piece of infrastructure and a cherished historical monument for future generations.

Notable Events

The Széchenyi Chain Bridge has witnessed numerous significant events throughout Budapest's history. During World War II, as German forces retreated, the bridge was heavily damaged, and its central span was destroyed. The destruction of the bridge was symbolic of the devastation wrought on Hungary during the war. However, the bridge's meticulous restoration in the post-war years highlighted the resilience of Budapest and its inhabitants. The bridge was reopened in 1949, and its reconstruction came to represent the city's determination to rebuild and recover. Over the years, the Széchenyi Chain Bridge has also served as the backdrop for various cultural events, celebrations, and national holidays.

Tourism

Today, the Széchenyi Chain Bridge attracts millions of tourists each year. Visitors come not only to cross the bridge but also to enjoy the spectacular views of the Danube River, the Hungarian Parliament, and the Buda Castle. The bridge is particularly beautiful at night when it is illuminated, casting a warm golden glow across the water and contributing to Budapest's enchanting atmosphere. Tourists flock to the bridge to take photographs, stroll across it, and enjoy the surrounding views. The bridge is a central point for walking tours of the city, often serving as the starting point for exploring Budapest's historic sites.

Legacy

The Széchenyi Chain Bridge is a symbol of Budapest's progress and resilience. It remains one of the most iconic structures in Hungary, representing the country's journey through history. Over the years, the bridge has become synonymous with Budapest itself, playing an integral role in both the city's development and its cultural identity. As one of the most well-known landmarks in Hungary, the Széchenyi Chain Bridge continues to serve as a reminder of the nation's historical milestones and its continued aspirations for the future.

Future Plans and Developments
As Budapest continues to grow and modernize, the Széchenyi Chain Bridge will remain a vital part of the city's infrastructure. Efforts are being made to modernize the bridge's facilities while preserving its historical features. Furthermore, as the city plans for increased tourism and urban development, the bridge will continue to serve as a key connection between the two sides of Budapest, ensuring that it remains a symbol of the city's enduring strength and beauty for generations to come.

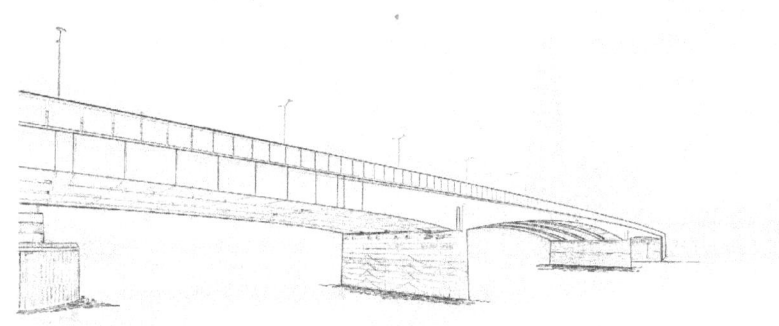

LONDON BRIDGE (UK)

London Bridge, one of the world's most famous and historically significant bridges, has played a central role in the development of London for over two thousand years. Spanning the River Thames, it has witnessed the transformation of the city from a Roman settlement to a modern metropolis. The bridge's history reflects the evolution of London itself, with multiple versions constructed to accommodate the growing needs of the city.

History

The first iteration of London Bridge was constructed around 50 AD by the Romans when they established Londinium on the banks of the Thames. This wooden bridge was crucial for connecting the settlement on the south bank with Roman-controlled territory to the north. It served both practical and symbolic purposes, facilitating trade and communication while asserting Roman authority over Britain.

By 1209, the growing city needed a more durable structure, and a stone bridge was built during King John's reign. The new bridge became a center of commerce and culture, housing shops, houses, and St. Thomas's Chapel. However, by the 16th century, the bridge was deteriorating. Various repairs were attempted under the Tudor monarchs, but by 1831, it was clear that a new bridge was necessary.

Design

The decision to replace the medieval bridge led to the construction of a new stone bridge designed by John Rennie, which was completed in 1832. However, this design quickly proved inadequate for the growing traffic demands of London. By the early 20th century, it became apparent that a more modern bridge was required. The bridge's replacement was planned in the 1960s, leading to the sale of the 19th-century structure to an American entrepreneur in 1968. The current London Bridge, designed by Sir Giles Gilbert Scott, was completed in 1973. Made from concrete and steel, this version is utilitarian in appearance and was designed primarily for function, lacking the grandiose features of its predecessors.

Cultural Significance

London Bridge holds immense cultural significance, appearing in art, literature, and folklore. The nursery rhyme "London Bridge is Falling Down" dates back to at least the medieval period, thought to reference the frequent damage and rebuilding of the bridge. The rhyme has become iconic, symbolizing the bridge's enduring legacy. Additionally, the bridge's name has become synonymous with the city of London itself, carrying a weight of cultural and historical meaning.

Functionality

The current London Bridge continues to serve as an essential part of the city's infrastructure. It provides a crucial connection between the City of London and Southwark, facilitating both vehicular and pedestrian traffic. The bridge remains integral to the flow of people and goods across the Thames, linking key areas of the city, including the financial district and London's South Bank. Despite its plain design, London Bridge is an essential transportation hub that supports modern London's fast-paced demands.

Renovations and Maintenance
Throughout its long history, London Bridge has undergone numerous renovations and reconstructions to maintain its structural integrity. The most significant of these occurred in the 19th and 20th centuries, with the medieval bridge being replaced in 1832 and the 19th-century bridge sold and relocated in 1968. The modern bridge, completed in 1973, has required ongoing maintenance to ensure its safety and functionality, especially given the heavy traffic it accommodates. Efforts continue to preserve the bridge for future generations, ensuring it remains a vital part of London's transportation network.

Notable Events
London Bridge has witnessed numerous historical events, including the rise and fall of monarchs, periods of war and peace, and cultural shifts. A pivotal moment occurred in 1968 when the old bridge was sold to Robert P. McCulloch and relocated to Lake Havasu City, Arizona. This event sparked public interest and raised questions about the preservation of historical landmarks. Over the centuries, London Bridge has stood as a silent witness to the transformation of London, with each iteration marking a new chapter in the city's history.

Tourism
Today, London Bridge remains a popular destination for tourists. Though it is often overshadowed by the nearby Tower Bridge, the bridge's long history and connection to the city's

past attract visitors from around the world. Tourists can walk across the bridge, taking in views of the Thames and the iconic landmarks of London, including the Shard, St. Paul's Cathedral, and the Tower of London. The bridge is also a key point for exploring London's South Bank, home to numerous cultural institutions such as the Tate Modern and Shakespeare's Globe Theatre.

Legacy
The legacy of London Bridge extends far beyond its function as a transportation link. It stands as a symbol of London's resilience, adaptability, and ability to evolve with the times. Its many iterations reflect the city's changing needs, from a wooden bridge for Roman traders to the modern stone and steel structure that serves today's commuters.

Future Plans and Developments
While the current London Bridge is expected to remain in service for the foreseeable future, the city of London continually assesses the need for future developments. Given the ongoing urban expansion and the increasing demands on the city's infrastructure, it is likely that London Bridge will undergo further maintenance and upgrades in the years to come. However, given the bridge's historical importance, any developments will need to balance modern requirements with the need to preserve the iconic structure. The future of London Bridge is intricately tied to the ongoing transformation of London, serving as both a link to the past and a foundation for the city's future.

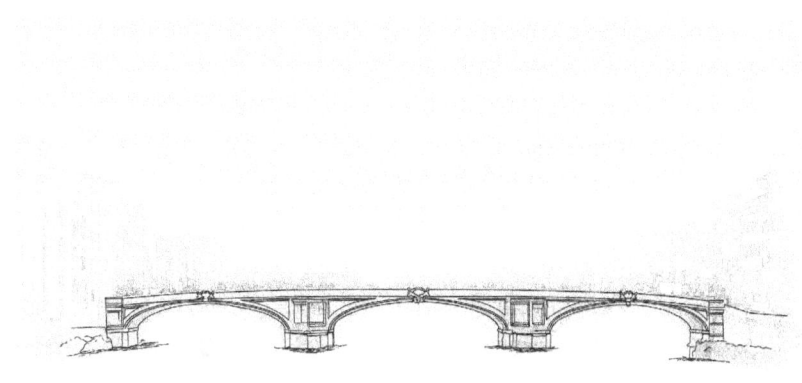

PONTE SANTA TRINITA (FLORENCE, ITALY)

Ponte Santa Trinita, located in the heart of Florence, Italy, is one of the city's most iconic and historically significant bridges. Spanning the Arno River, it connects the Oltrarno district on the southern bank with the central historical district, home to landmarks like the Piazza della Signoria and the Uffizi Gallery. Renowned for its elegance and architectural design, the bridge has become an essential part of Florence's cultural landscape, embodying the city's rich artistic heritage and wartime resilience.

History

The bridge was originally constructed in the 16th century, under the commission of the powerful Medici family, who ruled Florence at the time. The Medici sought a bridge that would serve both practical and aesthetic purposes, contributing to the city's architectural harmony. Architect Bartolomeo Ammannati was selected to design the bridge, and construction began in 1567, with its completion in 1571. Ponte Santa Trinita was quickly recognized as one of the most beautiful bridges in Florence, playing a vital role in connecting key areas of the city and contributing to its commercial growth.

However, its history was marked by tragedy during World War II, when retreating German forces destroyed several of Florence's bridges, including Ponte Santa Trinita, to slow the advancing Allied troops. The destruction of the bridge was a blow to the city, symbolizing the devastation of the war. For years, the bridge lay in ruins, leaving a gap in the city's architectural heritage.

Design

Ponte Santa Trinita's design reflects the ideals of the Renaissance, with its elegant symmetry and grace. The bridge features three large arches, which allow the Arno River to flow beneath unobstructed. Constructed using local stone, it blends seamlessly with the surrounding architecture of Florence, renowned for its Renaissance beauty. At the time of its completion, the bridge became a symbol of Florence's wealth and artistic accomplishment, standing as a testament to the city's intellectual and cultural achievements.

A distinctive feature of the bridge are its six statues, created by Giovanni Caccini. These statues, representing virtues such as Charity, Fortitude, Justice, and Prudence, add both decorative and symbolic value to the structure, further emphasizing the

Renaissance values upheld by the city's ruling elite. The statues also serve as a reminder of the city's moral ideals, reinforcing the cultural significance of the bridge.

Cultural Significance

Ponte Santa Trinita holds immense cultural significance in Florence, both as a functional structure and as a symbol of the city's artistic heritage. It was designed not only for utility but also to contribute to the city's architectural harmony. Its central location, near important cultural landmarks, further enhances its importance. The bridge has come to symbolize the city's wealth and artistic values, reflecting Florence's role as a center of art, architecture, and intellectual life. Its elegant design stands in contrast to the more utilitarian structures of the time, showcasing the Renaissance ideals of beauty and functionality.

Functionality

Ponte Santa Trinita serves as an important crossing over the Arno River, linking the Oltrarno district with the central city. In addition to its historical and aesthetic value, the bridge continues to serve a vital function in modern-day Florence. Locals use it as a crucial route for pedestrian traffic, while tourists flock to the bridge to admire its beauty and historical importance. Its central location in Florence makes it an essential part of the city's daily life, as well as a key point for sightseeing, offering panoramic views of the Arno River and the surrounding cityscape.

Renovations and Maintenance

The destruction of Ponte Santa Trinita during World War II led to a significant restoration effort. In 1958, plans to rebuild the bridge were set into motion, with great care taken to restore the bridge to its original design. Skilled artisans, engineers, and historians worked tirelessly to ensure that the bridge was rebuilt using materials that matched those used in the 16th century. By 1959, Ponte Santa Trinita was reopened, and its restoration was celebrated as a symbol of Florence's resilience. This post-war restoration was a major achievement, allowing the bridge to reclaim its place as a vital part of the city's cultural heritage.

Notable Events

Ponte Santa Trinita has witnessed several significant events throughout its history, particularly the devastation caused by World War II. The destruction of the bridge during the retreat of German forces marked a turning point in its history, leading to a long period of ruin. The subsequent restoration in 1959, however, was an important moment for Florence, symbolizing both the city's recovery from wartime destruction and its commitment to preserving its cultural heritage. The reopening of the bridge was widely celebrated, marking a triumph for the artisans and historians involved in the restoration.

Tourism

Today, Ponte Santa Trinita remains one of Florence's most beloved landmarks. It offers stunning views of the Arno River and the surrounding cityscape, including famous landmarks such as the Uffizi Gallery and Ponte Vecchio. Tourists from around the world visit the bridge, drawn not only to its beauty but also to its historical and cultural significance. The bridge is particularly popular for photography, as its location provides the perfect vantage point to capture the charm of Florence, especially at sunrise and sunset when the city is bathed in a golden light.

The bridge is also a popular spot for tourists wishing to enjoy Florence's vibrant atmosphere, with the bustling Oltrarno district and the central city nearby, offering a variety of cultural and historical attractions.

Legacy

Ponte Santa Trinita's legacy extends beyond its functionality as a bridge. It stands as a symbol of Florence's artistic and cultural heritage, embodying the city's history and the resilience of its people. Its Renaissance design and post-war restoration have solidified its place as one of Florence's most important cultural landmarks.

Future Plans and Developments
As a key cultural and architectural landmark, Ponte Santa Trinita is likely to undergo continued maintenance and preservation efforts to ensure its longevity. Given its status as a UNESCO World Heritage Site, efforts to protect and preserve Ponte Santa Trinita will remain a priority for Florence's authorities, ensuring that this iconic bridge continues to stand as a testament to the city's history and artistic legacy.

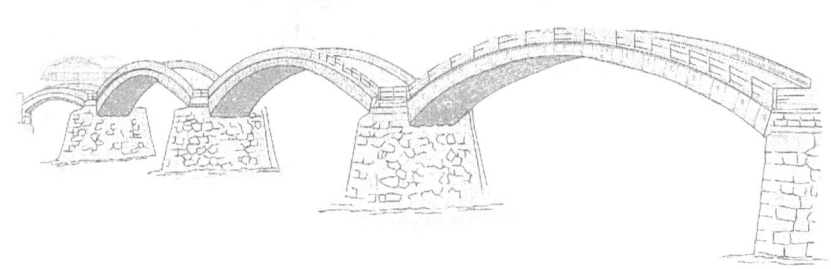

KINTAIKYO BRIDGE (JAPAN)

Kintai Bridge, located in Iwakuni, Japan, is one of the most iconic and historically significant bridges in the country. Spanning the Nishiki River, this picturesque wooden structure is renowned for its unique design, rich cultural history, and stunning natural surroundings. Kintai Bridge has become a symbol of the Iwakuni region and is celebrated as a marvel of traditional Japanese craftsmanship and engineering.

History
The origins of Kintai Bridge date back to 1673, when it was

first constructed under the guidance of the daimyo (feudal lord) Kikkawa Hiroyoshi of the Iwakuni Domain. The need for a bridge to connect Iwakuni Castle, which stood on a hill overlooking the town, to the area on the opposite bank of the Nishiki River, became apparent as the town grew. At the time, crossing the river was only possible by boat, which was inefficient and impractical. Kikkawa Hiroyoshi recognized the need for a permanent and functional bridge, symbolizing both the domain's power and prestige.

The bridge was designed by a skilled carpenter named Shinra, who was tasked with constructing the bridge using traditional wooden techniques passed down through generations. The design of the bridge is particularly notable for its five distinct arches, a feature that is both aesthetically pleasing and crucial for the bridge's structural integrity.

Design
Kintai Bridge is a wooden structure known for its five elegant arches that span the Nishiki River. The arches rise gradually from one side of the river to the other, contributing to the graceful and harmonious appearance of the bridge. Not only do these arches enhance the bridge's visual appeal, but they also play an essential role in its engineering. By distributing the weight of the structure, they help ensure stability against the river's currents.

The bridge is a remarkable feat of traditional Japanese engineering. It was built without nails or metal fasteners, relying instead on traditional Japanese joinery techniques known as "kigumi." This method uses interlocking wooden beams and columns, creating a sturdy and flexible structure. The wooden construction also allowed the bridge to blend seamlessly with the surrounding natural landscape, a key consideration in Japanese architecture.

Cultural Significance

Kintai Bridge has long been a symbol of Iwakuni, representing the craftsmanship of the people who built it and the resilience of the community that maintains it. Over the centuries, the bridge has been featured in numerous artistic works, including paintings, photographs, and literary references. It is often celebrated for its beauty and historical importance.

The bridge is closely associated with Iwakuni Castle, which was built in the early 17th century and served as the seat of the Iwakuni Domain. Kintai Bridge connected the castle to the town, allowing the lord and his family to travel between the two. Today, Iwakuni Castle is a popular tourist destination, offering sweeping views of the bridge and the surrounding landscape.

Functionality

Beyond its aesthetic appeal, Kintai Bridge has served as a critical infrastructure for Iwakuni, providing a reliable means of crossing the Nishiki River. The river, particularly during the rainy season, can swell dramatically, posing challenges to any bridge's stability. The bridge's design, featuring five arches, allows it to absorb the force of the river's current. Additionally, the flexible wooden structure moves with the water, reducing the risk of damage. This adaptability to natural forces has been crucial in preserving the bridge for centuries.

Renovations and Maintenance

Since its original construction, Kintai Bridge has undergone several reconstructions and repairs due to the vulnerability of wooden structures to weather and time. The original bridge was washed away in 1675 by a powerful flood, just two years after its completion. Despite this setback, it was rebuilt, and the bridge has been reinforced and repaired over the years to maintain its structural integrity.

In the early 20th century, Kintai Bridge was completely rebuilt, and it remains in its present form. Regular maintenance continues to ensure that the bridge remains safe for use and continues to represent the enduring craftsmanship of the Japanese people.

Notable Events

Kintai Bridge has become a focal point for various cultural events, particularly during the spring and autumn months. One of the most famous events is the cherry blossom viewing season. The surrounding landscape, including the bridge, is renowned for its breathtaking beauty during this time when the cherry blossoms are in full bloom. The bridge, with its elegant arches framed by the pink blossoms, is a favorite subject for photographers and artists.

Another notable event is the Kintai-kyo Fireworks Festival, held annually in August. The festival features a stunning display of fireworks, with the bridge illuminated by the colorful explosions. Thousands of spectators gather along the riverbanks to enjoy the spectacle, creating a magical atmosphere that draws visitors from across the world.

Tourism

Kintai Bridge has become a major tourist destination, attracting visitors from both Japan and abroad. The area surrounding the bridge is a popular spot for hanami (cherry blossom viewing) and offers picturesque views throughout the year. The bridge's beauty, particularly during the spring and autumn months, draws a large number of tourists.

In addition to its aesthetic appeal, the bridge's proximity to Iwakuni Castle makes it a popular spot for visitors interested in Japan's feudal history. Tourists can explore the castle, which offers a panoramic view of the bridge, and enjoy the surrounding parkland. Kintai Bridge has also been designated as an Important Cultural Property by the Japanese government, further boosting its tourism appeal.

Legacy

Kintai Bridge stands as a testament to the resilience of the people of Iwakuni and their commitment to preserving their cultural heritage. Over the years, the bridge has come to symbolize the strength and ingenuity of the local community. It has also become an enduring symbol of traditional Japanese craftsmanship, representing the values of harmony with nature and the importance of skilled craftsmanship in Japanese culture.

Future Plans and Developments

Looking forward, efforts are being made to ensure that Kintai Bridge remains a symbol of Iwakuni's heritage while also addressing the challenges of modern infrastructure needs. Regular maintenance and careful restoration work will continue to preserve the bridge's structure for future generations.

Moreover, as tourism to the area grows, there are plans to enhance the visitor experience while preserving the authenticity of the site. Future developments will focus on improving accessibility and expanding educational programs about the bridge's historical and cultural significance. Efforts will also be made to protect the bridge and its surrounding environment, ensuring that it continues to stand as a living monument to Japan's rich cultural history.

Kintai Bridge remains not just a functional bridge but a cultural treasure that connects generations and tells the story of Japan's ingenuity, resilience, and natural beauty.

INDUSTRIAL-ERA MARVELS

The Industrial Revolution brought with it an explosion of technological advancements, and nowhere is this more apparent than in the realm of bridge building. This era marked a significant shift from traditional materials like wood and stone to steel and iron, opening up new possibilities for the design and scale of bridges. Engineers began experimenting with larger spans, more intricate designs, and innovative construction techniques, resulting in iconic structures such as the Brooklyn Bridge and the Forth Bridge. These bridges were not just engineering feats but also symbols of the industrial age itself—monuments to progress, innovation, and the rise of modernity. The Industrial-Era Marvels category highlights the transformative period in bridge design when engineering techniques advanced rapidly, and bridges became bold, visible statements of industrial might.

BROOKLYN BRIDGE (NEW YORK CITY, USA)

The Brooklyn Bridge, one of the most iconic structures in the United States, has become synonymous with New York City itself. Connecting the boroughs of Manhattan and Brooklyn, this suspension bridge has stood as a testament to human ingenuity and perseverance since its completion in 1883. Known for its sweeping arches, intricate design, and historical significance, the Brooklyn Bridge is much more than just a transportation route—it is a symbol of New York City's resilience and transformation over time.

History

The Brooklyn Bridge was the brainchild of John A. Roebling, a German immigrant and renowned bridge engineer. The idea for the bridge arose in the mid-19th century when Brooklyn's rapid growth necessitated a more efficient means of crossing the East River. At the time, ferries were the primary means of transport, but with the population increasing, they were no longer sufficient. Roebling's vision was to construct a bridge that would not only serve as a vital connection between the two boroughs but also symbolize modern progress and engineering achievement.

Roebling's death in 1869, due to an accident while surveying the site, left his son, Washington Roebling, to oversee the project. Washington, despite lacking experience in large-scale bridge construction, faced several challenges, including severe health issues due to the deep underwater caissons. However, with the assistance of his wife, Emily Warren Roebling, he managed to complete his father's vision, and the bridge was finally completed in 1883.

Design

The Brooklyn Bridge was groundbreaking in both its engineering and aesthetic design. The bridge's central span stretches 1,595 feet (486 meters), making it the longest suspension bridge in the world at the time of its completion. The structure used a combination of steel cables for strength and granite masonry for the towers, both of which were innovative at the time. The Gothic-style arches, although decorative, played a critical role in the bridge's structural integrity, enhancing its overall strength while adding to its grandeur.

The bridge's suspension system, never before used on such a large scale, utilized steel cables to bear the weight of the bridge and its traffic. The design marked a significant advancement in bridge engineering and influenced the development of future suspension bridges.

Cultural Significance

The Brooklyn Bridge has become a symbol of New York City, embodying its spirit of ambition, resilience, and progress. Over the years, it has been featured in countless works of art, literature, and films, further cementing its place in American pop culture. The bridge's distinctive design—its massive stone towers, soaring arches, and criss-crossed cables—has made it one of the most photographed landmarks in the world.

Functionality

Since its completion, the Brooklyn Bridge has served as an essential transportation route, allowing for the easy movement of people and goods between Manhattan and Brooklyn. Initially, the bridge provided a crucial link for pedestrians and horse-drawn carriages, and later, as the city evolved, it accommodated increasing automobile traffic. Today, it is still a vital link in New York City's transportation infrastructure, used by commuters, cyclists, and pedestrians alike.

The bridge was the first to use steel cables in its construction, a design element that not only allowed it to span the East River but also ensured its ability to withstand the increasing weight of modern traffic. Over the years, it has adapted to changing needs, including the addition of dedicated lanes for pedestrians and cyclists.

Renovations and Maintenance

Given the Brooklyn Bridge's age, it has undergone several major repairs and upgrades to ensure its continued functionality. In the early 20th century, the bridge's cables were reinforced to accommodate the increasing weight of traffic. During the 1950s, extensive repairs were made to address wear and tear caused by the growing use of automobiles. These repairs included the replacement of old cables, reinforcement of the bridge's towers, and improvements to the deck to accommodate the increasing traffic load.

Notable Events

The Brooklyn Bridge has been the backdrop for numerous notable events throughout its history. Its opening in 1883 was celebrated with a grand ceremony, and it quickly became a central part of the city's infrastructure. Over the years, the bridge has witnessed parades, protests, and celebrations, with its status as a city icon drawing thousands of spectators.

One of the most famous events was the 1883 "Bridge Opening Day," when thousands of people crossed the bridge in celebration. The bridge has also served as the site of New York City's parades, political demonstrations, and public gatherings, symbolizing unity and progress.

Tourism

Today, the Brooklyn Bridge is not just a transportation route but also a popular tourist destination. Visitors from all over the world walk or cycle across the bridge, taking in breathtaking views of the Manhattan skyline, the Statue of Liberty, and the surrounding East River. The bridge has become a must-see landmark for tourists, with its historical significance and stunning views drawing millions annually.

Legacy

The Brooklyn Bridge's legacy extends far beyond its role as a physical connector between Brooklyn and Manhattan. It represents the culmination of a vision of innovation and progress and stands as a testament to the determination and perseverance of those who brought it to life. Its iconic design and enduring structure have influenced the development of modern suspension bridges and continue to inspire engineers and architects worldwide.

Future Plans and Developments

As the Brooklyn Bridge continues to serve as a vital link in

New York City's infrastructure, plans for its future focus on maintaining its structural integrity while ensuring it remains a safe and accessible route for pedestrians, cyclists, and motorists. Ongoing maintenance projects aim to address issues related to wear and tear, traffic congestion, and safety.

In addition to structural improvements, efforts are being made to enhance the visitor experience by improving access to the bridge and surrounding areas. This includes the development of new pedestrian pathways, improvements to the bridge's lighting, and enhancements to nearby parks and public spaces.

JOHN A. ROEBLING SUSPENSION BRIDGE (USA)

The Roebling Suspension Bridge, a historic engineering marvel, spans the Ohio River between Cincinnati, Ohio, and Covington, Kentucky. Completed in 1866, it was the first major bridge to use wire cables in its design and is considered the precursor to the more famous Brooklyn Bridge. Named after its visionary engineer, John A. Roebling, this bridge marked a significant advancement in bridge construction and continues to serve as a vital connection between the two cities more than 150 years later.

History

The idea for the Roebling Suspension Bridge emerged from the need for a reliable and safe crossing between Cincinnati and its neighboring city of Covington. Prior to the bridge's construction, the only method of crossing the Ohio River was by ferry, which was inefficient for the growing demands of trade and commerce in the region. Cincinnati, a hub of industrial and commercial activity, needed better connectivity to the growing Kentucky side of the river. John A. Roebling, a German immigrant renowned for designing suspension bridges, was selected to design the new crossing. His innovation lay in using wire cables to support the bridge, a technique previously untested on such a large scale. Roebling's vision was to create not only a functional crossing but also a structure that would stand the test of time, incorporating cutting-edge materials and technology.

Design

The Roebling Suspension Bridge was groundbreaking in both its design and materials. The bridge used cast iron for its towers and steel wire for the cables, allowing it to span a much greater distance than earlier bridges. The design, characterized by towering stone piers and elegant suspension cables, was both innovative and aesthetically pleasing. The bridge's overall length was 1,057 feet (322 meters), making it the longest suspension bridge in the world at the time of its completion. This design would go on to influence other notable bridges, including the Brooklyn Bridge, completed in 1883.

Cultural Significance

The Roebling Suspension Bridge played a crucial role in the development of Cincinnati and Covington, enhancing their economies and connectivity. By facilitating trade and transportation, it helped to establish Cincinnati as a major center of commerce and industry in the 19th and 20th centuries. Beyond its practical function, the bridge also became a cultural and architectural icon. Its striking silhouette, with massive stone towers and graceful cables, captured the imagination of those who saw it. The bridge's success also led to widespread recognition of John A. Roebling's expertise in suspension bridge engineering, which directly contributed to the later success of the Brooklyn Bridge.

Functionality

Initially designed to carry horse-drawn carriages and pedestrians, the Roebling Suspension Bridge quickly became vital for regional transport. It facilitated the movement of goods, services, and people between the two cities, strengthening the economic ties between Cincinnati and Covington. In later years, the bridge had to be upgraded to accommodate the increasing weight of automobiles and trucks. Despite these changes, the bridge has continued to serve its purpose as a key transportation link, offering pedestrian access as well as vehicular traffic.

Renovations and Maintenance

As with all significant infrastructure, the Roebling Suspension Bridge has required maintenance over the years to keep up with modern demands. In the 20th century, the bridge underwent several repairs and reinforcements to handle the increased weight of motor vehicles. In the late 20th century, the bridge faced the possibility of demolition as newer, larger bridges were built to accommodate growing traffic volumes. However, its historical significance and iconic status led to its preservation. In 1975, the Roebling Suspension Bridge was added to the National Register of Historic Places, ensuring its continued place in Cincinnati's history and safeguarding its future.

Notable Events

The Roebling Suspension Bridge has been the site of numerous notable events throughout its history. Its opening in 1866 was celebrated as a triumph of engineering, marking the beginning of a new era for the city. Over the years, the bridge has been a witness to Cincinnati's growth, serving as a vital link in the region's transportation network. It has also been featured in various cultural and historical contexts, solidifying its place as a landmark in both Cincinnati and American engineering history.

Tourism

Today, the Roebling Suspension Bridge serves not only as a functional piece of infrastructure but also as a popular tourist destination. Visitors from around the world come to admire its design and learn about its fascinating history. The bridge offers stunning views of the Ohio River and the Cincinnati skyline, making it a favorite spot for both tourists and locals. Its inclusion in Cincinnati's tourism circuit further highlights its importance as a symbol of the city's historical development and resilience.

Legacy

The legacy of the Roebling Suspension Bridge is far-reaching. It was the first major suspension bridge to use wire cables, a method that revolutionized bridge construction. Its successful implementation set the stage for the design of other iconic suspension bridges, including the Brooklyn Bridge. The Roebling Suspension Bridge remains a proud symbol of the Roebling family's engineering genius and the forward-thinking vision of its designer, John A. Roebling. It also continues to serve as a vital transportation route, connecting the cities of Cincinnati and Covington and contributing to the region's economy.

Future Plans and Developments

Despite its age, the Roebling Suspension Bridge continues to be a valuable part of Cincinnati's infrastructure. There are ongoing efforts to maintain and preserve the bridge, ensuring that it remains a safe and functional part of the region's transportation network. Future developments may include additional upgrades to accommodate modern traffic demands and further preservation efforts to ensure the bridge's longevity.

As part of its ongoing role in the city's development, the bridge may also continue to be celebrated as a historical landmark, drawing visitors and inspiring future generations of engineers and architects.

TOWER BRIDGE (LONDON, UK)

Tower Bridge, one of London's most iconic landmarks, spans the River Thames, connecting the boroughs of Tower Hamlets and Southwark. Known for its dual bascule (drawbridge) design and Gothic architecture, it is a symbol of British engineering innovation. Opened in 1894, it plays an essential role in London's transportation network and has become an internationally recognized symbol of the city, admired for its beauty and engineering complexity.

History

The need for Tower Bridge arose in the late 19th century, during a period of rapid industrial growth and urban expansion in London. With the city's population booming, there was an increasing demand for both river transport and more effective crossings over the River Thames. While other bridges like London Bridge and Westminster Bridge were already in place, none were situated near the Tower of London, one of the busiest areas in the city. By the 1870s, the idea for a new bridge in this location took form, but it presented an engineering challenge: how to span the busy, tidal River Thames while ensuring ships could pass through unhindered.

Sir Horace Jones, the City of London's surveyor, and civil engineer John Wolfe-Barry led the design and construction of the bridge. The challenge was solved with a hybrid bascule design that combined practicality with grandeur, allowing the bridge's roadbed to rise for ships, while still supporting heavy road traffic.

Design
Tower Bridge's design is a stunning combination of functionality and elegance. The bridge consists of two towers, rising 200 feet above the River Thames, designed in a Gothic style. This unique and majestic appearance was intended to blend harmoniously with the nearby Tower of London. The bascule mechanism, which allowed the roadbed to be raised for ship passage, was revolutionary at the time. The use of steel and stone ensured the bridge was not only durable enough to handle heavy traffic but also capable of withstanding the stresses of the mechanical system. Over 11,000 tons of steel and 70,000 tons of concrete were used during construction, which began in 1886 and was completed in 1894.

Cultural Significance
Tower Bridge quickly became more than just a functional piece of infrastructure; it became a cultural symbol of London. Its distinct design and stunning location made it a favorite subject

of photographers and filmmakers. The bridge has appeared in numerous films and television shows, further cementing its status as one of the city's most recognizable landmarks. Today, it stands as a symbol of London's resilience, creativity, and engineering prowess, representing not just the city's rich history but also its forward-thinking approach to innovation.

Functionality
When Tower Bridge opened, it provided a vital link between the northern and southern parts of London. The bascule mechanism allowed it to be raised and lowered quickly to accommodate large ships passing through the river. Over time, the bridge became an essential part of the city's transportation system, allowing both vehicular and pedestrian traffic to cross the Thames without interrupting river traffic. In the 20th century, the bridge underwent a modernization process, which included replacing the manual system for raising the bascules with hydraulic machinery, making the process more efficient.

Renovations and Maintenance
Tower Bridge has undergone several maintenance and renovation projects over its lifespan to ensure its continued functionality and safety. One major upgrade occurred in the 1970s when the original manual bascule operation system was replaced with automated hydraulic machinery. Additionally, in the early 2000s, the bridge underwent a comprehensive restoration to protect its structural integrity and maintain its aesthetic charm. This included repairs to its towers and restoration of its iconic blue color, which had started to fade over time. These efforts have ensured that the bridge remains a vital transportation route and an enduring symbol of London.

Notable Events
Over its history, Tower Bridge has been a part of numerous significant events. It has served as a ceremonial venue during royal events and state occasions, including the passage of the Royal Barge during the Queen's Diamond Jubilee celebrations

in 2012. The bridge has also been a popular location for commemorations and national holidays. Its role in facilitating trade and transport has been crucial throughout the years, especially during times of conflict, when it was crucial for the movement of goods and services.

Tourism
Today, Tower Bridge is a major tourist attraction, drawing visitors from around the world. The bridge's exhibition, located within the towers, offers an in-depth look into its history and construction. Visitors can explore the Victorian engine rooms, where the original hydraulic pumps used to raise the bascules were located. Tower Bridge also offers panoramic views of London from its glass-floored walkways, allowing tourists to look down on the river below. The bridge's stunning design and its place in London's historical landscape make it a must-see landmark for anyone visiting the city.

Legacy
The legacy of Tower Bridge extends far beyond its role as a functional transportation route. The bridge has become synonymous with London itself, embodying the city's spirit of innovation and progress. Its design and construction set new standards for bridge engineering and influenced the design of future bridges around the world. The bridge also contributed to the development of modern London, guiding the city through a period of rapid industrialization and urbanization. It has remained a crucial part of London's infrastructure while simultaneously growing in cultural and symbolic importance.

Future Plans and Developments
Looking to the future, Tower Bridge will continue to play an important role in the transportation network of London. However, as traffic patterns and demands evolve, the bridge will undergo further maintenance and improvements to adapt to modern needs. While the bridge itself will retain its iconic design, advancements in technology will ensure its continued

functionality and efficiency. Plans to enhance the visitor experience, including expanded exhibitions and interactive displays, will also ensure that Tower Bridge remains a key attraction for generations to come. The bridge will continue to stand as a testament to British engineering excellence and a symbol of London's enduring heritage.

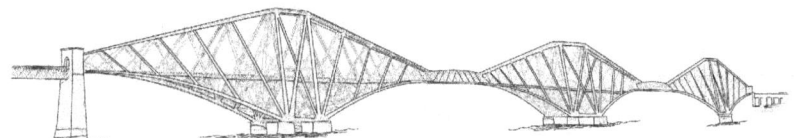

FORTH BRIDGE (SCOTLAND)

The Forth Bridge, an engineering marvel that spans the Firth of Forth in Scotland, is a symbol of the nation's industrial past and a testament to Victorian-era ingenuity. Opened in 1890, the cantilevered bridge continues to serve as a critical transportation link between Edinburgh and Fife. As a UNESCO World Heritage Site, the Forth Bridge is celebrated for its striking design and historical significance, representing the spirit of Scotland's industrial revolution.

History

The need for a bridge across the Forth River became apparent in the 19th century as the industrial revolution created a demand for efficient transportation. The ferry service connecting Edinburgh and Fife was no longer sufficient to handle the increasing railway traffic. In 1873, a competition was held to design a bridge to meet this need. Engineers Sir John Fowler and Sir Benjamin Baker won the competition with their proposal for a cantilevered bridge, which would minimize the need for supports in the river's estuary. Construction began in 1882, and after eight years of challenging work, the bridge was completed in 1890, quickly becoming a symbol of Scotland's industrial power.

Design

The Forth Bridge is a cantilevered bridge, designed to span the Firth of Forth with minimal support in the water. The structure features three massive steel towers, each 361 feet high, connected by steel beams that form triangular shapes, allowing the bridge to cover an expansive area without the need for multiple support piers. This innovative design was revolutionary at the time and allowed the bridge to carry heavy railway traffic. The deep red color, known as "Forth Bridge Red," adds to its visual impact, standing out against the river and sky. At the time of its completion, the Forth Bridge was the longest single cantilever bridge in the world.

Cultural Significance

The Forth Bridge is not only an engineering feat but also a cultural symbol of Scotland. It represents the progress and determination of the industrial era and showcases Scotland's role in advancing technology and construction. The bridge has become a national icon, celebrated for its bold design and its impact on the landscape. Its engineering achievements have inspired generations of engineers and architects, cementing its place in both the history of engineering and the cultural consciousness of Scotland.

Functionality
When completed, the Forth Bridge was the only railway crossing for the Firth of Forth, playing a crucial role in connecting Edinburgh and Fife. It remains an integral part of the UK's railway network, serving as one of the busiest railway bridges in the country. While other bridges have since been constructed, including the Forth Road Bridge and the Queensferry Crossing for road traffic, the Forth Bridge continues to handle substantial rail traffic, showcasing its enduring functionality and importance in the region's transportation network.

Renovations and Maintenance
Over the years, the Forth Bridge has required ongoing maintenance to ensure its structural integrity. The most significant maintenance task has been the constant repainting of the bridge to protect it from corrosion, a necessary effort due to the bridge's exposure to saltwater. The task of painting the entire bridge is often joked about as a never-ending process—once a section is completed, the painters begin again. This continuous upkeep is vital to preserving the bridge's structural health and ensuring its continued function for future generations.

Notable Events
One of the most notable events in the history of the Forth Bridge was its designation as a UNESCO World Heritage Site in 2015. This recognition highlighted the bridge's exceptional engineering and cultural significance, cementing its status as a symbol of Scotland's industrial heritage. The bridge continues to attract attention for its design and historical importance, frequently featured in various media and celebrations of Scottish culture.

Tourism
The Forth Bridge is a major tourist attraction, drawing visitors from around the world who come to admire its impressive

design and learn about its history. Tourists can enjoy views of the bridge from various vantage points along the Firth of Forth and take part in educational tours that highlight its engineering achievements. The bridge has become a popular subject for photographers and filmmakers, making it one of Scotland's most iconic landmarks. Its status as a UNESCO World Heritage Site further enhances its appeal as a destination for both local and international tourists.

Legacy
The legacy of the Forth Bridge extends far beyond its original purpose as a railway crossing. It has become a symbol of Scottish engineering excellence and national pride, inspiring future generations of engineers and architects. The bridge's bold design, once revolutionary, continues to influence the construction of modern bridges. Its status as a cultural and historical icon also ensures that it will remain an enduring symbol of Scotland's industrial past and its contributions to global engineering.

Future Plans and Developments
As the Forth Bridge continues to serve its purpose as a vital part of the UK's railway infrastructure, there are ongoing efforts to ensure its longevity. Future plans include continued maintenance and preservation to protect the bridge from the effects of time and weather. Given its status as a UNESCO World Heritage Site, the bridge is also subject to regulations that ensure any updates or changes are in line with its cultural and historical significance. The ongoing care and attention given to the bridge's upkeep will ensure that it remains a vital part of Scotland's transportation network and an enduring symbol of the nation's engineering prowess.

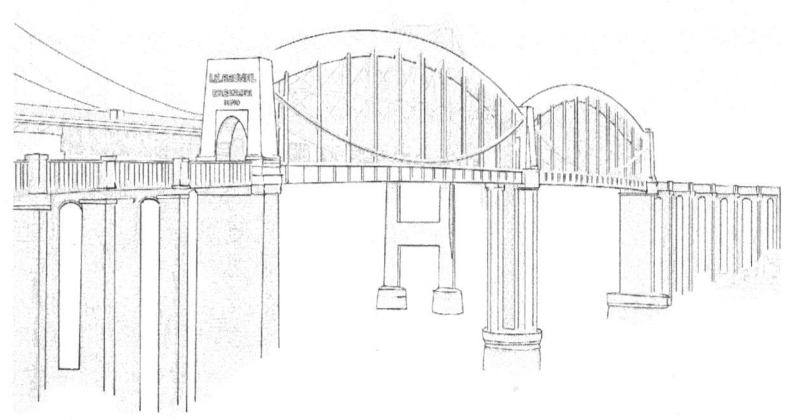

ROYAL ALBERT BRIDGE (UK)

The Royal Albert Bridge is a remarkable railway bridge that spans the River Tamar between Saltash in Cornwall and Plymouth in Devon, England. Completed in 1859, this iconic structure stands as a testament to Victorian engineering. Designed by the renowned civil engineer Isambard Kingdom Brunel, the bridge has become an enduring symbol of ingenuity, combining aesthetic beauty with technical functionality.

History
Before the construction of the Royal Albert Bridge, the River

Tamar was crossed only by ferry or the older ferry-powered chain bridge built in 1830. However, the rapid expansion of the railway network in the mid-19th century necessitated a reliable, permanent crossing for the region. The need for this crossing became increasingly urgent as the railway system expanded, prompting Brunel to design a bridge that would span the wide and deep river, while allowing ships to continue navigating the busy shipping route beneath. The construction of the Royal Albert Bridge was a major undertaking, and it dramatically improved transport links between Cornwall and the rest of Britain.

Design

The Royal Albert Bridge was an engineering marvel for its time. The structure stretches 1,480 feet across the River Tamar, with a central span of 450 feet, the longest in the world at the time. The bridge features five elegant but sturdy arches, with the central span allowing ships to pass under. Brunel's innovative use of iron and stone was groundbreaking; the combination of cast-iron components and durable stone masonry created a strong yet aesthetically pleasing structure. The bridge's design was not just functional but also artistic, with intricate wrought ironwork and graceful curves on the arches. The bridge's visual appeal, with its delicate ironwork and strong stone piers, made it a work of art in addition to a feat of engineering.

Cultural Significance

The Royal Albert Bridge holds deep cultural significance in the region. Named in honor of Prince Albert, consort to Queen Victoria, the bridge became a symbol of British pride during the height of the industrial revolution. It represented both the technological achievements of the era and the national pride associated with engineering feats. The bridge also serves as a lasting tribute to the genius of Isambard Kingdom Brunel, one of the most prominent engineers in history. The Royal Albert Bridge is often regarded as one of the finest examples of Victorian-era engineering and is frequently included in discussions of Britain's most important engineering achievements.

Functionality

The Royal Albert Bridge continues to serve a crucial role in the UK's railway infrastructure, linking Cornwall to the rest of the country. Although the demands of modern transportation have evolved, the bridge has withstood the test of time, maintaining its original purpose as a vital transport link. The structure is still in use today, carrying trains over the River Tamar, and remains one of the busiest railway bridges in the region.

Renovations and Maintenance

Over the years, the Royal Albert Bridge has undergone numerous renovations and maintenance works to preserve its structural integrity. The challenges posed by modern transport, especially the increased weight of trains, required modifications to ensure the bridge could continue to function safely. Despite these challenges, the bridge remains in excellent condition, thanks to regular maintenance and refurbishment efforts. The combination of iron and stone has proven remarkably durable, allowing the bridge to remain a key part of the UK's railway network.

Notable Events

The opening of the Royal Albert Bridge in 1859 marked a significant milestone in British transportation history. It allowed the Great Western Railway to expand its reach into Cornwall, creating a direct railway link between Plymouth and the rest of southern England. The bridge's completion was also a moment of immense pride for the region, highlighting the region's growing importance in Britain's industrial landscape. The bridge was also notable for its ability to combine function and beauty, setting a precedent for future engineering projects.

Tourism

The Royal Albert Bridge has become a popular landmark for both locals and visitors. Its graceful arches and intricate ironwork make it a favorite subject for photographers, while its location over the River Tamar provides breathtaking views. Tourists flock to the bridge to appreciate its architectural beauty, and it often features in travel guides and local tours. The bridge has also inspired numerous artists over the years, who have captured its elegance in their work.

Legacy
The legacy of the Royal Albert Bridge is immense. Not only does it remain a vital part of the UK's transport infrastructure, but it also serves as a symbol of the ingenuity and vision of Isambard Kingdom Brunel. The bridge continues to be celebrated as one of Britain's finest engineering achievements and serves as a reminder of the country's industrial heritage. It has influenced the design of subsequent bridges and structures, both in the UK and around the world. The Royal Albert Bridge is an iconic example of Victorian engineering that continues to inspire awe and admiration.

Future Plans and Developments
While the Royal Albert Bridge is still in use today, future plans aim to ensure its continued functionality and preservation. As the demands of modern rail traffic evolve, engineers are likely to explore further renovations and updates to the bridge. These developments will focus on maintaining the balance between preserving the bridge's historic integrity and meeting the demands of contemporary transport. Although new transportation technologies and infrastructure projects may change how people travel through the region, the Royal Albert Bridge will likely remain a key part of the historical fabric of Cornwall and the UK for many years to come.

GOLDEN GATE BRIDGE (SAN FRANCISCO, USA)

The Golden Gate Bridge is one of the most iconic and recognized structures in the world. Spanning the Golden Gate Strait, the bridge connects the city of San Francisco to Marin County, California, over a distance of 1.7 miles (2.7 kilometers). Completed in 1937, the bridge is not only an engineering marvel but also a symbol of progress, innovation, and the enduring human spirit.

History

Before the Golden Gate Bridge was constructed, the only way to cross the Golden Gate Strait was by ferry, a journey that could be both time-consuming and unreliable due to frequent fog and rough waters. The idea of building a bridge over the strait was initially met with skepticism. Many engineers doubted whether such a massive structure could be built in an area with strong currents, high winds, and frequent earthquakes. However, the persistence of Joseph Strauss, the chief engineer, along with the support of local residents and businesses, turned this ambitious vision into reality.

Construction of the Golden Gate Bridge began in January 1933 during the Great Depression, providing thousands of jobs to struggling workers. Strauss, an experienced engineer with a background in bridge-building, initially proposed a hybrid cantilever-suspension design. However, he later collaborated with other experts, including Leon Moisseiff, Irving Morrow, and Charles Alton Ellis, to finalize the bridge's suspension design. Morrow, an architect, also contributed the Art Deco aesthetic elements that define the bridge's unique appearance, such as the distinctive towers and railings.

Design

The Golden Gate Bridge's design is a suspension system, which uses two massive cables to support the weight of the roadway. These cables, made up of 27,572 strands of wire each, stretch over the top of the two main towers and anchor into enormous concrete blocks on either side of the bridge. The two towers rise 746 feet (227 meters) above the water, making them a striking visual feature of the bridge and an engineering achievement in their own right. At the time of its completion, the Golden Gate Bridge was the longest and tallest suspension bridge in the world, with a main span of 4,200 feet (1,280 meters) and a total height surpassing any other bridge of its kind.

One of the most visually striking aspects of the Golden Gate Bridge is its color, known as "International Orange." The color was chosen by Morrow to enhance the bridge's visibility in the frequent fog that envelops San Francisco Bay. While it was initially intended as a temporary primer, the color proved so popular that it became a defining feature of the bridge's identity. The bright orange-red hue not only provides a stark contrast to the surrounding natural landscape but also highlights the bridge's elegant lines and bold design.

Cultural Significance

The Golden Gate Bridge holds deep cultural and symbolic significance. It has been featured in countless films, television shows, books, and artworks, becoming a global icon synonymous with San Francisco and the broader American West. The bridge's sweeping views of the bay, Alcatraz Island, and the Pacific Ocean attract millions of tourists each year, making it one of the most photographed and visited landmarks in the world. It symbolizes the perseverance and vision of those who built it and continues to be a testament to the spirit of innovation and progress.

Functionality

Beyond its cultural significance, the Golden Gate Bridge serves a vital role in transportation. Since its opening in 1937, it has provided a critical link between San Francisco and Marin County, significantly reducing travel time between these two regions. The bridge accommodates millions of vehicles annually, allowing for the smooth flow of traffic and contributing to the economic vitality of the surrounding areas. Over the years, the bridge's design has also adapted to accommodate modern needs, including the addition of a dedicated walkway for pedestrians and cyclists.

Renovations and Maintenance

Maintaining a structure as large and exposed as the Golden

Gate Bridge is no small task. The bridge undergoes constant maintenance and repainting to protect it from corrosion caused by salt-laden air and moisture. Contrary to popular belief, the bridge is not continuously painted from end to end; instead, specific sections are repainted as needed to ensure the structure's longevity. The maintenance crews, often referred to as "bridge painters," play a crucial role in preserving the bridge's iconic appearance and structural integrity.

The bridge has also been the focus of significant retrofitting efforts to improve its earthquake resilience. Situated near the San Andreas Fault, the Golden Gate Bridge is exposed to the risk of powerful seismic activity. Engineers have worked to reinforce the bridge's towers, cables, and anchorage systems, ensuring that it can withstand even the most severe earthquakes. These retrofitting projects, undertaken over the past several decades, have ensured the bridge's continued safety and functionality in an ever-changing environment.

Notable Events
The Golden Gate Bridge officially opened to the public on May 27, 1937, with a day dedicated to pedestrian traffic. An estimated 200,000 people walked, ran, and even roller-skated across the bridge on that first day. The following day, President Franklin D. Roosevelt signaled the start of vehicular traffic by pressing a telegraph key in Washington, D.C. Since then, the bridge has been a site of numerous significant events, including its appearance in numerous films and its role in the cultural identity of San Francisco.

Tourism
The Golden Gate Bridge attracts millions of visitors each year, making it one of the most popular tourist destinations in the world. Tourists come from around the globe to photograph the bridge, enjoy panoramic views of San Francisco, or simply marvel at the design. The surrounding Golden Gate National Recreation Area provides opportunities for hiking, picnicking,

and sightseeing. Visitors can also take part in organized tours that provide historical insights into the bridge's construction and cultural impact.

Legacy

As the decades pass, the Golden Gate Bridge remains a testament to human creativity, determination, and innovation. Its elegant design, functional significance, and enduring symbolism continue to captivate those who visit and cross it. The bridge's legacy is woven into the fabric of San Francisco's identity and continues to inspire new generations of engineers, architects, and dreamers. While newer and longer suspension bridges have been built since 1937, none have surpassed the Golden Gate Bridge in terms of cultural impact and universal recognition.

Future Plans and Developments

Looking to the future, the Golden Gate Bridge will continue to be a critical component of the region's infrastructure. Efforts to improve the bridge's sustainability and further enhance its earthquake resilience are ongoing. Additionally, modern technological upgrades are being explored to improve traffic flow and integrate sustainable practices into its maintenance.

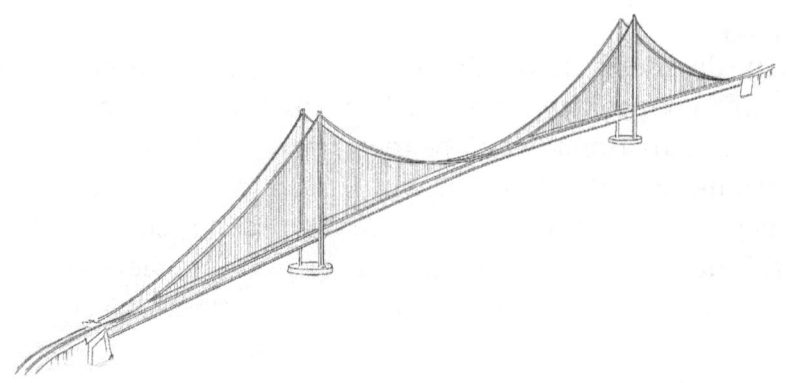

AKASHI KAIKYŌ BRIDGE (JAPAN)

The Akashi Kaikyō Bridge, often called the Pearl Bridge, stands as a modern engineering marvel and an iconic structure in Japan. Spanning the Akashi Strait, it connects Kobe on Honshu Island to Awaji Island and is an integral part of the Honshu-Shikoku Highway. As the world's longest suspension bridge, the Akashi Kaikyō Bridge reflects Japan's advanced engineering capabilities and resilience.

History
The idea for the Akashi Kaikyō Bridge was conceived after a

tragic ferry accident in 1955 that claimed the lives of over 160 passengers in the Akashi Strait. This disaster highlighted the need for a safer means of crossing the strait. The project was part of a broader effort to enhance infrastructure and connectivity between Japan's islands. After decades of planning, construction began in 1988, and the bridge was completed in 1998, overcoming numerous natural challenges, including earthquakes, typhoons, and tidal currents.

Design

The Akashi Kaikyō Bridge's main span of 1,991 meters (6,532 feet) is the longest of any suspension bridge in the world, while its total length stretches to 3,911 meters (12,831 feet). The bridge's design features a three-span continuous suspension system supported by two towering pylons, each 282.8 meters (928 feet) high. The towers are anchored deep in the seabed, ensuring stability even during seismic activity. A significant feature of the bridge is its flexibility to withstand earthquakes, particularly during the 1995 Great Hanshin Earthquake when the towers shifted slightly but the bridge remained operational.

Cultural Significance

The Akashi Kaikyō Bridge has become a symbol of Japan's engineering and architectural ingenuity. It stands as a representation of the nation's resilience, having been designed to withstand severe natural disasters. The bridge's aesthetic appeal also makes it an iconic structure, with its sleek design harmonizing with the surrounding landscape. At night, LED lights illuminate the bridge, further enhancing its visual impact. Over time, it has become a cultural landmark, inspiring various artists, photographers, and filmmakers to feature it in their works.

Functionality

The Akashi Kaikyō Bridge is not just an engineering marvel but also a vital transportation link. It significantly reduces travel time between Honshu and Shikoku, facilitating the efficient movement of goods and people. As a part of the Honshu-Shikoku Bridge Expressway, the bridge serves as a crucial part of the network connecting the islands, handling thousands of vehicles daily. Its strategic location also enhances disaster response capabilities, enabling swift evacuation and aid delivery in emergencies.

Renovations and Maintenance

Ongoing maintenance and inspections are essential to the bridge's longevity. The Akashi Kaikyō Bridge undergoes regular checks to ensure its safety, with advanced monitoring systems tracking its condition. Maintenance includes tasks like repainting, cable inspections, and deck repairs to maintain the bridge's structural integrity. Such measures ensure that the bridge continues to function as an essential transportation route and maintains its iconic appearance.

Notable Events

Since its opening in 1998, the Akashi Kaikyō Bridge has been the site of numerous events and developments. The bridge was a key factor in improving regional connectivity, and its construction was a significant achievement in overcoming the challenges posed by the Akashi Strait. In addition, the Great Hanshin Earthquake of 1995 proved the bridge's resilience, as it was designed to accommodate seismic shifts, demonstrating its robust construction and forward-thinking engineering.

Tourism

Tourists flock to the Akashi Kaikyō Bridge for its breathtaking views and historical significance. The Maiko Marine Promenade, located near the bridge, offers visitors a chance to observe the bridge from various angles and learn about its construction through interactive exhibits and historical displays. The Bridge World tour, which takes visitors inside the bridge for a unique engineering experience, is another popular attraction. This tour offers a chance to walk along the bridge's maintenance paths, guided by engineers who share insights into the structure's design and upkeep.

Legacy
The Akashi Kaikyō Bridge is more than just a bridge; it stands as a testament to human determination and technological advancement. It symbolizes Japan's ability to turn challenges into triumphs, and its successful completion has had a lasting impact on the country's infrastructure. The bridge has become not only an essential transportation link but also a cultural and architectural symbol of Japan's innovative spirit.

Future Plans and Developments
While the Akashi Kaikyō Bridge remains one of the most advanced bridges in the world, continued maintenance and technological upgrades are crucial to ensuring its future. Ongoing monitoring and retrofitting projects are in place to further enhance its earthquake resistance and ensure it remains safe and operational for years to come. As Japan continues to innovate in infrastructure, the bridge will undoubtedly play a role in shaping the future of engineering and transportation in the country.

In conclusion, the Akashi Kaikyō Bridge is not just a feat of engineering; it is a cultural landmark and an enduring symbol of Japan's resilience and innovation. It stands as a reminder of the power of vision and human effort, connecting people and inspiring future generations.

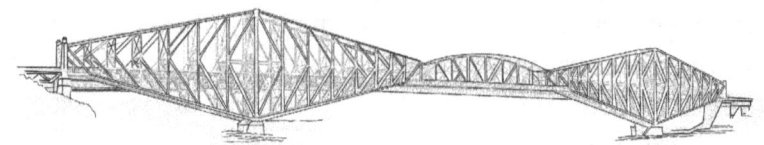

QUEBEC BRIDGE (CANADA)

The Quebec Bridge, spanning the Saint Lawrence River near Quebec City, Canada, stands as one of the most iconic cantilever bridges in the world. Completed in 1919, it holds the record for the longest cantilever span, measuring 549 meters (1,800 feet). However, the bridge's construction was marked by tragedy, triumph, and significant advancements in engineering practices. Today, it remains a vital transportation link and a symbol of resilience, determination, and innovation.

History

The Quebec Bridge's origins can be traced back to the late 19th century when the need for a reliable crossing over the Saint Lawrence River became apparent. Ferries, the primary means of transport, were no longer sufficient for the region's growing population and economy, particularly with the rise of rail transportation. Plans for the bridge began to take shape in the 1880s, but it wasn't until 1900 that serious construction efforts commenced. The bridge would not only facilitate the movement of people and goods but also cement Quebec City's role as a critical hub in Canada's national railway system.

Construction of the bridge officially began in 1904, overseen by the Quebec Bridge Company, with chief engineer Theodore Cooper at the helm. Unfortunately, the project's early years were plagued by challenges, including technical flaws in the original design and miscalculations. The first major setback occurred on August 29, 1907, when the southern arm of the bridge collapsed, resulting in the tragic deaths of 79 workers. The disaster halted the project and triggered an inquiry, which revealed critical errors in the planning and oversight of the construction. This tragedy was followed by another fatal accident in 1916, during the installation of the central span, claiming the lives of 13 workers.

Design
The Quebec Bridge is a cantilever bridge, a design chosen to address the challenges posed by the wide and deep Saint Lawrence River. The cantilever design allowed for a central span of 549 meters without the need for piers in the middle of the river, minimizing obstruction to shipping traffic. The bridge's total length measures 987 meters (3,239 feet), and it incorporates over 66,000 tons of steel, making it one of the heaviest and most robust bridges of its time. The structure consists of two large cantilever arms extending from the piers, supporting the central span, a remarkable feat of engineering.

Cultural Significance

The Quebec Bridge is more than just a transportation link—it is a cultural and historical landmark. The bridge was designated a National Historic Site of Canada in 1995, recognizing its significance as an engineering marvel and symbol of perseverance. The construction challenges, the tragic loss of life, and the subsequent triumph of completing the bridge have made it an enduring symbol of resilience and determination for both the engineering community and the people of Quebec. It has become a point of pride for locals, representing both the hardships of its creation and the triumph of human ingenuity.

Functionality
The Quebec Bridge has been an essential transportation link, particularly for rail traffic. It was originally designed to accommodate trains, and its strategic location made it an integral part of the Canadian National Railway network. The bridge also includes a roadway for cars and pedestrians, making it a versatile crossing for different modes of transportation. Over the years, the bridge has facilitated the movement of people, goods, and freight, contributing significantly to the economic development of the region.

Renovations and Maintenance
Maintaining a structure of this magnitude is an ongoing challenge. The Quebec Bridge's steel structure has required periodic maintenance, particularly to address wear and corrosion caused by exposure to harsh weather conditions and heavy use. Preservation efforts have focused on ensuring the bridge's continued functionality while preserving its historical and cultural significance. Regular inspections and restoration work are essential to maintaining the bridge's structural integrity and ensuring its safety for future generations.

Notable Events
The Quebec Bridge has been the site of several significant events, both tragic and triumphant. The two catastrophic collapses in 1907 and 1916 are the most notable and tragic events in the

bridge's history, leading to widespread scrutiny and changes in engineering practices. These events had a lasting impact on the field of civil engineering, emphasizing the need for rigorous safety standards and careful oversight. The bridge's eventual completion in 1919 marked a monumental achievement in engineering, and it has since played a central role in the transportation infrastructure of the region.

Tourism

Today, the Quebec Bridge is a popular tourist attraction, drawing visitors from around the world. Its iconic design and historical significance make it a must-see landmark in Quebec. Visitors often come to admire the bridge's engineering and to learn about its history at nearby informational displays. The bridge's massive steel arms and central span are particularly striking when viewed from various vantage points along the Saint Lawrence River. Local tours offer insights into the bridge's construction and its impact on the region's development.

Legacy

The Quebec Bridge's legacy extends beyond its physical presence. The lessons learned from its construction, especially the tragedies that occurred, have influenced modern bridge design and safety practices worldwide. The bridge has become a symbol of the resilience and perseverance of the engineers, workers, and community who overcame immense challenges to complete it. The Quebec Bridge also represents the progress made in engineering and the importance of safety in large-scale construction projects. Its enduring legacy is not just in its functionality but in the impact it had on the development of infrastructure and engineering standards.

Future Plans and Developments

The Quebec Bridge is still in use today, and efforts are underway to ensure its continued relevance and safety. As with any historic structure, maintaining the bridge's structural integrity is essential. Ongoing restoration and preservation work is focused on addressing wear and tear and updating the bridge to meet modern safety standards. While the bridge remains a crucial transportation link, future plans include ensuring that it remains an essential part of the region's infrastructure while preserving its historical significance. Continued monitoring and maintenance will ensure that the Quebec Bridge remains a symbol of innovation and resilience for generations to come.

The Quebec Bridge, spanning the Saint Lawrence River, continues to stand as a testament to human achievement, marking the progress of engineering and the resilience of those who brought it to life. Despite its troubled history, it remains one of the most remarkable engineering feats in the world. Its legacy will continue to inspire future generations, not only as a functional transportation link but also as a symbol of perseverance and ingenuity.

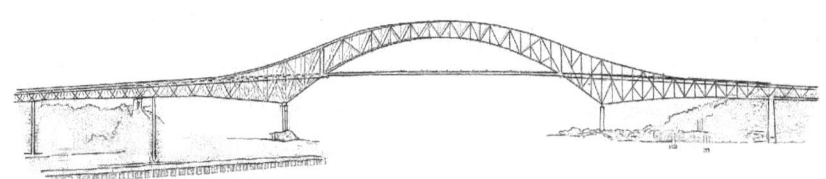

BRIDGE OF THE AMERICAS (PANAMA)

The Bridge of the Americas, or Puente de las Américas, is a vital transportation link connecting North and South America via the Pacific entrance to the Panama Canal. Spanning 1,654 meters (5,425 feet) with an arch that rises 61 meters (200 feet) above the canal, the bridge has served as a cornerstone of Panama's infrastructure since its completion in 1962. Not only does it facilitate commerce, tourism, and regional integration, but it has also become a symbol of Panama's strategic position between the continents. As a bridge that unites nations, it represents both engineering achievement and the enduring spirit of connection.

History

The history of the Bridge of the Americas is closely tied to the Panama Canal. By the mid-20th century, the canal had revolutionized global trade by allowing ships to bypass the lengthy and dangerous southern route around South America. However, the canal also divided Panama geographically, leaving limited crossing options over the waterway. Ferries and a small swing bridge were insufficient to meet the growing transportation needs of the region. The idea of constructing a permanent bridge over the canal was proposed in the 1950s, a project that was spearheaded by the United States, which controlled the canal at the time. The goal was to enhance the infrastructure of the Panama Canal Zone while also providing a direct road connection between the two halves of Panama.

Design

The design of the Bridge of the Americas was a feat of mid-20th-century engineering. A steel arch structure was chosen for its strength and durability, which allowed the bridge to span the canal without obstructing shipping traffic. The bridge's central arch measures 344 meters (1,128 feet), and the deck accommodates four lanes of traffic, providing a crucial route for vehicles and pedestrians. The clearance beneath the bridge was designed to ensure that even the largest ships could pass beneath it, an essential consideration given the importance of the canal. The structure was built using over 16,000 tons of steel, much of it fabricated in the United States before being assembled on-site in Panama.

Cultural Significance

The Bridge of the Americas holds a prominent place in Panama's national identity. It symbolizes the country's role as a bridge between North and South America and its unique connection to the Panama Canal, one of the world's most vital waterways. The bridge is more than just a transportation structure—

it represents Panama's development and modernization in the post-World War II era. Its towering arch and commanding presence at the entrance to the canal have become iconic, making the bridge a national symbol and a source of pride for Panamanians.

Functionality

The primary function of the Bridge of the Americas is to facilitate the movement of people, goods, and vehicles across the Panama Canal. The bridge provides a crucial road connection along the Pan-American Highway, linking the Americas from Alaska to Argentina. The bridge's strategic location makes it an essential artery for Panama, particularly for the movement of freight and passengers. Since its completion, it has been integral to Panama's economic development, enabling faster transportation across the country and reducing reliance on ferries. The bridge is also a critical part of Panama's integration into global trade networks.

Renovations and Maintenance

Over the years, the Bridge of the Americas has faced significant challenges due to increased traffic congestion and the wear and tear associated with heavy use. Efforts to maintain the structural integrity of the bridge have included regular inspections and repairs. The increasing volume of traffic has led to calls for upgrades and preservation work to ensure that the bridge remains safe and functional. In response, the opening of the Centennial Bridge in 2004 alleviated some of the traffic burden, but the Bridge of the Americas continues to handle tens of thousands of vehicles daily. Continued maintenance is necessary to ensure its long-term reliability and safety.

Notable Events

The Bridge of the Americas was inaugurated on October 12, 1962, in a ceremony attended by officials from Panama and the United States. Initially named the Thatcher Ferry Bridge in honor of the ferry it replaced, the bridge was later renamed to reflect its broader significance as a symbol of Panamanian-American cooperation and as a vital connection between the continents. The bridge's opening marked a transformative moment in Panama's history, greatly improving transportation links and helping the nation modernize.

The bridge also holds significant political importance, particularly with the eventual handover of the Panama Canal from the United States to Panama in 1999. The bridge became a symbol of Panama's sovereignty and independence, highlighting its ability to manage its critical infrastructure and its role in global trade.

Tourism
The Bridge of the Americas has become an important landmark for tourists and photographers. Visitors come from around the world to admire the bridge's impressive design and to take in panoramic views of the Panama Canal and the Pacific Ocean. The bridge's strategic location at the entrance to the canal also provides a unique vantage point to observe the steady stream of ships passing beneath it, which is an awe-inspiring sight for many tourists.

Legacy
The legacy of the Bridge of the Americas extends beyond its physical structure. It serves as a testament to Panama's growth and its key role in global trade. The bridge played a crucial part in Panama's development, facilitating commerce and uniting the country physically and economically.

Future Plans and Developments
As Panama continues to grow, there are plans to further upgrade and maintain the Bridge of the Americas to accommodate increasing traffic and to ensure its longevity. The development of additional transportation infrastructure, such as the Centennial Bridge and new roads, has already eased some of the strain on the Bridge of the Americas, but it remains a critical link

in Panama's transport network. Future developments may focus on enhancing the bridge's capacity, improving traffic flow, and preserving its structural integrity for generations to come.

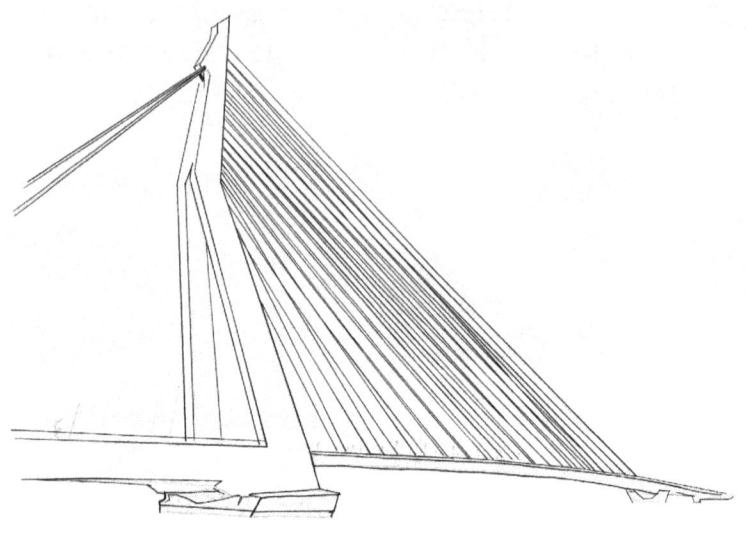

ERASMUSBRUG (ROTTERDAM, NETHERLANDS)

The Erasmusbrug, or Erasmus Bridge, is one of the most iconic structures in Rotterdam, Netherlands. Spanning the Nieuwe Maas River, it serves as a crucial transportation link while symbolizing the city's modernity and architectural innovation. Completed in 1996, the bridge, nicknamed "The Swan" for its elegant, asymmetrical pylon, embodies Rotterdam's resilience after its post-war rebuilding and its embrace of forward-thinking design. It is not just an engineering marvel but a cultural and architectural landmark that has come to define the city.

History

The idea for the Erasmusbrug emerged in the early 1990s during a period of transformation for Rotterdam. The city, known for its maritime history and modern architecture, sought to strengthen connections between its northern and southern districts, divided by the Nieuwe Maas River. With the south side undergoing rapid development, a new bridge was seen as both a practical necessity and a statement of Rotterdam's progressive architectural ambitions. Dutch architect Ben van Berkel was tasked with designing the bridge, which was officially opened on September 6, 1996, by Queen Beatrix of the Netherlands.

Design

The Erasmusbrug's design reflects Rotterdam's ethos of boldness and innovation. The bridge is a cable-stayed structure, with a 139-meter-high pylon tilted at an angle, resembling the graceful neck of a swan, hence the nickname. The bridge's span reaches 802 meters, supported by 40 steel cables, while its unique asymmetrical form makes it stand out against the city's skyline. The bridge also features a bascule section, allowing ships to pass under by lifting the central span, making it one of the largest and heaviest moveable bridges in the world. This innovative design combines form with function, making the Erasmusbrug both a visual and practical masterpiece.

Cultural Significance

The Erasmusbrug has become much more than just a transportation link. It is a cultural symbol of Rotterdam's post-war revival and its status as a hub of modern architecture. The bridge's sleek design has made it an icon, frequently appearing in photographs and media, symbolizing the city's dynamic and resilient spirit. Each year, the bridge serves as the starting point for the Rotterdam Marathon and is central to the city's New Year's Eve fireworks display. The Erasmusbrug has become a cultural landmark that fosters a sense of unity within the city and enhances Rotterdam's international reputation.

Functionality

As a major infrastructure piece, the Erasmusbrug plays a pivotal role in Rotterdam's daily functioning. The bridge accommodates vehicles, pedestrians, and cyclists, while also integrating into the city's public transport network with trams crossing it regularly. By connecting the northern and southern parts of Rotterdam, it has streamlined traffic flow and made the city's various districts more accessible. The bridge's design, which includes the bascule section, ensures that it can handle both pedestrian and vehicular traffic while allowing for the passage of large vessels beneath it, making it an essential piece of Rotterdam's infrastructure.

Renovations and Maintenance

Like any significant piece of infrastructure, the Erasmusbrug has undergone its share of challenges and maintenance efforts. Early on, the bridge faced issues such as vibrations caused by strong winds, which prompted design adjustments to improve stability. Over the years, various modifications have been made to ensure the bridge's structural integrity and improve its performance. These efforts underscore the importance of maintaining such a vital piece of infrastructure to accommodate the growing demands of the city's traffic and maritime activities.

Notable Events

The Erasmusbrug has been at the center of several significant events in Rotterdam. Its most notable role is as the starting point for the annual Rotterdam Marathon, one of the Netherlands' largest running events. The bridge is also featured prominently in the city's New Year's Eve fireworks display, drawing thousands of spectators each year. In addition, the Erasmusbrug's striking design has made it a popular subject for films, commercials, and television programs, further cementing its place as an icon of modern Rotterdam.

Tourism

The Erasmusbrug is a major tourist attraction in Rotterdam, drawing visitors from around the world who come to marvel at its architectural beauty and its significance to the city. The bridge's unique design and commanding presence on the skyline make it a favorite subject for photographers and tourists. It provides stunning views of the Nieuwe Maas River and the city, making it a must-visit landmark for anyone exploring Rotterdam. The bridge has also become a destination in its own right, often featured in tours of the city's architectural wonders.

Legacy

The Erasmusbrug holds a lasting legacy as one of Rotterdam's most recognizable landmarks. It stands as a testament to the city's resilience and its ability to reinvent itself after the devastation of World War II. As both an engineering marvel and a cultural symbol, the bridge has played a key role in shaping Rotterdam's modern identity. It has inspired other cities around the world to consider how infrastructure can be both functional and aesthetically pleasing. Its impact is felt not only in the city's physical landscape but also in the way it represents Rotterdam's spirit of innovation and forward-thinking design.

Future Plans and Developments

As Rotterdam continues to evolve, the Erasmusbrug remains an essential part of the city's infrastructure and skyline. Future plans for the bridge include continued maintenance and upgrades to ensure it meets the demands of modern traffic and maritime activity. The city's ongoing development of the Kop van Zuid district, once an industrial area and now a vibrant urban neighborhood, is closely tied to the presence of the Erasmusbrug. As Rotterdam continues to grow and evolve, the Erasmusbrug will undoubtedly remain a central symbol of the city's resilience, innovation, and forward-looking vision for the future.

MODERN AND INNOVATIVE DESIGNS

The 20th and 21st centuries have seen an explosion of creativity and innovation in the world of bridge construction. Modern bridges combine cutting-edge materials, such as high-strength steel, carbon fiber, and advanced composites, with innovative engineering techniques to create visually striking, functional, and highly efficient structures. These bridges are not merely functional—they are statements of human capability, defying both gravity and the natural environment to deliver unparalleled connections. They represent a marriage of technology, design, and ambition, with engineers seeking to design the next great architectural landmark.

HELIX BRIDGE (SINGAPORE)

The Helix Bridge in Singapore stands as a captivating example of the city-state's commitment to blending innovation, aesthetic beauty, and functional design. Spanning Marina Bay, this pedestrian bridge connects Marina Centre to Marina South, creating a vital link between landmarks such as the Marina Bay Sands and the ArtScience Museum. Opened in 2010, the Helix Bridge is a visual and engineering masterpiece, distinguished by its DNA-inspired design. It embodies Singapore's reputation for futuristic architecture, symbolizing the nation's progressiveness and its focus on sustainability and connectivity.

Its unique structure and design elements have made it one of the most iconic and visited landmarks in the city, cementing its place as a key element of the Marina Bay skyline.

History

The concept for the Helix Bridge emerged during Singapore's broader plans to transform Marina Bay into a world-class waterfront district. The bridge was designed not just to connect different parts of the area but to enhance the pedestrian experience and contribute to the aesthetic development of Marina Bay. The idea was born from the vision of creating an architectural landmark that would serve as a testament to human ingenuity and Singapore's future-oriented identity. The Helix Bridge was designed by the Australian architectural firm Cox Architecture, in collaboration with Singapore-based engineers from Arup. The bridge's construction marked a significant milestone in both the nation's engineering capabilities and architectural aspirations.

Design

The Helix Bridge's most striking feature is its double-helix structure, inspired by the geometry of DNA. This design represents more than just visual intrigue; it symbolizes themes of life, growth, and continuity, with its intertwining steel spirals resembling the structure of a DNA strand. This unique design required the innovative use of approximately 650 tons of stainless steel and a complex framework of triangular supports to ensure stability and lightness. The bridge spans 280 meters and accommodates pedestrians along a five-meter-wide walkway. The sophisticated use of lighting, which transforms the bridge into a glowing spectacle at night, and the interactive viewing pods along the walkway further enhance its aesthetic appeal.

Cultural Significance

The Helix Bridge is more than just a functional structure—it is a symbol of Singapore's cultural identity and aspirations. The

DNA-inspired design, with its pairs of colored letters embedded into the surface, references the scientific foundations of the structure, while also subtly hinting at the interconnectedness of life. This alludes to Singapore's focus on education, science, and research, positioning the country as a global leader in these fields. The bridge is a visible representation of the nation's drive for innovation, combining cutting-edge technology with cultural resonance, making it an important cultural landmark in Singapore's architectural landscape.

Functionality
While the Helix Bridge is undeniably beautiful, it also serves a practical purpose, enhancing pedestrian connectivity between key areas in Marina Bay. It provides an efficient and scenic route for those traveling between Marina Centre and Marina South, facilitating access to major attractions like Marina Bay Sands, Gardens by the Bay, and the Singapore Flyer. The bridge is designed to accommodate high foot traffic, with its wide walkway and ample space for pedestrians to move freely. Its positioning also offers breathtaking views of the surrounding urban landscape, making it not only a functional pedestrian bridge but also an immersive experience for those crossing it.

Renovations and Maintenance
Since its completion, the Helix Bridge has undergone regular maintenance to ensure its longevity and safety. The complex nature of its design means that meticulous care is required to preserve both its aesthetic qualities and structural integrity. Routine inspections ensure the bridge remains safe for use, especially given the tropical climate's potential impact on materials like stainless steel. While no significant renovations have been reported, the design's longevity reflects its high-quality construction and Singapore's commitment to maintaining its public spaces to the highest standards.

Notable Events
The Helix Bridge plays a central role in various events

throughout the year. It is often featured in the National Day Parade, providing a spectacular backdrop for the festivities. The bridge also serves as an ideal viewing platform for major celebrations, including the Marina Bay Singapore Countdown on New Year's Eve, where it offers unparalleled views of fireworks displays and other celebrations. Its role in public events elevates its cultural significance, making it not just a physical bridge but a gathering point for both locals and tourists during some of Singapore's most important events.

Tourism
The Helix Bridge has become a key destination for tourists visiting Singapore, drawing people from all over the world. Its stunning design and panoramic views of the Marina Bay area make it a favorite spot for photography and sightseeing. As part of the broader Marina Bay area, the bridge complements other attractions like Marina Bay Sands and Gardens by the Bay, enhancing the overall tourist experience. Its unique architecture, particularly the dynamic lighting that illuminates the structure at night, makes it one of the most photographed landmarks in the city. The bridge's appeal as both a functional walkway and a visual landmark makes it a must-see for visitors to Singapore.

Legacy
The Helix Bridge has made a lasting impact on Singapore's architectural landscape. It has been recognized globally for its innovative design and engineering, earning numerous awards, including the prestigious "World's Best Transport Building" at the 2011 World Architecture Festival. The bridge stands as a testament to Singapore's ability to combine artistic expression with technical expertise, becoming a lasting symbol of the nation's development. It represents not just a triumph in architectural and engineering terms but also Singapore's emergence as a global hub of innovation and modernity. Its legacy is reflected in its continued popularity and its influence

on future bridge designs worldwide.

Future Plans and Developments

While there are no immediate plans to alter the Helix Bridge, its presence in the Marina Bay area continues to influence future developments. As Singapore continues to evolve as a leading global city, the Helix Bridge remains a significant architectural and cultural landmark. Future plans for the surrounding area include the further development of Marina Bay as an integrated waterfront district, with the bridge playing a pivotal role in maintaining connectivity between new and existing landmarks. As Singapore's urban landscape continues to grow and innovate, the Helix Bridge is likely to remain a key part of the city's ever-evolving architectural identity, inspiring future generations of architects and engineers to push the boundaries of design.

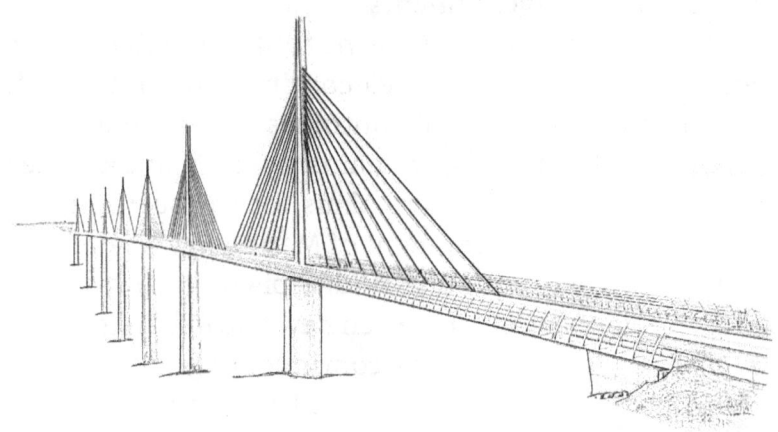

VIADUC DE MILLAU (FRANCE)

The Millau Viaduct in southern France is one of the tallest bridges in the world, celebrated for its striking design and innovative engineering. Spanning the Tarn Valley, it serves as a vital transportation link and a remarkable symbol of architectural achievement. Completed in 2004, it stands as a testament to human ingenuity, blending seamlessly into the dramatic landscape of the Massif Central. Designed by Sir Norman Foster and structural engineer Michel Virlogeux, the bridge is a bold statement of innovation, functionality, and aesthetic harmony.

History
The idea for the Millau Viaduct emerged as a solution to the transportation challenges faced by the A75 motorway, which connects Paris to the Mediterranean. Prior to its construction, the town of Millau experienced significant traffic congestion, particularly during the summer months, when tourism surged in the region. The French government sought to improve the flow of traffic by creating a direct route over the Tarn Valley while preserving the natural beauty of the area. The Millau Viaduct was conceived as the centerpiece of this solution, addressing both the functional needs of transportation and the desire to minimize environmental impact. The construction began in 2001 and took just over three years to complete.

Design
Designed by British architect Sir Norman Foster and French engineer Michel Virlogeux, the Millau Viaduct is a cable-stayed bridge with seven slender piers that rise dramatically from the valley floor. The bridge stretches 2.46 kilometers (1.53 miles) across the Tarn Valley, with the deck soaring 270 meters (890 feet) above the river below. The tallest pier, Pier P2, reaches an impressive height of 343 meters (1,125 feet), surpassing even the Eiffel Tower. The structure's design was carefully planned to ensure both structural efficiency and aesthetic elegance. The use of lightweight materials such as high-performance concrete and steel allowed the bridge to achieve its remarkable height without compromising stability. The cable-stayed design, where the deck is supported by cables fanning out from the pylons, provides a sense of lightness and visual grace while ensuring the necessary strength to withstand high winds and seismic activity.

Cultural Significance
The Millau Viaduct is not just a piece of infrastructure; it holds profound cultural significance. It has become a symbol of innovation and human achievement, representing the blend

of modern engineering with the natural landscape. Architect Sir Norman Foster described the viaduct as a "sculpture in the landscape," and its design philosophy reflects this idea. The bridge's presence in the Tarn Valley has transformed the region's identity, turning it into a symbol of French ingenuity. It also plays a role in reinforcing the country's cultural focus on blending cutting-edge technology with respect for the environment.

Functionality

The primary function of the Millau Viaduct is to facilitate smoother traffic flow across the Tarn Valley, alleviating congestion in the town of Millau. It serves as a vital link on the A75 motorway, connecting the southern regions of France to the rest of the country. By providing a direct crossing over the valley, the bridge has reduced travel time, particularly during peak tourist seasons, and has improved accessibility to the Mediterranean coast. Beyond its functional role in transportation, the viaduct has also become an important feature of the local economy, drawing in tourists who come to marvel at its engineering and the stunning views it offers of the surrounding landscape.

Renovations and Maintenance

Since its completion, the Millau Viaduct has required minimal maintenance due to its advanced design and the durable materials used in its construction. The bridge was built with longevity in mind, and its environmental integration has ensured it remains relatively low-maintenance. Routine inspections are conducted to ensure the continued safety and stability of the structure, and the bridge has been periodically updated with lighting and safety features to enhance its functionality for both drivers and visitors. The viaduct's design incorporates the latest technology to monitor its performance and make adjustments as needed.

Notable Events

The Millau Viaduct has hosted several significant events since its completion, most notably the ceremonial opening in December 2004, which was attended by French President Jacques Chirac. The viaduct has also become an iconic backdrop for a variety of cultural and artistic events, such as photography exhibitions and architectural tours. Its status as a symbol of engineering excellence has ensured that it remains in the global spotlight, celebrated for its beauty and functionality. The bridge is often included in discussions about the future of infrastructure and design, cementing its place as a major achievement in contemporary engineering.

Tourism
Tourism has flourished in the region due to the Millau Viaduct's unique appeal. Visitors from around the world come to experience the bridge, not only for its architectural wonder but also for the spectacular views it offers of the Tarn Valley and the surrounding Massif Central. Viewing platforms and visitor centers have been established to allow tourists to observe the viaduct from various perspectives. The surrounding area, rich in natural beauty and history, also attracts visitors who come to explore the region's landscapes, charming villages, and cultural heritage. The viaduct has undoubtedly become a major tourist attraction, contributing to the region's economy and global recognition.

Legacy
The legacy of the Millau Viaduct extends beyond its role as a functional bridge. It stands as a symbol of visionary design and the potential for architecture and engineering to blend with nature. The viaduct has inspired numerous other infrastructure projects around the world, demonstrating the possibilities that emerge when ambitious ideas are paired with cutting-edge technology. Its legacy is not just in its physical structure but in its ability to inspire a sense of wonder and admiration for the ingenuity of human creation.

Future Plans and Developments

Looking to the future, the Millau Viaduct will likely remain a crucial element of France's transportation infrastructure. Plans for its continued preservation and potential upgrades will focus on maintaining its structural integrity while ensuring that it meets the demands of modern traffic. The bridge's design, known for its efficiency and minimal environmental impact, could serve as a model for future infrastructure projects aimed at blending functionality with environmental consciousness.

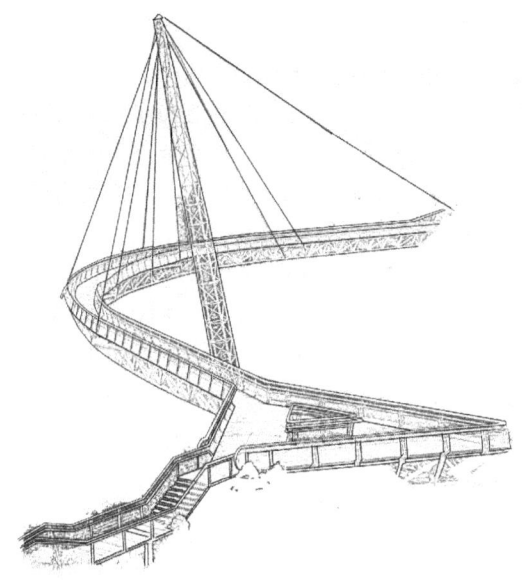

LANGKAWI SKY BRIDGE (MALAYSIA)

The Langkawi Sky Bridge, situated on Langkawi Island in Malaysia, is a stunning architectural and engineering feat that attracts visitors from around the world. Suspended high above the island's lush rainforests, the bridge offers breathtaking views and serves as an iconic symbol of the harmonious blend between human ingenuity and nature. Spanning 125 meters (410 feet), the Langkawi Sky Bridge provides not only a thrilling experience for adventure seekers but also a tranquil escape into the region's natural beauty.

History

The Langkawi Sky Bridge was constructed in 2004 as part of a broader initiative to develop Langkawi's tourism infrastructure while highlighting the island's natural beauty. The bridge was designed to be a focal point of the Langkawi Geopark, a UNESCO-recognized site, and to provide access to panoramic views of the island and the Andaman Sea. The ambitious project faced significant challenges due to its remote location and the rugged terrain of Gunung Mat Cincang, the second-highest mountain on Langkawi. Despite these obstacles, the bridge was completed in just over a year, showcasing the determination and skill of the engineers involved.

Design

The Langkawi Sky Bridge's design is remarkable for its unique curved structure and single towering pylon that supports the bridge. The pylon anchors suspension cables, allowing the bridge to span a vast distance with minimal environmental impact. The innovative design reduces the need for multiple supports, minimizing disturbance to the surrounding ecosystem. The bridge's graceful curve allows visitors to experience different views as they walk, with cantilevered platforms providing unobstructed vistas of the forest, the Andaman Sea, and the islands beyond.

Cultural Significance

Langkawi's rich cultural heritage is reflected in the Sky Bridge's surroundings. Gunung Mat Cincang, the mountain where the bridge is located, is named after a mythical warrior, lending the area an air of mystique and legend. Additionally, the Sky Bridge itself has become a cultural symbol for the island, representing Langkawi's commitment to blending tourism with sustainable development. Visitors not only come for the bridge but also to explore the rich folklore and natural wonders in the surrounding area, which includes attractions such as the Seven Wells Waterfall and local villages.

Functionality
The Langkawi Sky Bridge serves as both a tourist attraction and an architectural wonder. It offers visitors panoramic views and a unique experience of walking suspended above the rainforest. The bridge is designed to be both functional and aesthetic, with its minimalistic support structure enhancing the visual appeal while ensuring safety and stability. The addition of the SkyGlide elevator, which transports visitors to the bridge, makes it accessible to people of all ages and abilities, ensuring that the bridge is a welcoming experience for a diverse range of visitors.

Renovations and Maintenance
The Langkawi Sky Bridge continues to be maintained and upgraded to ensure its safety and accessibility. Regular maintenance is carried out to preserve the structural integrity of the bridge and to enhance the visitor experience. The introduction of the SkyGlide elevator is one of the significant upgrades aimed at improving accessibility. The focus on maintenance and upgrades highlights the commitment to preserving the bridge as a lasting attraction and a part of Langkawi's tourism infrastructure.

Notable Events
While the Langkawi Sky Bridge has not been the site of any specific historical events, it has gained international recognition and become a key part of Malaysia's tourism marketing. The bridge's opening in 2004 was celebrated as a monumental achievement in modern engineering, and since then, it has been featured in numerous travel magazines, websites, and social media platforms. Its inclusion in Langkawi Geopark further emphasizes its significance as a symbol of sustainable tourism in the region.

Tourism
Langkawi Sky Bridge is a must-see attraction for tourists visiting Langkawi Island. It draws visitors from around the

globe, offering an exhilarating experience with breathtaking views of the surrounding landscape. Tourists can access the bridge via the Langkawi Cable Car, which adds an element of excitement as it ascends the mountain slopes, providing stunning views of the island. Once on the bridge, visitors are treated to panoramic vistas of the Andaman Sea, the Langkawi archipelago, and the lush rainforest below. The bridge has significantly boosted Langkawi's tourism industry, elevating the island's status as a premier travel destination in Malaysia.

Legacy
The Langkawi Sky Bridge has left a lasting legacy on Langkawi Island. As a major tourist attraction, it has contributed to the growth of the island's economy by increasing visitor numbers and encouraging sustainable tourism. Its success has also led to the development of further infrastructure projects in Langkawi, reinforcing the island's reputation as a hub for eco-tourism and adventure tourism in Southeast Asia. The bridge's unique design and environmental consideration serve as a model for future projects that seek to combine tourism with environmental sustainability.

Future Plans and Developments
Looking ahead, the future of the Langkawi Sky Bridge appears bright. Plans for further improvements and additions aim to enhance the visitor experience while maintaining the bridge's environmental and cultural integrity. There are ongoing discussions about expanding the accessibility of the bridge through the use of new technology, such as mobile apps for guided tours and interactive displays. Efforts are also underway to increase public awareness about the importance of conservation and sustainable tourism in the region. With its enduring appeal and commitment to sustainability, the Langkawi Sky Bridge is likely to remain one of Malaysia's most iconic landmarks for years to come.

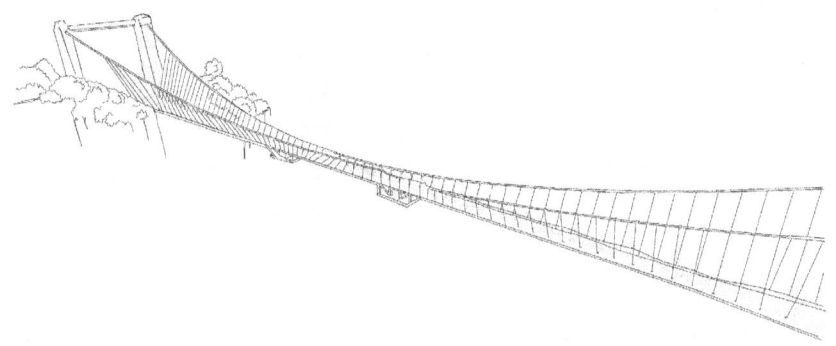

ZHANGJIAJIE GLASS BRIDGE (CHINA)

Suspended above the Zhangjiajie Grand Canyon in China, the Zhangjiajie Glass Bridge is a remarkable feat of modern engineering and architectural innovation. Spanning 430 meters (1,410 feet) in length and hanging 300 meters (984 feet) above the canyon floor, this transparent bridge offers an exhilarating experience. Made entirely of glass and steel, it is a testament to China's ambition, pushing the boundaries of what is possible in both structural and visual design. It has become a symbol of human ingenuity and an extraordinary addition to the already breathtaking scenery of the Zhangjiajie region.

History
The Zhangjiajie Glass Bridge, designed by Israeli architect Haim Dotan, was completed and opened to the public in 2016. Its construction was a significant engineering challenge due to the bridge's location in the remote Zhangjiajie Grand Canyon. The idea for the bridge emerged as part of China's broader goal to develop tourism in the region, capitalizing on the area's UNESCO World Heritage status and the world-renowned beauty of its sandstone pillars, which were famously portrayed as the floating mountains in the 2009 film *Avatar*. The bridge was conceived as part of a larger effort to increase tourism and enhance the region's global visibility.

Design
The Zhangjiajie Glass Bridge stands as a minimalist marvel. It features 99 panes of triple-layered tempered glass, which create a transparent walkway for visitors. The bridge's design emphasizes the concept of invisibility, blending seamlessly into the environment. It is supported by white steel suspension cables, almost invisible from a distance, allowing the focus to remain on the natural beauty of the canyon. The engineering required to build the bridge was complex due to the harsh terrain and remote location, but it successfully harmonizes the human-made structure with the awe-inspiring landscape.

Cultural Significance
Beyond its stunning design and engineering, the Zhangjiajie Glass Bridge has become a cultural icon in China. It frequently appears in films, advertisements, and social media, with its dramatic location and daring design attracting photographers and influencers. The bridge symbolizes China's growing global presence in innovation and its ability to combine cutting-edge technology with respect for nature. The bridge also highlights the country's commitment to sustainable tourism, as it aims to preserve the fragile ecosystems of the Zhangjiajie Grand Canyon while offering visitors a unique experience.

Functionality
The bridge serves as more than just a tourist attraction. It acts as a gateway for visitors to explore the vast Zhangjiajie Grand Canyon. Visitors can descend to the canyon floor via trails, discovering hidden caves, streams, and waterfalls. The bridge itself offers a thrilling experience, with its transparent glass floor creating the sensation of walking in mid-air, over the steep cliffs and valleys below. The bridge also boasts a bungee jump platform, which, at 260 meters (853 feet), offers the highest bungee jump in the world, making it an additional draw for adventure seekers.

Renovations and Maintenance
Since its opening, the Zhangjiajie Glass Bridge has undergone regular maintenance and safety checks to ensure its structural integrity. Given the exposure to natural elements, the glass panels and steel structure are frequently inspected for wear and tear. The bridge has been subjected to rigorous safety tests, including the use of sledge hammers and even a car to demonstrate its strength during its opening. These tests have reassured visitors about its safety, as the bridge can support up to 800 people at a time. Ongoing maintenance ensures the structure remains both safe and accessible to the growing number of tourists.

Notable Events
The opening of the Zhangjiajie Glass Bridge in 2016 attracted global attention, drawing visitors from around the world. During the first days of its opening, the bridge was subject to demonstrations that showcased its durability. For example, a sledgehammer was used to strike the glass to prove its strength. These demonstrations not only helped to quell any fears but also highlighted the bridge's remarkable engineering. Additionally, the addition of the bungee jumping platform turned the bridge into a major attraction for thrill-seekers, further cementing its place in global tourism and popular culture.

Tourism

The Zhangjiajie Glass Bridge has had a profound impact on tourism in the region, significantly boosting the local economy. It has become one of China's most visited landmarks, attracting millions of tourists annually. The bridge's dramatic design and its location above the Zhangjiajie Grand Canyon make it a perfect spot for photographers, filmmakers, and influencers. In addition to the bridge itself, the surrounding region offers a wealth of natural wonders, making it a key component of the broader tourism strategy in Zhangjiajie. As a result, the bridge has helped transform the area into a global travel destination.

Legacy

The Zhangjiajie Glass Bridge is more than just an architectural structure—it is a legacy of human creativity and engineering prowess. The bridge has changed the way we think about combining nature and human-made structures. It has become a symbol of innovation, inspiring similar projects around the world, and it has showcased China's capability in delivering world-class engineering feats. Moreover, it has raised awareness about the potential of architecture to enhance, rather than obscure, natural beauty. As such, it has left a lasting impact on both the architectural community and the public at large.

Future Plans and Developments

Looking to the future, the Zhangjiajie Glass Bridge is set to continue as a major tourist attraction. Efforts to ensure the safety and preservation of the structure are ongoing, with future renovations and upgrades aimed at improving the visitor experience while maintaining the integrity of the design. Plans to further develop the tourism infrastructure around the bridge are also in place, including expanding the range of activities available to visitors. These developments aim to ensure that the Zhangjiajie Glass Bridge remains a sustainable and iconic part of the region's appeal for years to come.

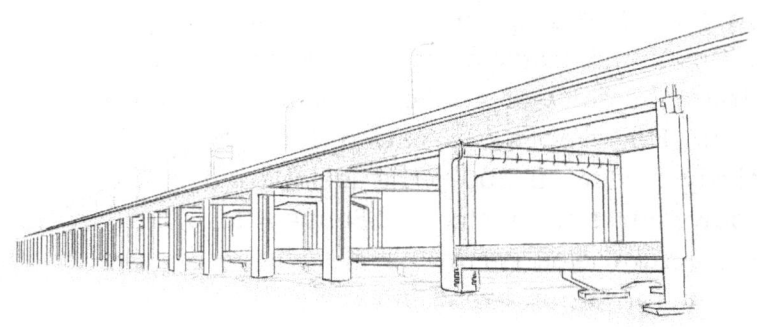

BANPO BRIDGE (SEOUL, SOUTH KOREA)

Banpo Bridge in Seoul, South Korea, is a striking fusion of engineering, artistry, and urban planning. Spanning the Han River, it has become an essential part of the cityscape, seamlessly blending functionality with aesthetic beauty. Opened in 1982, the bridge connects the districts of Seocho and Yongsan, serving as a crucial transportation link while also becoming a major cultural landmark thanks to its transformation into a multi-functional space, most notably with the addition of the

Moonlight Rainbow Fountain.

History
Banpo Bridge was constructed in response to Seoul's rapid urban growth during the 1980s. It was designed primarily as a functional transportation link to ease congestion and facilitate the flow of traffic between two of the city's key districts. However, its evolution into a cultural symbol is relatively recent. In 2009, the installation of the Moonlight Rainbow Fountain transformed Banpo Bridge from an ordinary infrastructural element into a globally recognized landmark. This transformation exemplifies the city's ability to combine modern functionality with artistic expression.

Design
The design of Banpo Bridge is a testament to the ingenuity of urban planning. The bridge features a dual-layer structure: the upper deck caters to vehicular traffic, while the lower deck, known as Jamsu Bridge, is dedicated to pedestrians and cyclists. One of the most innovative aspects of the design is the Jamsu Bridge's ability to submerge during periods of heavy rainfall or rising water levels, acting as a flood control measure. This design maximizes the bridge's usability while addressing environmental concerns. The bridge's elegant aesthetic is further enhanced by the Moonlight Rainbow Fountain, which stretches 1,140 meters and includes 380 nozzles capable of shooting water up to 20 meters in the air.

Cultural Significance
Banpo Bridge has become a symbol of Seoul's dynamic and forward-thinking spirit. Its Moonlight Rainbow Fountain is a major cultural and artistic addition to the city, drawing millions of visitors each year. The bridge is not just a functional piece of infrastructure but a central part of the city's identity, embodying both the technological prowess of South Korea and the nation's rich cultural heritage. The bridge's fountain, synchronized with music and LED lighting, represents the

harmonious blend of nature, technology, and art, reflecting the country's ability to marry tradition with modernity.

Functionality

While the beauty of Banpo Bridge cannot be overstated, its functionality is equally impressive. The bridge serves as a critical transportation link, facilitating smooth traffic flow across the Han River. The upper deck accommodates vehicular traffic, while the lower deck serves pedestrians and cyclists. This dual-purpose design maximizes space in one of the most densely populated cities in the world. Moreover, the lower deck's flooding mechanism offers a practical solution to the city's seasonal water level fluctuations, showcasing Seoul's commitment to resilient and sustainable infrastructure.

Renovations and Maintenance

Banpo Bridge has undergone minimal renovations since its completion, with the most significant change being the addition of the Moonlight Rainbow Fountain in 2009. The fountain has since become an integral part of the bridge's identity and is carefully maintained to ensure its smooth operation. The eco-friendly design of the fountain, which recycles water drawn from the Han River, is an example of how urban infrastructure can be both functional and sustainable. Regular maintenance is carried out to preserve the bridge's aesthetic appeal and structural integrity, ensuring that it remains both a transportation link and a popular tourist destination.

Notable Events

Banpo Bridge has been the backdrop for numerous cultural and social events. It plays a central role in the Hangang Summer Festival, an annual celebration of Seoul's river culture, featuring live performances, movie screenings, and water sports. During the spring, the cherry blossoms along the riverbanks enhance the bridge's beauty, making it a popular spot for both locals and tourists. The Moonlight Rainbow Fountain, with its captivating water, light, and music show, has become a key attraction during these festivals, drawing crowds to witness the spectacle that transforms the bridge into a work of art.

Tourism

Banpo Bridge is a must-visit destination for anyone traveling to Seoul. Its stunning Moonlight Rainbow Fountain, which features water jets synchronized with LED lights and music, has become one of the most photographed and visited sites in the city. The bridge's strategic location along the Han River offers spectacular views of Seoul's skyline, including iconic landmarks like Namsan Seoul Tower and the 63 Building. Visitors can enjoy the surrounding Banpo Hangang Park, which offers expansive green spaces, bike paths, and seating areas, creating a perfect place to relax and enjoy the beauty of the river and the bridge. The addition of the floating islands, Some Sevit, further enhances the area's appeal, providing cultural events, dining options, and exhibitions.

Legacy

Banpo Bridge holds a special place in the hearts of Seoul residents and international visitors alike. As a symbol of both the city's historical development and its modern achievements, the bridge represents Seoul's ongoing evolution. It stands as a testament to the city's commitment to blending functionality with beauty, creating public spaces that are both practical and inspiring. The bridge's design and its transformation into a cultural icon have influenced urban planning projects worldwide, showcasing the power of creativity in shaping cities that are as aesthetically pleasing as they are functional.

Future Plans and Developments

Looking ahead, Banpo Bridge is likely to continue playing a significant role in Seoul's urban development. While there are no immediate plans for major renovations, ongoing maintenance and improvements will ensure that the bridge remains a safe and reliable part of the city's infrastructure. As the city continues to grow, the bridge will likely remain a central feature of the Hangang Park system, contributing to the development of public spaces that enhance the quality of life for Seoul's residents. The Moonlight Rainbow Fountain will likely continue to evolve, with potential updates to the lighting and water displays, keeping the attraction fresh and appealing to future generations of visitors.

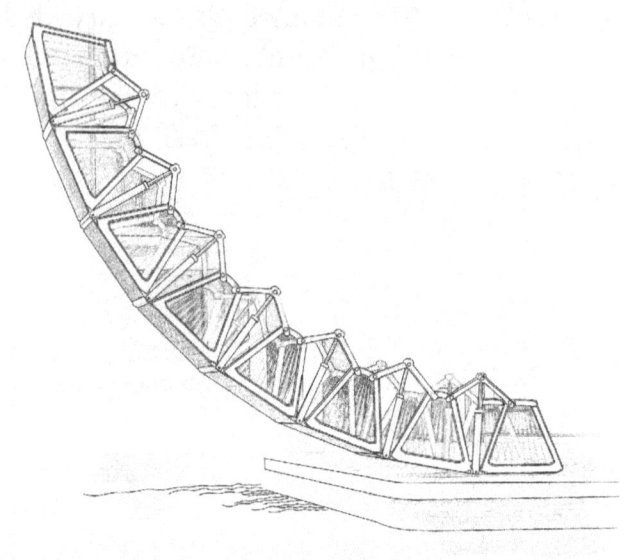

THE ROLLING BRIDGE (LONDON, UK)

The Rolling Bridge in London, UK, is an extraordinary example of modern engineering and innovative urban design. Located in the Grand Union Canal at Paddington Basin, this bridge is celebrated for its unique ability to curl and unfold like a living organism. Designed by renowned British architect Thomas Heatherwick, it combines art and functionality, offering a pedestrian crossing while serving as a striking visual spectacle. Completed in 2004, the bridge challenges conventional bridge design and stands as a testament to creativity in architecture.

History
The Rolling Bridge was conceived and designed by Thomas Heatherwick in the early 2000s. The idea for this unique structure came from Heatherwick's desire to rethink the traditional concept of a bridge. Rather than creating a static, utilitarian crossing, he aimed to design something dynamic and transformative. The bridge was completed in 2004, marking a significant moment in London's architectural history. Situated in Paddington Basin, the bridge was part of a larger regeneration project aimed at reviving the area. Once an industrial zone, Paddington Basin underwent a dramatic transformation, with the Rolling Bridge serving as both a functional and artistic landmark in the newly developed district.

Design
The Rolling Bridge's design is what sets it apart from conventional bridges. Spanning just 12 meters, it is constructed from a combination of steel and timber, chosen for both strength and aesthetic appeal. The bridge's most remarkable feature is its ability to fold up into an octagonal shape, resembling the movement of a caterpillar or an armadillo. This transformation occurs through a series of hydraulics and pistons embedded within the structure. Each of the bridge's eight triangular sections is hinged, allowing the bridge to curl up smoothly. The entire process of folding or unfolding takes about three minutes and is powered by a hydraulic system at the bridge's base.

Cultural Significance
The Rolling Bridge has become a symbol of innovation and creativity within London's architectural landscape. Its unique design challenges conventional ideas of infrastructure and bridges, combining artistic expression with functionality. It reflects the city's commitment to pushing the boundaries of design and engineering, as well as its focus on integrating creativity into everyday urban life. The bridge has also sparked

conversations about how architecture can contribute to a city's identity, encouraging people to view infrastructure not only as practical but also as a source of inspiration and beauty.

Functionality

Despite its unconventional form, the Rolling Bridge serves a very practical purpose. It facilitates pedestrian movement across the Grand Union Canal, providing a vital link between different parts of Paddington Basin. Its kinetic design ensures that boats and vessels can pass through the canal when necessary, as the bridge curls up to create an open waterway. This dual-purpose design enhances its functionality, allowing the bridge to transform between a pedestrian crossing and an open passage for boats, depending on the needs of the area. The hydraulic system powering the bridge ensures smooth and efficient operation, making the structure both functional and visually captivating.

Renovations and Maintenance

Since its completion, the Rolling Bridge has required minimal maintenance, thanks to the robustness of its design and the quality of its materials. The hydraulic system that powers the bridge's folding mechanism has been carefully maintained to ensure reliable performance. However, as with any mechanical structure, occasional checks and updates are necessary to keep the bridge functioning properly. Regular maintenance ensures that the bridge remains in optimal condition, preserving both its functionality and its role as a key architectural feature of Paddington Basin.

Notable Events

The Rolling Bridge has become a popular attraction in London, frequently featured in architectural tours and urban design discussions. It is especially well-known for its rolling motion, which attracts spectators who gather around Paddington Basin to witness the spectacle. The bridge performs its rolling motion at scheduled times each week, drawing crowds of locals and tourists eager to watch this kinetic masterpiece unfold. It has also been featured in various media outlets, further solidifying its reputation as a groundbreaking piece of engineering. The bridge's design has earned numerous accolades, including the British Structural Steel Award in 2005, which recognized its innovation in engineering and materials.

Tourism

The Rolling Bridge has significantly contributed to the popularity of Paddington Basin, drawing tourists and architecture enthusiasts from all over the world. As a distinctive example of contemporary design, it has become a must-see landmark for visitors to London. Tourists come to admire not only the Rolling Bridge but also other architectural gems in the area, such as the nearby Fan Bridge. Paddington Basin, once a neglected industrial site, is now a vibrant and thriving district, with the Rolling Bridge serving as a focal point for both locals and tourists alike. Its presence has revitalized the area, making it a key destination for those interested in cutting-edge design and urban development.

Legacy

The Rolling Bridge has had a lasting impact on both the architectural community and the public. It has redefined what a bridge can be, offering a fresh perspective on how infrastructure can be both functional and artistic. The bridge's combination of practicality and creativity has made it an influential model for future architectural projects. Its success has also demonstrated the importance of integrating innovative design into urban spaces, encouraging cities around the world to explore new ways to combine utility with beauty. The Rolling Bridge has become a celebrated symbol of London's forward-thinking approach to urban design, leaving a lasting legacy in the city's architectural history.

Future Plans and Developments

Looking ahead, the Rolling Bridge is likely to continue serving as a benchmark for innovative urban design. Its presence in Paddington Basin is part of a broader trend in the city towards embracing bold, dynamic architecture. As London continues to evolve, the Rolling Bridge will remain an important part of the city's landscape, symbolizing the intersection of art, engineering, and urban life. There are no specific plans to alter or replace the bridge in the immediate future, as its design continues to meet the needs of both pedestrians and boat traffic. However, as technology advances, there may be opportunities to further enhance the bridge's functionality or sustainability, ensuring that it remains a relevant and admired piece of infrastructure for years to come.

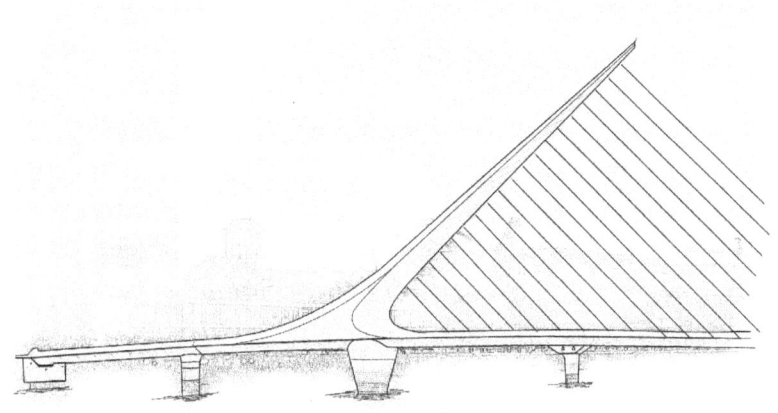

PUENTE DE LA MUJER (BUENOS AIRES, ARGENTINA)

Puente de la Mujer, or "The Bridge of the Woman," stands as one of Buenos Aires' most iconic landmarks, symbolizing the city's contemporary spirit and its ongoing transformation into a global urban hub. Located in the revitalized Puerto Madero district, the bridge serves both as a pedestrian crossing and a striking architectural piece. Designed by renowned Spanish architect Santiago Calatrava, it has garnered widespread acclaim for its unique design and mechanical functionality, making it a must-visit spot for locals and tourists alike.

History

Completed in 2001, Puente de la Mujer is the only work by Santiago Calatrava in Latin America. The bridge was constructed as part of a larger effort to revitalize the Puerto Madero district, which had previously been an underutilized port area. The transformation of Puerto Madero into a bustling area with luxury apartments, restaurants, art galleries, and cultural spaces helped position the bridge as a symbol of the district's rejuvenation. The bridge's construction was funded by local businessman Alberto L. González, who sought to enhance Buenos Aires' international image through a world-class architectural feat. Calatrava's appointment as the designer was a natural choice, given his reputation for creating iconic structures worldwide.

Design

The design of Puente de la Mujer is a striking example of Calatrava's signature style, blending art with engineering. The bridge spans 170 meters across the Río de la Plata dock, connecting the eastern and western sides of Puerto Madero. The most distinctive feature of the bridge is its asymmetrical design, dominated by a towering steel pylon that tilts at a sharp 39-degree angle. This pylon serves both as a structural element and a visual focal point. Supporting the bridge via steel cables, the pylon is meant to represent a man, while the curving walkway symbolizes the graceful movement of a woman's dance. The entire structure evokes the image of a tango dancer, a tribute to Argentina's national dance, adding cultural depth to the design.

Cultural Significance

Puente de la Mujer's name reflects the cultural importance of women in Argentine society. It is part of Puerto Madero's thematic naming convention, where streets and structures are named after prominent women in Argentine history. The bridge, though not named after an individual, pays homage to the many women who have shaped the country's culture and history. Its design and location further underscore Buenos Aires' commitment to blending modernity with cultural respect.

Functionality
Functionally, Puente de la Mujer is a swing bridge that can rotate 90 degrees to allow boats to pass through the dock. This rotation is powered by a sophisticated mechanical system located at the base of the pylon. The process takes only a few minutes, creating an interesting spectacle for onlookers. While the bridge is primarily a pedestrian crossing, its ability to rotate adds a dynamic element, making it both a practical structure and a visual attraction. The bridge connects busy commercial areas with quieter residential zones in Puerto Madero, enhancing connectivity and accessibility within the district.

Renovations and Maintenance
Though Puente de la Mujer is relatively young, it has required periodic maintenance to preserve its mechanical system and aesthetic appeal. The rotation mechanism, which is a crucial part of the bridge's functionality, has undergone several repairs and updates over the years to ensure it remains operational. The bridge's exposure to the elements, including saltwater from the Río de la Plata, necessitates regular maintenance to prevent corrosion and wear. Despite these challenges, the bridge continues to be a reliable and iconic feature of Buenos Aires' urban landscape.

Notable Events
Puente de la Mujer has become an integral part of Buenos Aires' cultural life, hosting various events and celebrations. The bridge has served as a backdrop for tango performances, which tie into the cultural significance of the bridge's design, as well as art installations that take advantage of its striking form. Over the years, the bridge has also hosted music festivals, public gatherings, and even light displays, further cementing its role as a cultural landmark in Buenos Aires. Its unique design and

function have made it a frequent subject of media coverage, enhancing its visibility in the global cultural scene.

Tourism

Since its completion, Puente de la Mujer has become a major tourist attraction in Buenos Aires. Situated in the heart of the redeveloped Puerto Madero district, the bridge draws visitors who come to admire its elegant design and witness its rotation. The bridge's striking appearance and location make it a popular spot for photographers, particularly at sunset or when illuminated at night. Tourists often visit the bridge as part of a walking tour of Puerto Madero, a district known for its blend of modern architecture and historical charm. Whether crossing the bridge, taking photos from the waterfront, or simply admiring it from a nearby café, Puente de la Mujer has become an essential stop for anyone visiting Buenos Aires.

Legacy

Puente de la Mujer has left an indelible mark on the architectural landscape of Buenos Aires. It stands as a symbol of the city's commitment to innovation, blending functional infrastructure with artistic expression. The bridge has helped to transform Puerto Madero from an industrial wasteland into one of the city's most sought-after districts. It is also an emblem of Buenos Aires' cultural identity, connecting the past with the present through its reference to the tango, one of the city's most famous cultural exports. The bridge's legacy lies in its ability to merge utility with beauty, setting a precedent for future urban development in Buenos Aires.

Future Plans and Developments

Looking ahead, there are no major changes planned for Puente de la Mujer itself, but its place within Puerto Madero will continue to evolve. As the district further develops into a high-end cultural and residential area, the bridge is likely to play an even more prominent role in the area's identity. Ongoing maintenance and preservation efforts will ensure that the bridge remains a functional and aesthetically pleasing part of the city's landscape. Additionally, there are plans to enhance the pedestrian experience around the bridge, with new public spaces and facilities expected to be added in the surrounding area. The bridge's continued popularity is expected to drive further investment in Puerto Madero, cementing its status as a key destination for both locals and tourists.

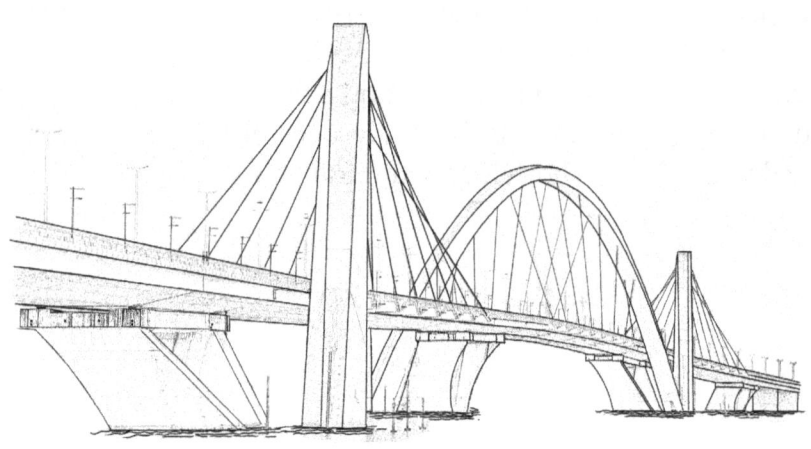

JUSCELINO KUBITSCHEK BRIDGE (BRASÍLIA, BRAZIL)

The Juscelino Kubitschek Bridge (JK Bridge) is a prominent architectural and engineering landmark that has become synonymous with the modern city of Brasília, Brazil. Spanning the waters of Lake Paranoá, the bridge is celebrated for its dynamic design and its symbolic connection to the forward-thinking spirit of Brasília. Named after the visionary president Juscelino Kubitschek, who played a crucial role in the creation of the city, the JK Bridge is a testament to the ambition and progress that defines the capital. Completed in 2002, the bridge stands as a functional piece of infrastructure while also serving as a visual masterpiece that integrates seamlessly with the city's modernist landscape.

History

The Juscelino Kubitschek Bridge was officially inaugurated in December 2002, contributing to Brasília's evolving infrastructure. Named in honor of President Juscelino Kubitschek, who championed the creation of Brasília as a symbol of Brazil's future, the bridge was conceived as part of the city's expansion. Its construction addressed the city's need for a reliable and efficient route between the southern residential areas, such as Lago Sul and Paranoá, and the central districts. Prior to its completion, residents had to navigate lengthy routes around Lake Paranoá, but the bridge significantly shortened travel times, enhancing the city's connectivity.

Design

The JK Bridge's striking design was the work of architect Alexandre Chan and structural engineer Mário Vila Verde. The bridge spans 1,200 meters across Lake Paranoá and is supported by three large, asymmetrical steel arches that rise to 60 meters. These arches, which criss-cross diagonally over the bridge's deck, create a sculptural effect that appears to be in constant motion. This dynamic form is complemented by the pristine white color of the steel, which contrasts beautifully with the natural surroundings of the lake and the city's modernist architecture. The bridge's unusual diagonal arches are a bold departure from traditional bridge designs, creating a visual rhythm that captivates onlookers from every angle.

Cultural Significance

The JK Bridge is not just an engineering feat; it is also a cultural symbol that reflects the ideals and aspirations of Brasília. Named after Juscelino Kubitschek, the bridge embodies his vision of progress and modernization, serving as a tribute to his role in the development of Brasília. Its bold design captures the city's commitment to innovation, while its integration with the natural beauty of Lake Paranoá symbolizes Brasília's balance between modernity and nature. The bridge has become a key element in the city's identity and is featured prominently in promotional materials, photographs, and films, further cementing its place in the cultural landscape of Brazil.

Functionality

Functionally, the JK Bridge serves as a crucial transportation link, connecting Brasília's southern districts with its central areas. Before the bridge was built, residents had to take long detours around the lake, increasing commute times significantly. The JK Bridge now allows for a faster, more efficient route, providing three lanes of traffic in each direction and pedestrian walkways on both sides. These walkways are particularly popular among joggers, cyclists, and tourists, offering stunning panoramic views of the lake and the surrounding city. The bridge not only facilitates everyday travel but also enhances the city's overall transportation infrastructure.

Renovations and Maintenance

Since its inauguration, the JK Bridge has required regular maintenance to ensure its continued safety and functionality. The unusual design, including its steel arches and suspension system, demands specialized care and attention. Routine inspections and maintenance of the steel cables, road surface, and lighting systems are necessary to keep the bridge in optimal condition. Given the heavy traffic it carries, maintaining the bridge's structural integrity is a priority for city officials. Over the years, the bridge has undergone periodic updates, including lighting enhancements and minor repairs, ensuring it remains a safe and vibrant part of Brasília's urban landscape.

Notable Events

The JK Bridge has become a focal point for various

cultural and public events in Brasília. Its striking design and prominence in the city have made it a natural backdrop for celebrations and gatherings. The bridge has been the site of numerous cultural exhibitions, performances, and even political events, reinforcing its role as a public space that reflects Brasília's cultural vibrancy. Photographers and filmmakers also frequently use the bridge as a subject, drawn to its sculptural quality and picturesque setting. Its status as a cultural landmark means it continues to play a central role in the city's artistic and public life.

Tourism
Tourism has become an essential part of the JK Bridge's legacy. As one of Brasília's most recognizable landmarks, the bridge attracts both local and international visitors. Tourists often stop to admire its unique design and capture photographs of the bridge set against the serene waters of Lake Paranoá. The pedestrian walkways provide a perfect vantage point for those wishing to experience the bridge from different perspectives. At night, when the bridge is illuminated, it transforms into a spectacular sight, drawing even more visitors. The JK Bridge is considered one of Brasília's must-see attractions, further solidifying its position as a key part of the city's tourism offerings.

Legacy
The JK Bridge holds an enduring legacy in Brasília and Brazil as a symbol of innovation, progress, and the harmonious relationship between modernity and nature. Its design, which merges architectural elegance with engineering excellence, serves as a model for future infrastructure projects. The bridge's cultural significance is equally important, as it embodies the ideals of Brasília's founder, Juscelino Kubitschek, and continues to represent the aspirations of the city and the nation. The JK Bridge is an enduring symbol of Brasília's commitment to becoming a modern, forward-thinking city that embraces both

beauty and functionality.

Future Plans and Developments

Looking to the future, the JK Bridge is expected to continue playing a central role in Brasília's urban development. Although the bridge's structure is robust, it will require ongoing maintenance and potential upgrades to keep pace with the growing population and increasing traffic in the city. As Brasília continues to evolve, the JK Bridge may also serve as the inspiration for new infrastructure projects that prioritize both innovation and aesthetic appeal. Additionally, the city may explore ways to enhance the bridge's role as a cultural landmark, integrating it further into public events and celebrations that highlight Brasília's vibrant cultural scene.

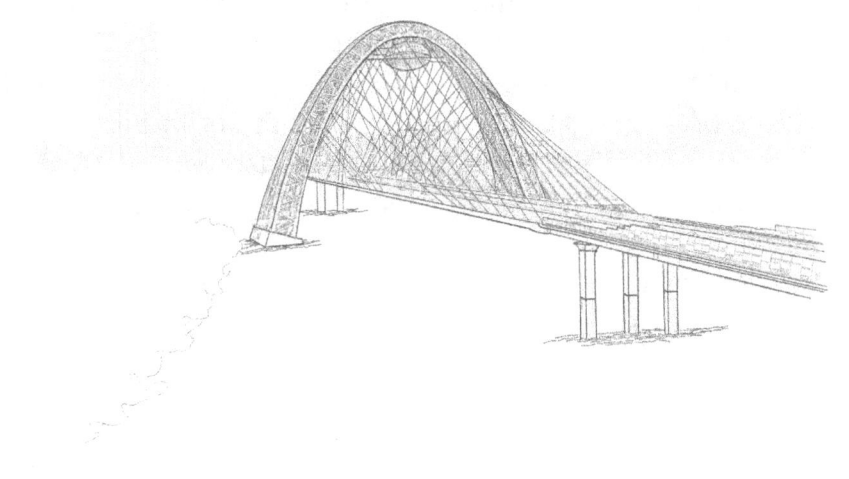

ZHIVOPISNY BRIDGE (MOSCOW, RUSSIA)

The Zhivopisny Bridge, located in Moscow, Russia, is a striking example of modern engineering and architectural design. Completed in 2007, this bridge spans the Moscow River, connecting the districts of Krylatskoye and Strogino. Known for its bold, aesthetic qualities, the Zhivopisny Bridge blends functionality with artistic brilliance, earning its place as one of Moscow's most iconic landmarks. The bridge stands as a symbol of the city's progressive approach to urban infrastructure and its evolving skyline.

History

The Zhivopisny Bridge was conceived as part of a broader initiative to enhance Moscow's infrastructure and accommodate the growing demands of urban traffic. Designed by architect Andrei Volkov, it was the city's answer to both functional transportation needs and the desire to incorporate modern artistic elements into its urban landscape. Construction began in 2003 and was completed in 2007, a relatively quick timeline given the bridge's complex design. Over the years, it has become a key feature in Moscow's urban development, symbolizing the city's embrace of innovation.

Design

The design of the Zhivopisny Bridge is both futuristic and harmonious with its natural surroundings. The defining feature of the bridge is its vibrant red steel arch, which rises 105 meters and stretches 410 meters in length, making it one of the tallest cable-stayed arches in Europe. This dramatic arch is not only a feat of engineering but also gives the bridge a dynamic and graceful appearance. The roadway is suspended from the arch by a series of steel cables, giving the bridge a sleek, modern look. Its curved design follows the natural contours of the river, creating a seamless connection between the urban and natural environments.

At the apex of the arch is a futuristic oval-shaped capsule, which was originally intended to house a restaurant or an observation deck. However, it has remained unused since the bridge's completion. Despite this, the capsule adds an element of intrigue to the bridge's design and enhances its iconic status. The unique combination of bold structural design with functional engineering makes the Zhivopisny Bridge a standout feature in Moscow.

Cultural Significance

The Zhivopisny Bridge has become an integral part of Moscow's identity. It represents the city's shift toward modernity and its willingness to embrace innovative design. The bridge's artistic and architectural qualities have made it a cultural symbol, widely recognized not only in Russia but internationally as well. Its striking red arch has appeared in various media outlets and films, cementing its place as a prominent landmark in Moscow. It is a symbol of the city's ambitions to blend functionality with creativity in the urban landscape.

Functionality
Functionally, the Zhivopisny Bridge serves as a crucial transportation link in Moscow. It connects the Krylatskoye and Strogino districts, two major areas in western Moscow, and is part of the busy Krasnopresnensky Prospekt. The bridge alleviates traffic congestion in this part of the city, providing a smoother and more efficient route across the Moscow River. The bridge accommodates thousands of vehicles daily, significantly improving traffic flow in the area. Although primarily functional, the bridge's unique design elevates it beyond the utilitarian role of a typical transportation structure.

Renovations and Maintenance
Since its completion, the Zhivopisny Bridge has been well-maintained, ensuring its longevity and functionality. Given the complexity of its design and the harsh Moscow climate, regular maintenance and inspection are essential to keep the structure in good condition. There have been no major renovations or structural changes to the bridge, but occasional updates to its lighting and other aesthetic features have enhanced its nighttime appearance. Its ongoing maintenance ensures that it continues to serve both as a vital transportation link and a cultural icon.

Notable Events
Over the years, the Zhivopisny Bridge has been featured in numerous events and celebrations in Moscow. Its stunning design has made it a popular backdrop for festivals, exhibitions,

and media productions. The bridge's prominent location along the Moscow River makes it an ideal site for various public events, including outdoor concerts and city celebrations. Additionally, the bridge has been featured in several documentaries and films, further solidifying its place in popular culture.

Tourism

The Zhivopisny Bridge has become a popular destination for both locals and tourists. Its location along the Moscow River offers visitors spectacular views of the surrounding cityscape and natural beauty. The bridge's design and its elevated position provide an ideal spot for photography, especially at sunrise or sunset, when the lighting accentuates its dramatic arch. The bridge's pedestrian walkways are popular among walkers, cyclists, and photographers, offering stunning views of the river and the surrounding parklands. Additionally, the unused capsule at the top of the bridge has sparked interest among tourists, who are intrigued by its potential and unique design.

Legacy

The Zhivopisny Bridge has left a lasting legacy in Moscow, both as an architectural achievement and as a symbol of the city's modernity. It represents the shift towards innovative, visually striking designs in Russian infrastructure. The bridge's unique combination of aesthetic appeal and functional utility has made it a source of pride for Moscow residents and a symbol of the city's growth as a global metropolis. Over the years, it has become a defining feature of Moscow's skyline, embodying the city's evolution from its Soviet past to its present as a forward-thinking urban center.

Future Plans and Developments

There are currently no major plans for renovations or structural changes to the Zhivopisny Bridge. However, its future role in Moscow's infrastructure remains significant. As the city continues to grow, the bridge will likely play an important part in improving traffic flow and connecting different parts of the city. There has been ongoing discussion about the potential development of the capsule at the top of the bridge, which could one day be repurposed as an observation deck or restaurant. This future development would further enhance the bridge's role as a cultural and tourist landmark, adding another layer to its already impressive legacy.

PONT DE NORMANDIE (FRANCE)

The Pont de Normandie, a monumental cable-stayed bridge spanning the Seine River in northern France, connects the cities of Le Havre and Honfleur. Completed in 1995, it was the longest cable-stayed bridge in the world at the time and became a symbol of modern engineering excellence. The bridge not only serves as an essential transportation link but also stands as a testament to France's dedication to both progress and aesthetic appeal. It is considered one of the most iconic structures in the region and continues to play a significant role in the local economy and tourism.

History

The Pont de Normandie's creation was driven by the need to improve transportation between the cities of Le Havre and Honfleur. Prior to its completion, travelers had to rely on a ferry service that was often delayed due to weather conditions. The decision to build a bridge was made after extensive research and planning, with the goal of providing a more reliable and efficient transportation link. French civil engineer Jean Muller and architect Philippe Maillet were tasked with designing a bridge capable of withstanding the specific challenges of the Seine River, including its wide expanse, strong tidal currents, and the need to accommodate large vessels passing underneath.

Construction of the bridge began in 1988, and despite several challenges, it was completed in 1995. Upon completion, it was the longest cable-stayed bridge in the world, a record it held until it was surpassed by other bridges in later years. The Pont de Normandie quickly became an iconic symbol of modern French engineering.

Design

The design of the Pont de Normandie is both innovative and aesthetically pleasing, combining functionality with beauty. The bridge spans 856 meters (2,808 feet) for its main span, supported by two towering pylons that rise to a height of 214 meters (702 feet). These pylons hold the steel cables that support the bridge's roadbed, creating a graceful yet powerful structure. The overall length of the bridge is 2,143 meters (7,031 feet), making it one of the most impressive structures in the region.

Its sleek, streamlined design, with its soaring towers and elegant cables, creates a striking silhouette against the sky. The use of high-tensile steel cables and reinforced concrete not only ensures the bridge's strength but also contributes to its visual appeal. The curves and lines of the structure evoke a sense of lightness, making it a work of art as well as a functional piece of infrastructure. The bridge was designed to be both practical and symbolic, reflecting France's commitment to progress while honoring its rich engineering heritage.

Cultural Significance

The Pont de Normandie is more than just a functional bridge; it has become an important cultural symbol for the region and for France as a whole. The bridge embodies the country's dedication to innovation, showcasing cutting-edge engineering while maintaining a connection to the past. Its location, spanning the Seine River, links two historic cities and continues the tradition of the river as a vital waterway for trade and cultural exchange.

Functionality

The Pont de Normandie has dramatically improved the flow of traffic between Le Havre and Honfleur, replacing the slow and often unreliable ferry service. The bridge allows for continuous movement of vehicles across the Seine, significantly reducing travel times between the two cities. The efficient transportation link has helped foster economic growth in the region, making it easier for goods and people to move between the cities and beyond.

In addition to its role in improving local transportation, the bridge also supports heavy traffic, as it is a vital component of the transportation network for both local residents and visitors. Its design allows for smooth and safe passage for vehicles while withstanding the forces of nature and heavy use. This functionality has made the Pont de Normandie an essential part of daily life in the region.

Renovations and Maintenance

As a major piece of infrastructure, the Pont de Normandie requires ongoing maintenance to ensure its safety and durability. Over the years, several renovations and improvements have been made to maintain the bridge's structural integrity and to adapt it to changing transportation needs. These upgrades have included strengthening cables and pylons, enhancing safety features, and updating the bridge's lighting systems.

Despite these challenges, the bridge remains in excellent condition and continues to serve its purpose as an essential transportation link. Its maintenance is crucial in preserving its status as a modern engineering marvel while ensuring that it remains a safe and reliable structure for future generations.

Notable Events
Since its completion, the Pont de Normandie has been a key part of regional life and has played host to various notable events. Its inauguration in 1995 marked a milestone in French engineering and transportation history, and over the years, the bridge has been the focal point of numerous celebrations, including national holidays and local festivals.

Tourism
The Pont de Normandie has become a major tourist attraction, drawing visitors from around the world who come to admire its grandeur and beauty. The bridge's unique design and its location along the picturesque Seine River make it a popular stop for tourists exploring the region. Visitors can capture stunning photographs of the bridge, especially at sunrise and sunset, when the changing light creates dramatic effects on the structure.

The bridge also plays a role in promoting tourism in both Le Havre and Honfleur. Its presence has helped highlight the historical and cultural significance of these two cities, drawing travelers who are interested in exploring the rich heritage and natural beauty of the area. The bridge's status as a symbol of modern engineering also attracts those with an interest in architectural and engineering marvels.

Legacy
The Pont de Normandie stands as a lasting symbol of modern

France, embodying the country's commitment to progress and innovation. Its engineering and design are admired worldwide, and its influence can be seen in other bridges built after its completion. The bridge's legacy extends beyond its role as a transportation link, as it has become an emblem of French creativity and technological achievement.

Future Plans and Developments

Looking ahead, there are ongoing discussions about how to maintain and improve the Pont de Normandie to meet the growing demands of modern transportation. Plans for future upgrades may include expanding the bridge's capacity to accommodate increasing traffic volumes and enhancing its environmental sustainability. As the bridge continues to play a central role in the region's economy and culture, it will remain an essential part of France's transportation infrastructure for years to come.

ENGINEERING FEATS

Some bridges are built to challenge the limits of engineering, pushing the boundaries of design and construction techniques. These engineering feats are often solutions to particularly difficult problems—bridges built in places where geography, weather, or technological limitations seemed to make construction impossible. The story of each of these bridges involves overcoming significant obstacles, whether that be difficult terrain, environmental considerations, or the need to develop new construction methods. The bridges in this category continue to inspire the next generation of engineers to dream bigger and bolder.

CHARILAOS TRIKOUPIS RIO-ANTIRRIO BRIDGE (GREECE)

The Charilaos Trikoupis Bridge, or Rio-Antirrio Bridge, is a landmark in Greek engineering, connecting the Peloponnese Peninsula with mainland Greece across the Gulf of Corinth. Officially inaugurated in 2004, it stretches 2.9 kilometers (1.8 miles) and is one of the world's longest cable-stayed bridges. This architectural marvel represents not only a functional triumph but also an iconic symbol of Greece's modern aspirations.

History

The bridge's construction was a response to decades of demand for a reliable and efficient connection between the Peloponnese and mainland Greece. Before its completion, the Gulf of Corinth was crossed solely by ferries, which were vulnerable to weather conditions and inefficiency. The idea for a permanent crossing dates back to the 19th century, championed by then-Prime Minister Charilaos Trikoupis, after whom the bridge is named.

Construction began in the late 1990s, led by a consortium of Greek and international engineers. Despite challenges posed by the gulf's depth, unstable seabed, and seismic activity, the project was completed on time and within budget. The bridge was officially opened on August 7, 2004, just days before the Athens Olympics, serving as a symbol of modern Greece's progress.

Design

The Rio-Antirrio Bridge's design combines beauty and cutting-edge technology. Its most prominent features are its four pylons, standing 220 meters (720 feet) tall, which are among Europe's tallest bridge supports. These pylons anchor a network of cables, creating an elegant silhouette reminiscent of ship sails, reflecting Greece's maritime heritage.

The bridge incorporates advanced engineering to tackle the region's challenges. Its foundation uses caissons—large concrete structures resting on the seabed—designed to stabilize the pylons in shifting soils. The structure is equipped with seismic shock absorbers and base isolators to withstand powerful earthquakes. This blend of innovation and resilience sets a global benchmark for seismic-resistant bridge construction.

Cultural Significance

Beyond its practical use, the Rio-Antirrio Bridge has become a symbol of modern Greece. It embodies the nation's ability to overcome adversity, embrace innovation, and look toward the future. The bridge's opening marked a moment of national pride, celebrating Greek ingenuity and resilience.

Its architectural elegance has cemented its status as a cultural icon. At night, its illuminated pylons and cables cast a striking reflection over the Gulf of Corinth, creating a mesmerizing image that resonates with both locals and tourists. The bridge has become an integral part of Greece's modern identity, blending functionality with aesthetic and symbolic value.

Functionality

The Rio-Antirrio Bridge has revolutionized transportation in the region. Previously reliant on ferries, the crossing now takes mere minutes by car, compared to over an hour by boat. This has improved daily commutes, facilitated trade, and opened up the region to increased tourism.

The bridge is a vital link in the European route E65, connecting the Peloponnese to central Greece and beyond. Its reliable year-round accessibility has enhanced the flow of goods and services, fostering regional economic growth and integration.

Renovations and Maintenance
Maintaining such a significant structure in a seismically active region requires constant vigilance. The bridge undergoes regular inspections and upgrades to ensure its resilience. Advanced monitoring systems track structural integrity, allowing for early detection of potential issues.

In addition to seismic considerations, the bridge is subject to harsh environmental conditions, including strong winds and saltwater exposure. Specialized coatings and materials are used to minimize corrosion, ensuring the bridge remains operational and safe for decades to come.

Notable Events
The Rio-Antirrio Bridge has hosted several notable events since its inauguration. Its opening ceremony in 2004 was a grand affair, attended by national leaders and international dignitaries. The bridge also played a key role in the Athens Olympics, facilitating efficient transport between venues.

In subsequent years, the bridge has become a venue for cultural and sporting events, including marathons and cycling races. These activities underscore its dual role as a functional infrastructure and a gathering place for the community.

Tourism
The Rio-Antirrio Bridge has become a major tourist attraction. Its striking design and scenic surroundings draw visitors from around the world. Photographers and artists are particularly captivated by its graceful curves and nighttime illumination.

Viewing platforms on either side of the bridge offer spectacular perspectives of the structure and the Gulf of Corinth. Guided tours provide insight into its engineering and cultural significance, making it a must-visit destination for tourists exploring Greece.

Legacy

The Rio-Antirrio Bridge stands as a testament to Greece's engineering prowess and cultural resilience. It has redefined the region's infrastructure, providing a reliable connection between the Peloponnese and mainland Greece.

Beyond its functional achievements, the bridge has become a national symbol, representing modernity, progress, and innovation. Its successful construction has inspired future infrastructure projects, showcasing Greece's ability to undertake and complete ambitious ventures.

Future Plans and Developments

As Greece continues to modernize its infrastructure, plans are underway to enhance the bridge's functionality further. Proposals include integrating advanced traffic management systems and exploring renewable energy solutions to reduce its environmental footprint.

Efforts are also being made to develop the surrounding areas, improving access roads and facilities to accommodate increasing tourism. These developments aim to ensure the Rio-Antirrio Bridge remains a cornerstone of Greek infrastructure and a symbol of progress for generations to come.

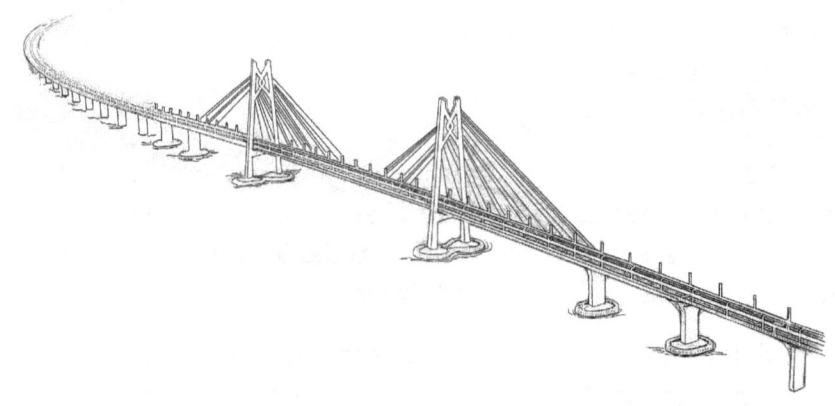

DANYANG–KUNSHAN GRAND BRIDGE (CHINA)

The Danyang–Kunshan Grand Bridge in China is a marvel of modern engineering, holding the distinction of being the longest bridge in the world. Stretching an astounding 164.8 kilometers (102.4 miles), it connects the cities of Danyang and Kunshan in Jiangsu Province. Completed in 2010 and opened in 2011, this bridge is an integral part of China's high-speed rail network, showcasing the country's ambition to create some of the most advanced infrastructure systems globally. Beyond its engineering significance, the bridge serves as a critical link in one of the busiest rail routes in the world: the Beijing–Shanghai High-Speed Railway.

History

The Danyang–Kunshan Grand Bridge was conceived as part of China's efforts to modernize its infrastructure and improve connectivity between major economic regions. Construction began in 2006, employing tens of thousands of workers over nearly four years. The project was part of the broader development of the Beijing–Shanghai High-Speed Railway, a route designed to bolster economic growth by improving transportation efficiency. At a cost of approximately $8.5 billion, the bridge represented one of the largest infrastructure investments in modern history.

The bridge was officially recognized as the longest in the world upon its completion, surpassing the Tianjin Grand Bridge. Its construction marked a turning point in large-scale infrastructure projects, demonstrating China's capability to execute ambitious engineering endeavors on a global scale.

Design

The sheer scale of the Danyang–Kunshan Grand Bridge is its most striking feature. Composed of viaducts, trestle bridges, and overpasses, it traverses various terrains, including rice paddies, swamps, lakes, and urban areas. Its elevated design, primarily supported by trestles, addresses the challenge of unstable soil and soft ground common in the region. The bridge incorporates flexible joints and shock absorbers to mitigate seismic risks, ensuring safety and stability.

The materials used, including steel and reinforced concrete, were chosen for their durability and ability to withstand natural forces like wind and rain. Prefabrication methods were integral to the project, enabling rapid assembly of bridge sections with the help of advanced machinery.

Cultural Significance

The Danyang–Kunshan Grand Bridge stands as a symbol of China's technological and engineering prowess. It reflects the nation's aspirations to lead in infrastructure development while fostering economic growth. The bridge also represents the harmony between human ingenuity and nature, as its design integrates seamlessly with the surrounding landscapes. Its aesthetic curves and arches have become iconic symbols of modern Chinese engineering.

Functionality

Functionally, the bridge is an essential component of the Beijing–Shanghai High-Speed Railway. It facilitates the rapid transit of passengers and goods between two of China's most important cities, reducing travel times and enhancing economic efficiency. Trains travel across the bridge at speeds of up to 350 kilometers per hour (217 miles per hour), making it a critical part of the high-speed rail system.

The bridge also minimizes environmental disruptions, particularly in areas where agriculture is a significant economic activity. Its elevated structure ensures that watercourses and ecosystems remain largely undisturbed.

Renovations and Maintenance

Given its massive scale, the Danyang–Kunshan Grand Bridge requires ongoing maintenance to ensure its structural integrity and safety. Regular inspections are conducted to monitor the condition of the bridge's components, including its concrete foundations, trestles, and seismic features. Advanced monitoring systems are in place to detect any signs of wear or damage, allowing for timely repairs. These efforts are essential to maintaining the bridge's functionality and extending its lifespan.

Notable Events

The bridge's opening in 2011 was celebrated as a milestone

in global engineering. It not only set a new record for length but also underscored China's ability to execute projects of unprecedented scale and complexity. Over the years, the bridge has withstood natural challenges, including heavy rainfall and seismic activity, proving the efficacy of its design and construction.

Tourism
While primarily functional, the Danyang–Kunshan Grand Bridge has become a point of interest for engineering enthusiasts and tourists alike. Its status as the longest bridge in the world attracts visitors eager to witness this modern marvel. The bridge's sweeping views of the Jiangsu countryside and its integration into China's high-speed rail network make it an appealing feature for those traveling the route.

Legacy
The Danyang–Kunshan Grand Bridge is a testament to the possibilities of modern engineering and infrastructure development. It represents a shift toward large-scale, efficient transportation systems designed to meet the demands of rapidly growing economies. As part of the high-speed rail network, the bridge has played a significant role in transforming China's transportation landscape, setting a benchmark for future projects worldwide.

Its completion marked a new era in bridge construction, demonstrating how technological advancements and innovative thinking can create infrastructure that is not only functional but also monumental in scope and ambition.

Future Plans and Developments
As China continues to expand its high-speed rail network, the Danyang–Kunshan Grand Bridge is expected to remain a critical component of the country's transportation infrastructure. Future plans include upgrading monitoring systems and integrating new technologies to enhance the bridge's safety and

efficiency. Additionally, the bridge serves as a model for similar projects in other regions, both within China and internationally.

The Danyang–Kunshan Grand Bridge exemplifies the future of large-scale infrastructure: ambitious, innovative, and transformative. As global demand for efficient transportation systems grows, this engineering marvel will continue to inspire and influence projects around the world.

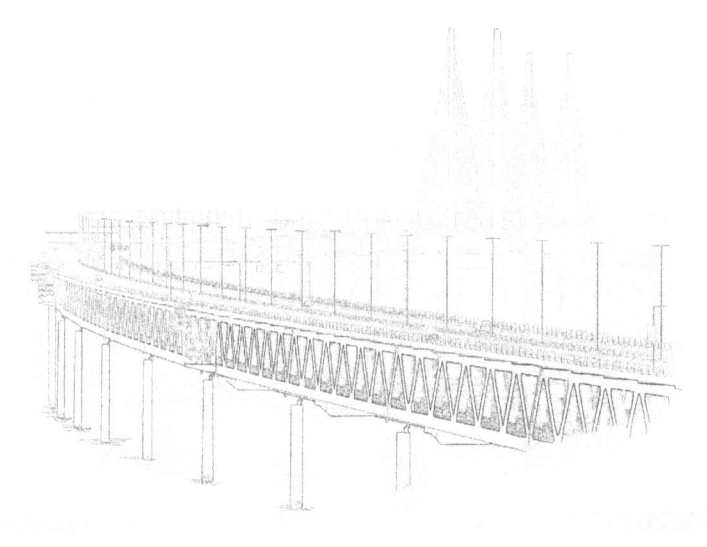

ØRESUND BRIDGE (DENMARK-SWEDEN)

The Øresund Bridge, spanning the Øresund Strait, is an architectural and engineering marvel linking Denmark and Sweden. This combined bridge and tunnel system, operational since 2000, connects Copenhagen and Malmö. Beyond serving as a vital transportation route, it stands as a symbol of international collaboration and innovation. Its design and construction have earned global recognition, making it one of Europe's most iconic landmarks.

History

The concept of the Øresund Bridge emerged in the 1980s as a response to the growing need for better connectivity between Denmark and Sweden. Official plans materialized after the Øresund Agreement was signed in 1991, laying the foundation for enhanced regional integration. Construction began in the mid-1990s, spearheaded by a joint Danish-Swedish venture. The project faced challenges, including adverse weather, deep waters, and environmental concerns, but meticulous planning and advanced engineering overcame these hurdles. Completed in 2000, the bridge fulfilled its mission of fostering cross-border cooperation and economic growth in the Øresund region.

Design
The Øresund Bridge features a unique combination of a cable-stayed bridge and an underwater tunnel. The bridge spans 8 kilometers (5 miles), while the entire structure, including the tunnel and connecting viaducts, measures 16 kilometers (10 miles). Its striking cable-stayed design includes a central span of 490 meters (1,608 feet) and pylons rising 204 meters (669 feet) above the water, ensuring structural stability and visual grandeur.

The Drogden Tunnel, an integral part of the design, spans 4 kilometers (2.5 miles) underwater and connects the bridge to Peberholm, an artificial island created for the project. The tunnel's prefabricated concrete sections were sunk into place, ensuring safe maritime passage and minimizing environmental disruption. This dual-purpose design accommodates a four-lane highway and dual railway tracks, serving cars and high-speed trains alike.

Cultural Significance
The Øresund Bridge symbolizes unity and cooperation between Denmark and Sweden. It facilitates daily commutes, cultural exchanges, and economic ties, effectively bridging physical and societal gaps. By enabling seamless interaction between Copenhagen and Malmö, the bridge fosters a sense of regional

identity while highlighting the interconnectedness of modern Europe.

The bridge has also gained cultural prominence through its role in the Swedish-Danish television series *The Bridge (Bron/Broen)*. The show, which features the bridge as a central setting, has garnered international acclaim, elevating the structure's status as a cultural icon and drawing attention to its symbolic representation of collaboration.

Functionality
The Øresund Bridge serves as a critical transportation link for both passenger and commercial traffic. Part of the E20 highway and a high-speed rail network, the bridge enhances mobility, enabling smooth travel between Denmark and Sweden. The dual infrastructure design ensures that cars and trains can operate simultaneously, streamlining the movement of goods and people.

Additionally, the bridge's proximity to Copenhagen Airport bolsters its functionality, making it a key transit route for international travelers. This connectivity has strengthened trade, tourism, and business relations between the two nations, contributing to regional economic growth.

Renovations and Maintenance
Maintaining a structure as significant as the Øresund Bridge requires ongoing efforts. Regular inspections ensure the bridge's safety and functionality, with attention given to its pylons, cables, and underwater tunnel. Advanced monitoring systems detect wear and tear, enabling timely repairs. Environmental concerns, such as the impact on surrounding marine ecosystems, are also carefully managed, showcasing a commitment to sustainable infrastructure management.
Notable Events

Since its inauguration in 2000, the Øresund Bridge has been the site of several notable events. The opening ceremony was a grand celebration attended by dignitaries, including Sweden's King Carl XVI Gustaf and Denmark's Queen Margrethe II. The bridge also gained international attention during the filming of *The Bridge (Bron/Broen)*, solidifying its cultural legacy.

In times of emergency, such as extreme weather conditions or regional crises, the bridge has demonstrated its resilience and importance as a lifeline between the two countries. Its dual-functionality as a road and rail link has ensured uninterrupted connectivity during critical moments.

Tourism
The Øresund Bridge has become a major tourist attraction, drawing visitors eager to marvel at its design and significance. Tourists can drive across the bridge, take a train ride, or enjoy boat tours around the structure to experience its architectural splendor from different perspectives.
The surrounding areas of Copenhagen and Malmö have also benefited from increased tourism. Both cities offer a wealth of cultural attractions, from museums and historic landmarks to vibrant culinary scenes, creating a dynamic tourism hub in the Øresund region.

Legacy
The Øresund Bridge stands as a testament to human ingenuity and international cooperation. It has redefined the concept of regional connectivity, making the Øresund region one of Europe's most dynamic economic zones. Its construction and subsequent success have inspired other large-scale infrastructure projects worldwide, solidifying its place in the annals of modern engineering.

Moreover, the bridge's role in uniting Denmark and Sweden goes beyond transportation. It has fostered a shared cultural identity, strengthened economic ties, and demonstrated the transformative power of visionary infrastructure projects.

Future Plans and Developments

Looking ahead, plans are underway to enhance the Øresund Bridge's efficiency and sustainability. Upgrades to rail and road systems aim to accommodate increasing traffic while reducing environmental impact. Green energy initiatives, such as integrating renewable power sources and reducing carbon emissions, are being explored to align with global sustainability goals.

Discussions about expanding cross-border collaborations and developing the Øresund region further underscore the bridge's role as a catalyst for growth. As a symbol of progress, the Øresund Bridge continues to inspire future projects, ensuring its relevance for generations to come.

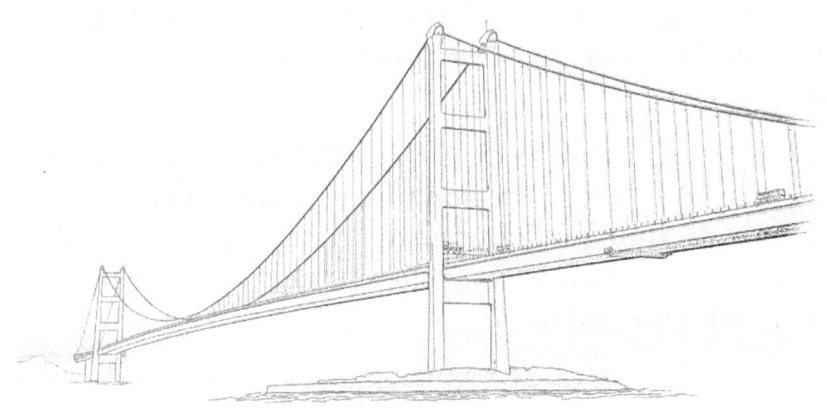

TSING MA BRIDGE (HONG KONG)

Hong Kong's Tsing Ma Bridge is a modern engineering marvel and an iconic landmark. Spanning the Ma Wan Channel, it connects Tsing Yi and Ma Wan Island, forming an integral part of the transportation network linking Hong Kong's Kowloon Peninsula to Lantau Island and the Hong Kong International Airport. Opened in 1997, the bridge represents Hong Kong's commitment to innovation, symbolizing the region's growth as a global hub for commerce and travel.

History

The concept for the Tsing Ma Bridge emerged in the late 1980s as part of Hong Kong's broader infrastructure development plan, necessitated by the construction of the new Hong Kong International Airport on Lantau Island. Prior to the bridge, ferry services and long, winding roads were the primary means of travel between Kowloon and Lantau, which were prone to weather disruptions and inefficiency. The project began in the early 1990s, aiming to create a seamless connection for both passengers and goods.

Named after the Tsing Yi and Ma Wan islands it connects, the Tsing Ma Bridge was completed in time for Hong Kong's 1997 handover to China, symbolizing progress and economic promise under Chinese sovereignty. Its completion marked a turning point in Hong Kong's transportation infrastructure, providing a direct, efficient route that drastically reduced travel times.

Design
The Tsing Ma Bridge stands as a testament to modern engineering. Its cable-stayed suspension design incorporates a central span of 1,377 meters (4,518 feet), making it one of the longest suspension bridges in the world at the time of completion. Towering 206 meters (676 feet) above the Ma Wan Channel, the bridge's twin pylons support a complex network of cables, balancing structural strength with visual elegance.

A distinctive feature of the Tsing Ma Bridge is its dual-purpose deck system. The upper deck accommodates six lanes of vehicular traffic, while the lower deck contains a double-track railway and a protected area for vehicles during typhoons. This innovative design ensures functionality even in extreme weather, a necessity given Hong Kong's susceptibility to typhoons and heavy rain.

Cultural Significance
Beyond its physical function, the Tsing Ma Bridge symbolizes Hong Kong's resilience and growth. Completed during the

politically significant period of the 1997 handover, it became a symbol of the city's ambition and commitment to maintaining its position as a global economic powerhouse.

Its dual-purpose design also highlights Hong Kong's ability to adapt to its unique geographic and environmental challenges, blending functionality with aesthetic appeal. The bridge has become a point of pride for the region, reflecting Hong Kong's engineering expertise and innovative spirit.

Functionality
The Tsing Ma Bridge serves as a vital artery in Hong Kong's transportation network. It links the Kowloon Peninsula to Lantau Island, connecting urban centers with residential areas, the airport, and industrial zones. The upper deck facilitates the movement of goods and passengers, while the lower deck accommodates the Airport Express rail line and the Tung Chung MTR line, ensuring seamless transit.

The bridge's capacity to handle both road and rail traffic has made it a cornerstone of Hong Kong's logistics and transportation infrastructure. It supports thousands of daily commuters and facilitates the efficient movement of cargo to and from the airport, which is among the world's busiest.

Renovations and Maintenance
Given its strategic importance, the Tsing Ma Bridge undergoes regular inspections and maintenance to ensure safety and functionality. The bridge's design incorporates features to withstand high winds and typhoons, but routine structural checks and reinforcements are essential to maintaining its integrity.

Advanced monitoring systems have been installed to detect stress or strain on the structure, enabling early intervention when necessary. The bridge has also undergone updates to its lighting systems, further enhancing its visual appeal, especially at night.

Notable Events
The Tsing Ma Bridge gained global attention upon its completion in 1997, coinciding with the handover of Hong Kong. It has since been featured in various cultural moments, including Jackie Chan's 1997 film Mr. Nice Guy, where it served as the backdrop for a high-octane car chase.

During major typhoons, the bridge's ability to maintain railway operations while closing the upper deck to vehicles has been tested and proven, showcasing its resilience. Its adaptability under extreme weather conditions underscores its importance to Hong Kong's infrastructure.

Tourism
The Tsing Ma Bridge has become a popular tourist attraction, drawing visitors who marvel at its engineering and scenic views. Ma Wan Park offers panoramic vistas of the bridge, set against a backdrop of mountains and the sea. Nighttime illuminations add to its allure, with lights accentuating the structure's elegant cables and massive pylons.

Observation tours and photography opportunities have made the bridge a staple of Hong Kong tourism. Its role as both a functional infrastructure project and an aesthetic landmark highlights its dual significance in the region.

Legacy
The Tsing Ma Bridge has left an indelible mark on Hong Kong's development. It has redefined transportation within the region, reducing travel times and facilitating economic growth. The bridge stands as a testament to Hong Kong's capacity for innovation, symbolizing the city's resilience and adaptability.

Culturally, the bridge represents Hong Kong's transition during a pivotal era in its history. Its inclusion in films and media has further cemented its status as an icon of modern infrastructure, blending utility with artistry.

Future Plans and Developments

As Hong Kong continues to grow, the Tsing Ma Bridge remains a critical component of its infrastructure. Future plans include enhancing the bridge's capacity to accommodate increasing traffic volumes and integrating it with other transportation projects, such as the Hong Kong-Zhuhai-Macau Bridge network.

Technological advancements may also play a role in maintaining the bridge's longevity. The use of artificial intelligence and advanced monitoring systems will likely improve maintenance efficiency and ensure its continued functionality for decades to come.

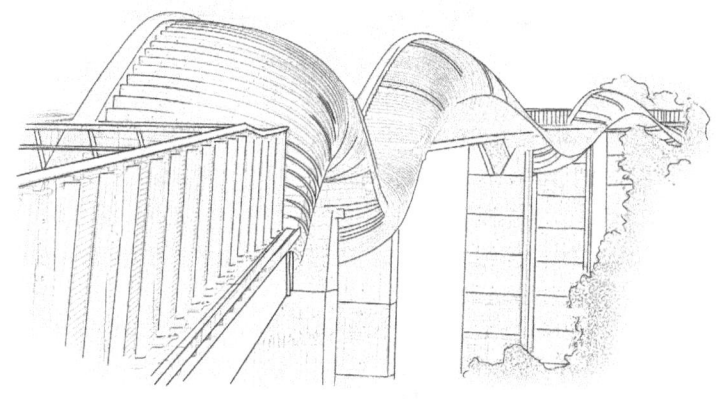

HENDERSON WAVES BRIDGE (SINGAPORE)

The Henderson Waves Bridge is one of Singapore's most iconic architectural marvels, seamlessly blending modern design with its lush natural surroundings. As the highest pedestrian bridge in Singapore, it offers an elevated vantage point for visitors to admire the city's skyline and verdant landscapes. Connecting Mount Faber Park and Telok Blangah Hill Park, the bridge provides more than just a route—it's a destination celebrated for its beauty, functionality, and cultural significance.

History

Completed in 2008, the Henderson Waves Bridge was part of Singapore's broader initiative to enhance green spaces and improve connectivity between its parks. Designed by IJP Corporation, the bridge's purpose extended beyond utility; it was meant to embody Singapore's commitment to integrating nature with urban development. The project's inception was driven by the desire to create a pedestrian route that would link two major green spaces while serving as a symbol of modernity and sustainability. Over time, the bridge has transformed into a prominent landmark and a testament to Singapore's dedication to innovative infrastructure.

Design
The Henderson Waves Bridge is renowned for its wave-like design, which combines aesthetic appeal with structural ingenuity. Its undulating curves are formed by arched steel ribs that rise and fall in a wave pattern, creating a visually striking silhouette. These ribs support the bridge's decking, made from sustainably sourced teak wood, which complements the natural environment. Spanning 274 meters and rising 36 meters above the valley below, the bridge's design ensures both strength and elegance. At night, the structure is illuminated with soft, warm lights that highlight its curvaceous form, further enhancing its allure. The blend of steel and wood not only makes the bridge durable but also harmonizes it with the surrounding greenery, creating a structure that feels like a natural extension of the landscape.

Cultural Significance
The bridge holds a special place in Singapore's cultural and architectural identity. It exemplifies the nation's vision of urban planning, which prioritizes the coexistence of modernity and nature. Frequently featured in the media and celebrated for its innovative design, the Henderson Waves Bridge has become a symbol of Singapore's forward-thinking approach to infrastructure. It's more than just a bridge—it's a representation

of the country's efforts to foster connectivity, sustainability, and aesthetic excellence in its public spaces.

Functionality

As part of the Southern Ridges trail, the Henderson Waves Bridge connects Mount Faber Park and Telok Blangah Hill Park, creating a vital pedestrian link between two of Singapore's major green spaces. It serves as a safe, scenic route for walkers and cyclists, encouraging outdoor activities and promoting green transportation. The bridge also acts as a connector between Singapore's Central Business District and the southern part of the city, offering both residents and tourists a tranquil escape from urban life. Its elevated path minimizes disruption to the natural environment below, ensuring that wildlife and vegetation are preserved.

Renovations and Maintenance

Since its completion, the Henderson Waves Bridge has undergone routine maintenance to ensure its safety and longevity. The teak wood decking is periodically treated to protect it from weathering, while the steel components are inspected for structural integrity. The lighting system, which plays a crucial role in enhancing the bridge's nighttime appeal, is regularly upgraded to use energy-efficient technology. These efforts reflect Singapore's commitment to preserving its landmarks and maintaining high standards for public infrastructure.

Notable Events

The Henderson Waves Bridge has been a backdrop for numerous events and activities over the years. Its picturesque setting has made it a popular venue for outdoor yoga sessions, nature walks, and even art installations. The bridge is also frequently featured in photography contests and promotional campaigns, showcasing its stunning design to a global audience. Additionally, its strategic location within the Southern Ridges trail has made it a key highlight for annual events like the Green

Corridor Run and other eco-themed initiatives.

Tourism

As one of Singapore's most Instagrammable spots, the Henderson Waves Bridge attracts a steady stream of tourists and locals. Visitors are drawn to its unique design, panoramic views, and serene ambiance. The viewing platforms integrated into the bridge's structure provide ideal spots for sightseeing and photography, offering breathtaking vistas of the city skyline, southern coastline, and nearby islands. The bridge's nighttime illumination further enhances its appeal, making it a must-visit destination for evening strolls.

Legacy

The Henderson Waves Bridge has left an indelible mark on Singapore's architectural and cultural landscape. It exemplifies how thoughtful design can enhance the natural environment while serving practical purposes. Recognized as one of the world's most beautiful pedestrian bridges, it continues to inspire architects and engineers worldwide. Its success has also reinforced Singapore's reputation as a global leader in sustainable urban planning, demonstrating the potential of integrating infrastructure with nature.

Future Plans and Developments

Looking ahead, the Henderson Waves Bridge is expected to remain a cornerstone of Singapore's green infrastructure initiatives. Future developments may include enhancements to the Southern Ridges trail to improve accessibility and connectivity, ensuring that the bridge continues to serve as a vital link in the network. Upgrades to the lighting and materials may also be considered to align with evolving sustainability standards. As Singapore expands its efforts to create greener, more inclusive public spaces, the Henderson Waves Bridge will undoubtedly remain a shining example of what's possible when innovation meets environmental stewardship.

ESHIMA OHASHI BRIDGE (JAPAN)

The Eshima Ohashi Bridge in Japan is a marvel of engineering and an iconic piece of modern infrastructure. Renowned for its steep gradient and dramatic appearance, it spans the Nakaumi Sea to connect the cities of Matsue in Shimane Prefecture and Sakaiminato in Tottori Prefecture. Dubbed the "roller coaster bridge," it is both a critical transportation link and a significant tourist attraction, showcasing Japan's commitment to innovative design and functionality.

History

Constructed between 1997 and 2004, the Eshima Ohashi Bridge was built to address the growing demand for an efficient transportation link between Matsue and Sakaiminato. Prior to its completion, travelers relied on ferries or long detours to cross the Nakaumi Sea, which was both inconvenient and time-consuming. The bridge was envisioned to reduce travel time, alleviate congestion, and improve regional economic connectivity. Its construction marked a milestone in infrastructure development for the area, cementing its role as an essential transportation corridor.

Design

The bridge's design is bold and functional, combining aesthetic appeal with practical engineering. Its most distinctive feature is its steep incline, which rises to a height of 44.7 meters at its peak. This dramatic elevation allows large ships to pass beneath without requiring a movable bridge. Spanning 1.7 kilometers, the structure is made of reinforced concrete, ensuring durability and stability against heavy traffic and harsh weather conditions.

The incline, while visually striking, was carefully engineered to balance load capacity and weather resilience. Its curvature facilitates a smooth flow of vehicles, despite its steep gradient. The bridge's design achieves harmony between the natural landscape and the human-made structure, offering a unique visual and functional experience.

Cultural Significance

The Eshima Ohashi Bridge has transcended its role as mere infrastructure to become a cultural landmark. Its steep gradient creates optical illusions that make vehicles appear as though they are driving vertically, earning it global recognition through viral images and videos. These visual effects, combined with its architectural boldness, symbolize Japan's innovative spirit.

The bridge is also a testament to Japan's ability to blend modern engineering with local geography. It reflects the country's commitment to creating infrastructure that is not only functional but also resonates with the natural and cultural environment.

Functionality

Despite its striking appearance, the Eshima Ohashi Bridge is a fully operational transportation link that handles significant daily traffic. It connects two vital economic hubs, facilitating the movement of goods and people. By reducing travel time and offering an alternative to ferries, it has improved regional accessibility and strengthened economic ties between the Shimane and Tottori Prefectures.

The bridge plays a crucial role in local commerce, enabling efficient transportation of goods and services. It exemplifies Japan's dedication to creating infrastructure that supports both local economies and national connectivity.

Renovations and Maintenance

Given its critical role in the transportation network, the Eshima Ohashi Bridge undergoes regular maintenance to ensure its structural integrity and safety. The steep gradient and exposure to maritime weather conditions necessitate ongoing inspections and occasional renovations. These efforts focus on preserving the bridge's durability and functionality while maintaining its iconic design.

The use of reinforced concrete and advanced construction techniques has minimized the need for frequent repairs. However, proactive maintenance remains essential to address wear and tear caused by heavy traffic and natural elements.

Notable Events

The Eshima Ohashi Bridge has been the site of numerous events that highlight its cultural and engineering significance. It frequently features in advertisements, films, and media showcasing Japan's technological achievements. The bridge's unique optical illusion has made it a viral sensation, attracting attention from photographers, filmmakers, and social media users worldwide.

Its inclusion in promotional campaigns and documentaries has solidified its status as a symbol of modern Japan. The bridge has also hosted community events and activities that celebrate its role in connecting local communities.

Tourism
The Eshima Ohashi Bridge is a major tourist attraction, drawing visitors who are eager to experience its dramatic incline firsthand. Tourists often stop to photograph the bridge from specific angles that exaggerate its steepness, creating striking visual effects. These optical illusions have become a focal point for tourism marketing, enticing visitors from around the globe.

In addition to its visual appeal, the bridge offers breathtaking views of the surrounding Nakaumi Sea and nearby landscapes. Visitors often combine a trip to the bridge with explorations of Matsue and Sakaiminato, making it a central feature of regional tourism.

Legacy
The Eshima Ohashi Bridge has become an enduring symbol of Japan's engineering excellence and innovative spirit. Its design and functionality have inspired architects and engineers worldwide, earning it recognition as a masterpiece of modern infrastructure. The bridge's ability to blend practicality with dramatic aesthetics has set a benchmark for future projects.

Beyond its architectural significance, the bridge has contributed to regional development and cultural identity. It stands as a testament to Japan's ability to create infrastructure that enhances both human connectivity and the natural environment.

Future Plans and Developments
As a vital transportation link, the Eshima Ohashi Bridge is

likely to remain a focal point of infrastructure planning in the region. Future developments may include enhancements to its surroundings, such as improved access roads, viewing platforms, and facilities for tourists.

Innovations in materials and engineering may also influence maintenance strategies, ensuring the bridge continues to serve its purpose efficiently. As Japan advances its efforts in sustainable infrastructure, the Eshima Ohashi Bridge may see adaptations that further integrate it with environmental and technological advancements.

CONFEDERATION BRIDGE (CANADA)

The Confederation Bridge, connecting Prince Edward Island to the mainland province of New Brunswick, is a marvel of modern engineering and ingenuity. Spanning 12.9 kilometers (8 miles), it holds the title of the longest bridge over ice-covered waters in the world. Since its completion in 1997, it has transformed the economic, social, and cultural fabric of the region.

History

For decades, Prince Edward Island relied on ferries to traverse the Northumberland Strait. While functional, this mode of transportation was prone to delays and cancellations, particularly during harsh winters when the waters froze. The idea of a fixed crossing emerged as demand grew for a more dependable link. However, debates regarding environmental, financial, and cultural implications delayed its approval until the 1980s. Construction commenced in 1993, culminating in the bridge's grand opening on May 31, 1997, after four years of meticulous work.

Design

The construction of the Confederation Bridge was a monumental feat. Designed to endure extreme weather and powerful ice floes in the Northumberland Strait, it features 44 main piers uniquely shaped to deflect ice and safeguard the structure. These piers were constructed onshore and floated into position, showcasing advanced logistics and engineering. Built primarily of reinforced concrete for its resilience, the bridge rises to a height of 60 meters (197 feet) above water at its peak, allowing large vessels to pass beneath.

The bridge's gently curving design ensures a smooth drive for vehicles and offers stunning views of the surrounding waters. Planners aimed to create a structure that harmonized with the natural beauty of the area, balancing functionality with environmental sensitivity.

Cultural Significance

For Prince Edward Islanders, the Confederation Bridge represents both progress and a redefinition of identity. It has eased access to essential services like healthcare, education, and employment, enhancing the quality of life for residents. However, the transition from the ferry system, which symbolized the island's unique character and traditions, to a fixed crossing was met with mixed emotions. While some mourned the loss of the ferry's cultural legacy, others embraced the bridge as a symbol of connection and progress.

The bridge's name, chosen through a national contest, reflects its role as a unifying structure, both physically and symbolically, linking Prince Edward Island to the mainland and strengthening its ties to the rest of Canada.

Functionality

Driving across the Confederation Bridge offers a unique experience, with breathtaking views of the Northumberland Strait. Clear days provide expansive horizons, while foggy mornings lend the bridge a mystical appearance as it fades into the mist. Beyond its aesthetic appeal, the bridge handles over a million vehicles annually, providing a reliable, year-round connection for residents and businesses.

Renovations and Maintenance

Maintaining the Confederation Bridge is an ongoing, complex process. Equipped with advanced monitoring systems, the bridge undergoes regular inspections to track structural integrity, traffic flow, and weather conditions. Repairs are carried out as needed to ensure safety and durability, preserving the bridge's functionality for future generations.

Notable Events

The Confederation Bridge's opening on May 31, 1997, was a historic moment, marked by celebrations and festivities. It symbolized the culmination of decades of planning, debate, and engineering excellence. Since then, it has been a venue for various events, including marathons and promotional campaigns that highlight its status as an iconic landmark.

Tourism

The Confederation Bridge is not just a transportation link but a major tourist attraction. Visitors are drawn to its engineering marvel, panoramic views, and the experience of crossing one of Canada's most remarkable structures. The bridge also serves as a gateway to Prince Edward Island's natural beauty, cultural sites, and renowned culinary scene, further bolstering the region's tourism industry.

Legacy
The Confederation Bridge stands as a testament to human ingenuity and perseverance. Its construction, though controversial, has reshaped the region's economic and social landscape. It is widely recognized as one of Canada's most significant engineering achievements, symbolizing the power of innovation to overcome barriers and connect communities.

Future Plans and Developments
Looking ahead, there are discussions about further enhancing the bridge's infrastructure to incorporate renewable energy solutions, such as wind or solar power, and improving its environmental sustainability. These plans aim to ensure that the Confederation Bridge remains a vital and progressive part of Canada's transportation network, serving as a beacon of modern engineering for generations to come.

SEVEN MILE BRIDGE (FLORIDA KEYS, USA)

The Seven Mile Bridge is an iconic symbol of the Florida Keys, serving as both a vital transportation link and a breathtaking visual marvel. Stretching across turquoise waters, the bridge connects Knight's Key in Marathon to Little Duck Key and is an integral part of the Overseas Highway. This modern bridge runs parallel to an older structure that was initially part of the Florida East Coast Railway, reflecting a rich history of progress and resilience. The Seven Mile Bridge stands as a testament to human ingenuity, blending engineering brilliance with the natural beauty of its surroundings.

History

The story of the Seven Mile Bridge begins with the vision of industrialist Henry Flagler, who extended the Florida East Coast Railway to Key West in the early 20th century. Known as the "Eighth Wonder of the World," this railway was a monumental achievement, linking the mainland to the Keys for economic and strategic purposes. Constructed between 1909 and 1912, the original bridge was a key component of this ambitious project.

However, the Labor Day Hurricane of 1935 inflicted devastating damage on the railway, leading to its abandonment. In the years that followed, the bridge was repurposed into a highway, allowing for vehicular traffic. By the 1970s, the need for a safer and more efficient structure became apparent, prompting the construction of the modern Seven Mile Bridge, which was completed in 1982.

Design

The current Seven Mile Bridge is a masterpiece of modern engineering, designed to withstand the harsh conditions of a marine environment. Spanning 6.79 miles (approximately 11 kilometers), it is constructed from precast concrete spans supported by robust piers. This design ensures resilience against strong winds, waves, and saltwater corrosion, making the bridge a durable and reliable structure.

The bridge's aesthetic appeal is enhanced by its gentle curve, which provides drivers with panoramic views of the ocean. Elevated to allow boats to pass beneath, the bridge seamlessly integrates functionality with beauty. Its construction required advanced techniques, reflecting the ingenuity and precision that went into its creation.

Cultural Significance

The Seven Mile Bridge has transcended its role as a transportation link to become a cultural and cinematic icon. Its striking design has made it a sought-after location for filmmakers, with movies like True Lies and Licence to Kill showcasing its dramatic expanse. Artists and photographers are similarly drawn to its elegance and the stunning natural backdrop of the Florida Keys.

Moreover, the bridge holds a special place in the hearts of locals and visitors alike. It symbolizes the spirit of adventure, connection, and resilience that defines the region, serving as a reminder of the ingenuity that made its construction possible.

Functionality
As a vital artery of the Overseas Highway, the Seven Mile Bridge facilitates the movement of people, goods, and services throughout the Florida Keys. It provides a reliable connection between the islands and the mainland, significantly enhancing the region's economic and social connectivity.

The bridge also serves as an important corridor for marine traffic. Its height ensures unobstructed passage for boats, making it an essential link for both vehicular and maritime transportation. For residents and visitors alike, the bridge is more than a structure—it is a lifeline that supports daily life and commerce in the Keys.

Renovations and Maintenance
Building and maintaining a bridge in a marine environment presents unique challenges. Engineers had to consider factors like saltwater corrosion, hurricanes, and tidal currents during its construction. Regular inspections and maintenance efforts are critical to preserving the bridge's integrity and ensuring its continued safety and functionality.

The old Seven Mile Bridge, though no longer in use for vehicular traffic, has undergone preservation efforts to maintain sections of it as a pedestrian and cycling pathway. This repurposing highlights the commitment to preserving the bridge's historical and recreational value for future generations.

Notable Events

The Seven Mile Bridge Run, an annual foot race held since 1982, is one of the most celebrated events associated with the bridge. This unique race attracts runners from around the world, offering them the chance to test their endurance while enjoying the breathtaking scenery of the Florida Keys. Limited to 1,500 participants, the event temporarily closes the bridge to vehicles, allowing runners to fully immerse themselves in its majesty.

This event is more than a race—it is a celebration of community and the adventurous spirit that defines the Florida Keys, making it a highlight of the region's calendar.

Tourism

The Seven Mile Bridge is a major draw for tourists, offering one of the most picturesque drives in the world. Visitors flock to the bridge to experience its stunning views of the Atlantic Ocean and Gulf of Mexico. The vibrant shades of blue and green, coupled with the expansive horizon, create a sense of tranquility and awe for those who cross it.

The old bridge, now a pedestrian and cycling pathway, offers an additional attraction. Visitors can walk or bike along its spans, enjoying panoramic views and access to Pigeon Key, a small island with historical significance. Pigeon Key, once a base camp for railway workers, now serves as a museum and educational center, adding depth to the visitor experience.

Legacy

The Seven Mile Bridge is more than an engineering marvel; it is a symbol of connection, progress, and resilience. It has transformed the Florida Keys, making them accessible and fostering economic growth through tourism and commerce. The bridge stands as a testament to human determination and the ability to overcome environmental challenges, bridging not only physical distances but also historical and cultural divides.

For locals and visitors alike, the bridge represents the enduring relationship between people and the environment. Its legacy is one of innovation, beauty, and the unwavering spirit of the Florida Keys.

Future Plans and Developments
Efforts to preserve and enhance the Seven Mile Bridge continue, ensuring its relevance for future generations. Maintenance and preservation projects focus on combating the effects of time and the marine environment, safeguarding the bridge's structural integrity and historical significance.

Plans to further develop the surrounding areas, including improved visitor facilities and interpretive centers, aim to enhance the tourism experience. These initiatives reflect a commitment to honoring the bridge's legacy while adapting to the evolving needs of the region.

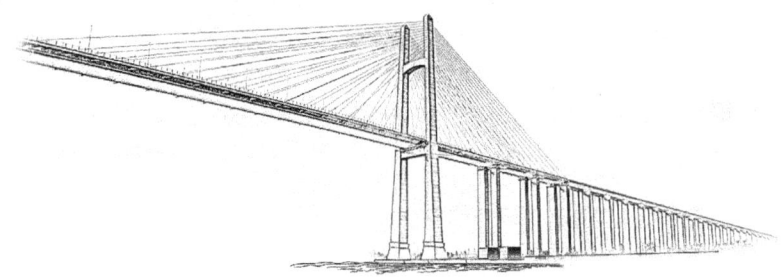

SUEZ CANAL BRIDGE (EGYPT)

The Suez Canal Bridge, also referred to as the Mubarak Peace Bridge or Al-Salam Bridge, is a remarkable infrastructure project connecting the continents of Africa and Asia. Situated near El Qantara in Egypt, this cable-stayed bridge serves as a critical artery for transportation and global trade. Beyond its architectural and logistical significance, the bridge embodies the intersection of modern engineering and international collaboration.

History

Completed in 2001, the Suez Canal Bridge was a joint endeavor between Egypt and Japan, with the Japanese government funding a significant portion of the project. The bridge emerged from Egypt's broader ambition to modernize its infrastructure and enhance connectivity within the Suez Canal region. Before the bridge's construction, movement across the canal relied on ferries and tunnels, which were often inefficient and time-consuming.

The bridge's location is strategic, spanning the Suez Canal—a waterway that has been a focal point of global trade since its completion in 1869. The canal links the Mediterranean Sea to the Red Sea, eliminating the need for ships to navigate the lengthy and dangerous route around Africa's southern tip. The construction of the bridge marked a modern chapter in the canal's long history, enhancing its role as a critical trade corridor.

Design
The Suez Canal Bridge's design is a combination of practicality and elegance. The structure stretches approximately 3.9 kilometers (2.4 miles) and features a vertical clearance of 70 meters (229 feet) to accommodate the massive ships that traverse the canal. Two towering pylons, each 154 meters (505 feet) high, anchor the main span and support the roadway with a fan-shaped arrangement of cables.

The bridge's white pylons and cables contrast strikingly against the canal's blue waters, creating an iconic silhouette. Its sleek aesthetic complements the surrounding arid landscapes, demonstrating how engineering can harmonize with the environment. Moreover, its design incorporates resilience to withstand the harsh climatic conditions of the region, including high temperatures and frequent sandstorms.

Cultural Significance
The Suez Canal Bridge carries profound cultural and geopolitical

significance. As a symbol of Egypt's modernization, it showcases the nation's ability to execute large-scale infrastructure projects. The collaboration between Egypt and Japan in constructing the bridge also highlights the importance of international partnerships in achieving shared development goals.

Furthermore, the bridge underscores the enduring importance of the Suez Canal in global trade and Egypt's central role in facilitating maritime commerce. By linking Africa and Asia, the bridge is a physical manifestation of the region's strategic significance, connecting continents, cultures, and economies.

Functionality
The Suez Canal Bridge plays a crucial role in Egypt's transportation network and the global trade ecosystem. Its integration with Egypt's national road system facilitates the movement of goods and people between the Nile Delta and the Sinai Peninsula, reducing dependence on ferries and tunnels.

For local residents and businesses, the bridge offers faster, more reliable access to markets, resources, and services. It also reduces transportation costs and travel times, enhancing regional economic integration. On a global scale, the bridge supports the uninterrupted flow of goods through the Suez Canal, a waterway that handles approximately 12% of the world's total trade volume.

Renovations and Maintenance
To ensure its longevity and functionality, the Suez Canal Bridge undergoes regular inspections and maintenance. Engineers have implemented advanced monitoring systems to track the bridge's structural integrity, traffic conditions, and environmental impacts. These measures address potential wear and tear caused by high temperatures, sandstorms, and the heavy volume of vehicles using the bridge daily.

Renovations and repairs are carefully planned to minimize disruptions to the critical trade and transportation activities that the bridge supports. These efforts are essential for maintaining its role as a vital link within Egypt and the global economy.

Notable Events

Since its completion, the Suez Canal Bridge has been a site for various significant events. It has hosted ceremonies celebrating milestones in Egypt-Japan relations and served as a backdrop for initiatives promoting the Suez Canal region's development.

In 2015, the bridge was prominently featured during the inauguration of the New Suez Canal expansion project, which aimed to increase the canal's capacity and reinforce its position as a global trade hub. The bridge's visibility during these events underscores its importance as both a functional structure and a symbol of progress.

Tourism

The Suez Canal Bridge has also become an attraction for tourists interested in its engineering marvel and its scenic surroundings. Visitors can appreciate the bridge's impressive scale and design while exploring the historical significance of the Suez Canal itself.

Nearby attractions, including industrial zones, trade hubs, and cultural landmarks, further enhance the area's appeal. For travelers, the bridge is a gateway to exploring the rich history and modern development of the Suez Canal region.

Legacy

The Suez Canal Bridge stands as a testament to human ingenuity and the power of collaboration. It is an enduring symbol of Egypt's ambition to connect its regions and foster economic growth. Its role in facilitating trade and transportation has cemented its place as one of the country's most important infrastructure achievements.

Future Plans and Developments

Looking ahead, the Suez Canal Bridge is poised to remain an integral part of Egypt's development strategy. Plans for the region include further expansion of industrial zones, logistics hubs, and trade facilities to capitalize on the enhanced connectivity the bridge provides.

As Egypt continues to modernize its infrastructure, additional projects may complement the bridge's functionality, ensuring that it remains a cornerstone of the Suez Canal region's growth. These developments aim to attract investment, create job opportunities, and reinforce the area's position as a global trade nexus.

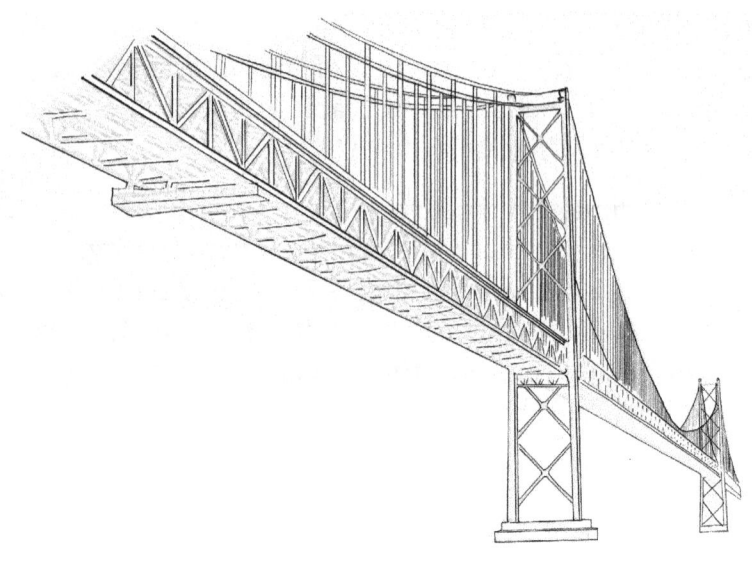

25 APRIL BRIDGE (LISBON, PORTUGAL)

The 25 de Abril Bridge, known locally as Ponte 25 de Abril, is one of Lisbon's most recognizable landmarks. Spanning the Tagus River, this iconic suspension bridge connects the city of Lisbon on the north bank to Almada on the south. Stretching 2,277 meters (7,470 feet), the bridge is not only a vital transportation link but also a symbol of Portugal's modernization and resilience. Its striking red color and elegant design draw comparisons to San Francisco's Golden Gate Bridge while embodying its own unique historical and cultural identity.

History
Construction on the bridge began in 1962 during Portugal's Estado Novo regime, under the leadership of Prime Minister António de Oliveira Salazar. Originally named Ponte Salazar in his honor, the bridge was designed to connect the expanding Lisbon metropolitan area with suburbs south of the Tagus River. The American Bridge Company, which had contributed to iconic structures like the San Francisco-Oakland Bay Bridge, oversaw the construction, bringing cutting-edge suspension bridge technology to Portugal.

The bridge officially opened to traffic on August 6, 1966, marking a milestone in Portuguese engineering and infrastructure development. At its inauguration, it was the longest suspension bridge in Europe. However, its name was changed to Ponte 25 de Abril following the Carnation Revolution of April 25, 1974, which ended Portugal's dictatorship. This renaming symbolized a break from the past, honoring the peaceful uprising that brought democracy to the country.

Design
The 25 de Abril Bridge is a marvel of engineering and aesthetics. Its bold red color, chosen for its visibility and vibrancy, complements Lisbon's cityscape and the natural beauty of the Tagus River. While comparisons to the Golden Gate Bridge are inevitable due to their shared suspension bridge technology, the 25 de Abril Bridge is distinct in its streamlined, lightweight design.

The bridge features a steel framework comprising over 54,000 tons of metal, and its towers rise 190 meters (623 feet) above the water. Its 1,013-meter (3,323-foot) main span remains one of the longest in the world. Originally designed to carry only road traffic, the bridge was adapted in 1999 to include a lower deck for rail traffic, significantly increasing its capacity and functionality.

Cultural Significance
The 25 de Abril Bridge has become an enduring symbol of Lisbon and Portuguese identity. Its image is prominently featured in films, postcards, and advertisements, representing the city's blend of tradition and modernity. The bridge also serves as a backdrop for significant cultural events, including the Lisbon Marathon, where thousands of participants have the rare opportunity to traverse its span on foot.

The bridge is more than just a functional structure—it is a source of pride for Lisbon's residents. Its renaming after the Carnation Revolution further solidified its status as a symbol of freedom and democracy, connecting not just two sides of a river, but also Portugal's historical and cultural narratives.

Functionality
The 25 de Abril Bridge is a critical transportation link, facilitating the movement of commuters, tourists, and freight between Lisbon and Almada. The upper deck accommodates six lanes of road traffic, while the lower deck supports a double-track railway. This dual-purpose design reflects the bridge's adaptability to Lisbon's growing population and increasing transportation needs.

Travelers crossing the bridge are treated to spectacular views of Lisbon, Almada, and the expansive Tagus River. The elevated position offers a unique perspective on the city's landmarks, including the towering Cristo Rei statue and the historic Belem district, making the bridge a highlight of many journeys.

Renovations and Maintenance
Maintaining a structure of this scale requires rigorous inspections and upkeep. Regular maintenance includes repainting sections of the steel framework, replacing worn components, and upgrading systems to ensure safety and efficiency. These efforts are crucial for protecting the bridge from the harsh maritime environment, including saltwater

corrosion and strong winds.

Despite these challenges, the bridge has proven remarkably durable, thanks to the high standards of its original construction. Its longevity and resilience are testaments to the ingenuity and expertise of the engineers who designed it.

Notable Events
The 25 de Abril Bridge has been the site of numerous notable events, reinforcing its role as a cultural and civic hub. The Lisbon Marathon is one such event, drawing thousands of runners who get to experience the rare thrill of crossing the bridge on foot.

Additionally, the bridge has hosted various ceremonies and celebrations, including those marking its anniversaries and the introduction of the railway deck in 1999. These events highlight the bridge's ongoing significance to the community and its adaptability to changing needs over time.

Tourism
The 25 de Abril Bridge is a major tourist attraction, offering visitors an unparalleled experience of Lisbon's skyline and waterways. Many choose to view the bridge from the water on Tagus River cruises, which provide a stunning perspective of its architectural elegance. Others cross it by car or train, enjoying the dramatic views from high above the river.

Its proximity to landmarks such as the Cristo Rei statue and Belem Tower enhances its appeal, making it a must-see for tourists exploring Lisbon. The bridge's blend of functionality and beauty ensures that it leaves a lasting impression on all who encounter it.

Legacy
As a symbol of Lisbon's resilience and innovation, the 25 de Abril Bridge holds a unique place in Portugal's history. Its construction during the Estado Novo regime reflected the nation's aspirations for progress, while its renaming after the

Carnation Revolution symbolized a new era of democracy and freedom.

The bridge also stands as a testament to the power of engineering to connect people and places, transcending physical and cultural divides. It continues to inspire awe and admiration, serving as both a vital piece of infrastructure and a beloved landmark.

Future Plans and Developments
Looking ahead, the 25 de Abril Bridge is expected to remain a cornerstone of Lisbon's transportation network. Plans for future developments may include further modernization of its systems to accommodate increasing traffic and ensure continued safety and efficiency.

Additionally, efforts to enhance its integration with Lisbon's broader transportation infrastructure, including improved connections to public transit, may further solidify its role as a vital link in the city's development. As Lisbon continues to grow, the bridge will undoubtedly play a central role in shaping its future.

CULTURAL AND NATURAL WONDERS

Bridges don't just serve as functional pathways—they are also deeply embedded in the cultural and natural landscapes they occupy. In many instances, bridges are not just physical structures but are intertwined with the identity of the communities they connect. The cultural and natural significance of certain bridges cannot be understated. Additionally, many bridges are set against breathtaking natural backdrops, where the combination of human craftsmanship and the beauty of the natural world creates a powerful visual and emotional experience. These bridges are often seen not just as utilities but as integral parts of the environment they inhabit.

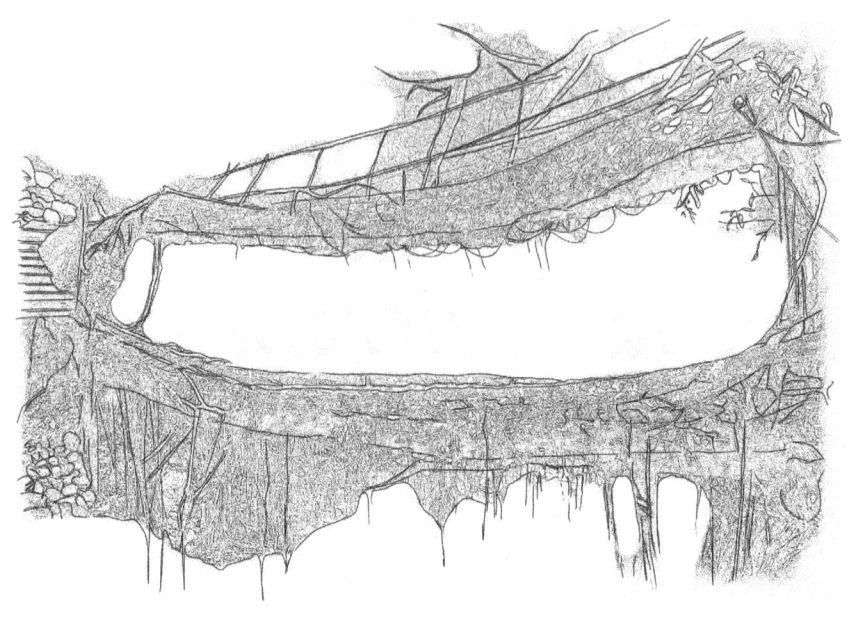

LIVING ROOT BRIDGES (MEGHALAYA, INDIA)

Living Root Bridges in Meghalaya, India, represent a remarkable fusion of human ingenuity and nature. These natural bridges, grown over decades rather than constructed, embody the symbiosis between the Khasi and Jaintia tribes and the rubber fig trees (Ficus elastica). Over centuries, these bridges have helped locals navigate the region's dense rainforests, where rainfall is abundant and rivers flood during the monsoon. More than functional structures, they showcase resilience, sustainability, and cultural continuity in one of the world's wettest places.

History

The creation of the Living Root Bridges dates back centuries, originating with the Khasi and Jaintia tribes, who developed techniques to cultivate the roots of rubber fig trees into bridges. This process was not accidental but rather a cultivated art passed down through generations. The roots of the rubber fig trees, known for their strength and flexibility, naturally grow in the direction of the riverbanks, and the tribes guide these roots across streams and gorges using bamboo scaffolding. The creation of these bridges is slow—taking 15 to 20 years for a bridge to fully mature. The oldest of these bridges are estimated to be over 500 years old, demonstrating the extraordinary durability and timeless quality of this method.

Design

The design of these bridges is a testament to the patience and ingenuity of the local tribes. The aerial roots of the rubber fig trees are initially guided over bamboo scaffolding to form a structure, and over time, the roots grow stronger and fuse into a resilient bridge. The most notable example is the double-decker root bridge in Cherrapunji. This unique design has two levels, with one often used for crossing and the other as a backup during times of heavy rainfall. The bridges are flexible and can adapt to the changing environmental conditions, making them particularly suitable for the steep, hilly terrain and the frequent, heavy rainfall of the region.

Cultural Significance

Living Root Bridges are more than just functional pathways; they hold deep cultural and spiritual significance for the Khasi and Jaintia tribes. For these communities, the bridges are considered living entities that must be cared for, respected, and maintained through communal effort. They symbolize the tribes' deep connection to nature and the environment, as well as their sustainable way of life. Oral traditions and rituals surrounding the cultivation and care of these bridges are integral to the identity of these communities, ensuring the continuation of this knowledge and practice for future generations.

Functionality

The primary function of the Living Root Bridges is to provide safe passage across the rivers and ravines in Meghalaya's rugged landscape. These bridges are especially crucial during the monsoon season when heavy rains cause river levels to rise rapidly, making traditional wooden or metal bridges unviable. Unlike conventional bridges, the Living Root Bridges become stronger with age, as the roots continue to grow and thicken, allowing them to carry heavy loads even during the most challenging weather conditions. This durability ensures that the bridges can withstand the test of time, far outlasting man-made structures that may erode or collapse over the years.

Renovations and Maintenance

The maintenance of Living Root Bridges requires ongoing care and attention from the local communities. As living structures, they are dynamic and require regular nurturing to ensure their continued growth and stability. The process involves guiding the roots, removing any obstructions, and ensuring that the natural materials continue to grow as needed. Since the bridges are essentially living organisms, they can regenerate and adapt over time, making them far less prone to decay than conventional infrastructure. Nonetheless, the communities must remain vigilant to ensure that the bridges remain functional and continue to serve their purpose.

Notable Events

Living Root Bridges have gained international recognition not only for their ecological and engineering ingenuity but also as cultural icons of Meghalaya. The bridges have been featured in various documentaries, publications, and studies on sustainable engineering and environmental preservation. In addition, these bridges have been integral to the lives of the local tribes, who have relied on them for generations. They also draw attention during community events and rituals, where people may cross the bridges as part of cultural celebrations. The bridges' most famous example, the double-decker root bridge in Cherrapunji, has become an enduring symbol of Meghalaya's traditional wisdom and sustainable practices.

Tourism
In recent years, the Living Root Bridges have become a major attraction for eco-tourists, trekkers, and nature enthusiasts. Villages like Nongriat and Mawlynnong, where several of these bridges are located, have become popular destinations for those looking to experience the serene beauty of Meghalaya's rainforests and witness the bridges firsthand. The bridges offer an immersive experience that connects visitors to the natural environment in a way that few modern tourist attractions can. However, increased tourism has brought concerns about the preservation of the bridges, and local communities, along with conservationists, are working to implement sustainable tourism practices. Measures include limiting visitor numbers, creating awareness of the cultural importance of the bridges, and ensuring that tourism benefits local communities without degrading the structures.

Legacy
The Living Root Bridges hold immense cultural and historical value, both for the local tribes and for the world. They serve as living symbols of sustainable engineering, environmental stewardship, and the enduring relationship between humans and nature. These bridges also represent a unique form of indigenous knowledge that is being recognized globally for its innovative approach to infrastructure. As the world faces environmental challenges, the Living Root Bridges offer valuable lessons in working with, rather than against, nature. They

are not just physical structures but also embodiments of the enduring wisdom and resilience of the Khasi and Jaintia tribes.

Future Plans and Developments
The future of the Living Root Bridges is intertwined with the future of the communities that maintain them. As interest in these natural wonders grows, it is crucial that steps are taken to ensure their preservation. Sustainable tourism, community involvement, and ongoing research into the ecological benefits of the Living Root Bridges will play key roles in protecting these bridges for future generations. There is also a growing interest in applying the principles of living infrastructure to other parts of the world, using these ancient techniques to create sustainable solutions to modern environmental challenges. As such, the Living Root Bridges stand not only as a remarkable achievement of the past but also as a beacon of innovation and sustainability for the future.

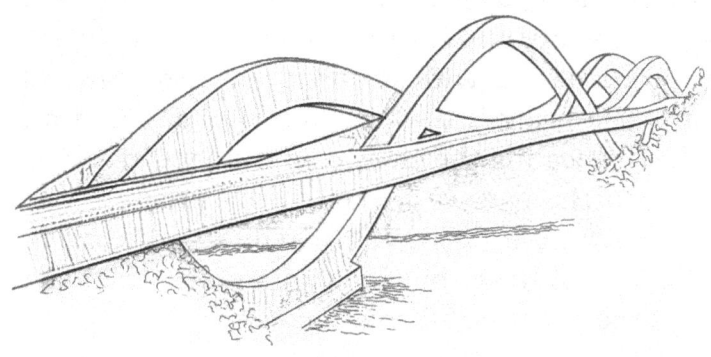

LUCKY KNOT BRIDGE (CHINA)

The Lucky Knot Bridge in Changsha, China, is a striking architectural feat that serves as both a functional transportation link and a symbol of cultural unity. Completed in 2016, it spans the Dragon King Harbour River in the city's New Lake District, connecting various sections of the city while embodying the fusion of tradition and modernity. This pedestrian bridge has become a prominent landmark due to its unique design and cultural resonance, playing an important role in the city's urban regeneration efforts and contributing to its growing reputation as a hub for architectural innovation.

History

The Lucky Knot Bridge is part of a larger urban regeneration project undertaken in Changsha's New Lake District, an area that has witnessed rapid development in recent years. Changsha, known for its history and cultural heritage, sought to integrate modern infrastructure with elements of traditional Chinese symbolism. The bridge's construction was a significant step in this effort, reflecting the city's commitment to maintaining connections to the past while embracing progress. Designed by the Dutch-Chinese firm NEXT Architects, the bridge was officially opened to the public in 2016 and has since become a landmark of the city's transformation.

Design

The Lucky Knot Bridge is renowned for its innovative design, inspired by the traditional Chinese art of knot tying. The knot symbolizes unity, good fortune, and eternity in Chinese culture, and this symbolism is directly reflected in the bridge's intricate, twisting structure. The bridge is composed of three steel ribbons that intertwine and loop, creating a knot-like shape that stretches 185 meters in length and rises 24 meters above the Dragon King Harbour River. This design not only provides a visually striking feature but also integrates seamlessly into the urban landscape, with elevated walkways offering pedestrians panoramic views of the surrounding area.

The bridge's form is supported by an innovative steel structure that ensures stability despite the complex design. The use of steel was key to achieving both strength and flexibility, allowing the bridge to withstand environmental challenges such as wind and rain, while maintaining its graceful, twisted appearance. The design prioritizes human-scale interaction, with spaces designed for leisurely walking and viewing, providing a stark contrast to the speed of the city's traffic.

Cultural Significance

The Lucky Knot Bridge carries profound cultural symbolism. In Chinese culture, knots are not only decorative but also hold deep meaning, representing eternal bonds, prosperity, and a sense of community. By integrating this traditional symbol into a modern architectural project, the bridge links Changsha's rich cultural heritage with its future aspirations. The use of the knot design serves as a reminder of the importance of unity, reinforcing the city's desire to bridge the old and the new in both architecture and spirit. The structure's visual language speaks to the city's ongoing efforts to retain its cultural identity while modernizing to meet the demands of a growing, dynamic metropolis.

Functionality

Beyond its symbolic value, the Lucky Knot Bridge is primarily a pedestrian bridge, designed to enhance connectivity across the Dragon King Harbour River. Its primary function is to link various parks and recreational areas in the New Lake District, providing a scenic and enjoyable route for pedestrians. The bridge also serves a practical purpose by encouraging walking and cycling, reducing the need for cars, and alleviating traffic congestion. This emphasis on non-motorized transportation aligns with global trends in sustainable urban development, aiming to create a more environmentally friendly and pedestrian-friendly city.

Renovations and Maintenance

Since its completion, the Lucky Knot Bridge has undergone minimal renovation, as it was constructed with durable materials designed to withstand the test of time. However, regular maintenance is conducted to ensure the bridge remains in optimal condition, particularly given its exposure to weather elements and its high volume of foot traffic. Maintenance focuses on preserving the structural integrity of the steel ribbons, ensuring that the bridge continues to serve as both a functional piece of infrastructure and an enduring architectural marvel.

Notable Events

The Lucky Knot Bridge has quickly become a cultural landmark, drawing attention from architects, tourists, and media outlets around the world. It has been featured in numerous architectural magazines and exhibitions, celebrated for its innovative design and integration of cultural motifs. The bridge's stunning appearance, especially when illuminated at night, has made it a popular subject for photographers and tourists alike. Its significance as both a transportation link and an artistic icon has made it a key feature in Changsha's ongoing development, symbolizing the city's aspirations for future growth and international recognition.

Tourism

Tourism has flourished around the Lucky Knot Bridge since its completion, with the structure becoming a must-see attraction for visitors to Changsha. The bridge's unique design and aesthetic appeal have made it a favorite for photographers, and it has frequently appeared on social media, attracting global attention. Tourists flock to the area, particularly during the evening when the bridge is illuminated, creating a mesmerizing visual display. The bridge's location in the New Lake District, a rapidly developing area of the city, has further boosted local tourism, with visitors exploring nearby parks, shopping areas, and cultural landmarks.

Legacy

The Lucky Knot Bridge stands as a testament to the blending of art, culture, and infrastructure. It represents the city's desire to create spaces that are not only functional but also visually captivating and culturally resonant. The bridge has significantly enhanced the city's architectural landscape, transforming the surrounding New Lake District into a vibrant public space where people can gather, relax, and interact with their environment. As such, the bridge has become a lasting symbol of Changsha's commitment to creating a city that honors its heritage while embracing modernity.

Future Plans and Developments

As Changsha continues to grow and develop, the Lucky Knot Bridge will remain a central feature in the city's urban planning. Future developments in the New Lake District are likely to build upon the success of the bridge, with further efforts to integrate green spaces, sustainable infrastructure, and cultural landmarks into the city's expanding urban fabric. The bridge's design has set a high standard for future projects, encouraging other cities to consider the role of architecture in shaping public spaces and enhancing the quality of life for residents. The ongoing preservation of the Lucky Knot Bridge, coupled with its integration into future developments, will ensure its continued significance in the urban landscape for years to come.

The Lucky Knot Bridge is more than just a piece of infrastructure; it is a symbol of how cities can embrace both tradition and innovation in creating spaces that serve functional, aesthetic, and cultural purposes. As Changsha evolves, this architectural wonder will remain a beacon of the city's creative spirit and its forward-thinking approach to urban development.

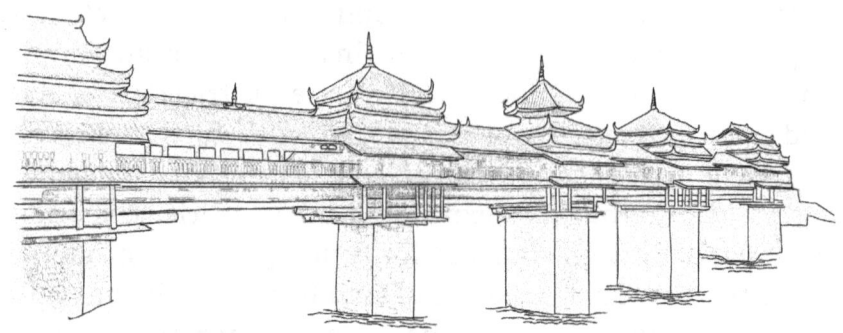

CHENGYANG BRIDGE (CHINA)

The Chengyang Bridge, located in Sanjiang Dong Autonomous County in Guangxi Zhuang Autonomous Region, China, is an awe-inspiring piece of traditional architecture. Known as a "wind and rain bridge," this structure represents the ingenuity and cultural identity of the Dong people. Spanning the Linxi River, it serves as both a functional pathway and a cultural icon that embodies the rich heritage of its creators.

History
Constructed in 1916, the Chengyang Bridge is one of the

most renowned examples of Dong architecture. The Dong people, an ethnic minority with deep-rooted traditions, have a long history of building wooden bridges without nails, using only interlocking wood and mortise-and-tenon joints. This innovative technique has been passed down through generations, ensuring the longevity of their creations. The bridge has withstood over a century of use, making it not just a functional structure but also a historical landmark symbolizing the enduring craftsmanship of its builders.

Design

The Chengyang Bridge is a 64.4-meter-long wooden marvel with a height of 10 meters. Its design features a series of pavilions with sweeping, curved rooftops that resemble the surrounding hills. These pavilions serve as shelters from rain and sun for travelers and enhance the bridge's aesthetic appeal. Every pavilion is adorned with intricate carvings that depict scenes from the daily lives, beliefs, and traditions of the Dong people. The use of locally sourced wood and the absence of nails highlight the sustainability and ingenuity behind its construction.

Cultural Significance

Beyond its architectural brilliance, the Chengyang Bridge holds profound cultural importance for the Dong people. Traditionally, it served as a communal gathering spot for villagers to share stories, celebrate festivals, and hold ceremonies. The bridge is also a symbol of unity, strength, and harmony, representing the collective efforts of the community in its construction and maintenance. Its role in local traditions underscores the Dong people's reverence for their cultural heritage and environment.

Functionality

The Chengyang Bridge is more than a piece of art; it is a vital piece of infrastructure. Connecting two sides of Chengyang Village, it facilitates daily life by allowing villagers to cross the

Linxi River on foot or by bike. Its robust wooden construction enables it to withstand the region's heavy rains and other natural elements, ensuring safe passage even during adverse weather conditions. Its design also makes it a comfortable resting place for travelers, blending practicality with cultural richness.

Renovations and Maintenance
Despite being over a century old, the Chengyang Bridge remains in excellent condition due to consistent maintenance by the local community. Preservation efforts include regular inspections and repairs to its wooden framework to ensure structural integrity. The villagers' commitment to its upkeep reflects their dedication to preserving their heritage. This ongoing maintenance ensures the bridge continues to serve its dual purpose as a functional pathway and a cultural treasure.

Notable Events
The Chengyang Bridge has played host to various significant events in the Dong community's history. It has been the venue for weddings, festivals, and traditional ceremonies, making it a focal point of communal life. Celebrations held on the bridge often feature Dong music and dance, further enriching its cultural significance. Its presence in local folklore and art solidifies its role as a cultural and historical beacon for the region.

Tourism
In recent years, the Chengyang Bridge has become a popular tourist destination, attracting visitors from around the world. Its stunning design and historical importance make it a must-visit site for those exploring traditional Chinese architecture and Dong culture. Tourism has brought economic benefits to the region, with many local families offering homestays, guiding services, and traditional crafts. However, the influx of visitors has also raised concerns about the potential impact on the bridge's preservation. To address this, efforts have been made

to promote sustainable tourism, balancing visitor access with conservation.

Legacy

The Chengyang Bridge stands as a timeless symbol of Dong culture and craftsmanship. It represents the resilience, creativity, and unity of the Dong people, serving as a tangible link to their history and traditions. Its recognition as a cultural heritage site underscores its significance in China's architectural and cultural landscape. For the Dong community, the bridge is not merely a structure but a living testament to their values, artistry, and enduring connection to their environment.

Future Plans and Developments

To ensure the Chengyang Bridge's longevity, local authorities and cultural organizations are exploring initiatives to enhance its preservation. These include advanced methods for monitoring its structural health and implementing stricter guidelines for tourism management. There are also plans to integrate the bridge into broader cultural heritage tours, highlighting its importance alongside other Dong architectural marvels. Such developments aim to protect this iconic structure while sharing its beauty and significance with future generations.

The Chengyang Bridge remains a shining example of traditional craftsmanship and sustainable architecture. As it continues to stand proudly over the Linxi River, it symbolizes the enduring power of cultural heritage and the harmonious relationship between humanity and nature.

DA VINCI-BROEN (NORWAY)

Da Vinci-broen, or the Da Vinci Bridge, stands as a shining example of modern engineering and architectural ingenuity in Norway. Located in Kongsvinger, a town known for its rich history and scenic landscapes, this pedestrian bridge elegantly spans a small river, blending the realms of art, history, and functional design. Named after Leonardo da Vinci, the Renaissance genius renowned for his diverse contributions to science, art, and engineering, the bridge encapsulates the visionary spirit of his work. It serves not only as a testament to his timeless influence but also as a symbol of how historical ideas can merge seamlessly with contemporary innovation.

History

The concept of the Da Vinci Bridge traces its origins to a public art initiative designed to enhance the urban landscape of Kongsvinger. The idea stemmed from an exploration of Leonardo da Vinci's own designs for bridges, specifically his 1502 sketches for a self-supporting, curved bridge. While da Vinci's original designs were never realized in his time, they inspired generations of architects and engineers. His vision of a bridge that would be both beautiful and functional resonated through the centuries, becoming an enduring symbol of human creativity.

In 2001, Norwegian architect Vebjørn Sand brought this historical vision to life. Sand, known for his work in bridging the gap between art and architecture, sought to reinterpret da Vinci's concept with modern materials and construction techniques. The result was a bridge that both honored da Vinci's genius and embraced the spirit of contemporary design. Sand's creation marked a significant moment in the celebration of da Vinci's legacy, showcasing the potential for historical ideas to influence and shape the future.

Design

The Da Vinci Bridge's design is a masterful interpretation of Leonardo da Vinci's original sketches, featuring a sweeping, graceful arch that appears to float above the landscape. This minimalist structure eschews the need for additional supporting elements, such as cables or pillars, by relying on the innovative use of tension and compression. The bridge's central arch, crafted from steel and reinforced concrete, provides the necessary stability while maintaining an elegant, lightweight aesthetic.

The design of the Da Vinci Bridge reflects da Vinci's philosophy of blending form and function. The sleek curves and flowing lines of the bridge not only enhance its visual appeal but also serve a practical purpose, making it both a functional pedestrian route and an artistic landmark. The curvature of the arch is not only a visual delight but also plays a key role in distributing the forces exerted on the bridge, ensuring that it remains sturdy and secure.

The bridge's integration with its natural surroundings is another remarkable aspect of its design. The curved form of the bridge complements the river beneath it, creating a harmonious relationship between human construction and the natural landscape. The sleek, modern materials used in its construction contrast beautifully with the lush greenery of Kongsvinger's countryside, offering a striking visual experience for both locals and visitors.

Cultural Significance
Beyond its engineering and architectural achievements, the Da Vinci Bridge holds profound cultural significance. It serves as a cultural landmark for Kongsvinger, symbolizing the town's connection to the global heritage of art, architecture, and engineering. The bridge stands as a metaphorical link between the past and the future, representing the enduring influence of Leonardo da Vinci and the continuing importance of creativity and innovation in shaping the world.

For the people of Kongsvinger, the bridge is a source of pride. It highlights their town's role in preserving and celebrating global cultural achievements, while also contributing to the local identity. The Da Vinci Bridge has become a symbol of the town's commitment to fostering creativity and progress, making it an integral part of Kongsvinger's cultural fabric.

The bridge also attracts visitors from around the world, many of whom come to admire its innovative design and learn more about da Vinci's legacy. It serves as a focal point for tourism and is frequently featured in architectural exhibitions and publications, further establishing its place as a key cultural landmark.

Functionality
While the Da Vinci Bridge's aesthetic appeal is undeniable, it is equally important as a functional structure. The bridge serves as a vital pedestrian route, connecting two parts of Kongsvinger

that would otherwise be separated by the river. This makes it an essential part of the town's infrastructure, facilitating movement and reducing the reliance on vehicles.

The bridge's design encourages walking and outdoor activity, promoting a healthier and more sustainable lifestyle. By providing a safe and scenic route for pedestrians, the bridge fosters a sense of community and encourages social interaction. Its central location ensures that it is a well-traveled path, contributing to the vitality of the surrounding area.

The elevated design of the bridge offers stunning views of the river valley below, making it a popular spot for recreational activities such as hiking and photography. The bridge not only serves as a pathway but also as a destination in its own right, enhancing the daily lives of residents and visitors alike.

Renovations and Maintenance
Since its completion in 2001, the Da Vinci Bridge has required minimal maintenance, a testament to the durability and longevity of its design and materials. Steel and reinforced concrete were carefully chosen for their strength and ability to withstand the harsh weather conditions typical of Norway. These materials ensure that the bridge remains functional and safe, even in the face of challenging environmental factors.

Periodic inspections are conducted to ensure the bridge's continued safety, and any necessary repairs are carried out promptly. The simplicity of the design, with its few structural components, makes the bridge easier to maintain, reducing the need for extensive upkeep.

Notable Events
The unveiling of the Da Vinci Bridge in 2001 was a highly anticipated event, drawing attention from both local and international audiences. The bridge's innovative design and historical inspiration made it a subject of fascination for architects, engineers, and art enthusiasts. Since its completion, the bridge has been featured in numerous exhibitions and publications, solidifying its reputation as a modern engineering

marvel.

Tourism

The Da Vinci Bridge has become a major tourist attraction, drawing visitors from across Norway and beyond. Its unique design, inspired by the visionary concepts of Leonardo da Vinci, makes it a must-see destination for architecture lovers and casual tourists alike. Visitors are often captivated by the bridge's graceful form and its harmonious integration with the surrounding landscape.

The popularity of the bridge has boosted local tourism, contributing to Kongsvinger's economy and cultural identity. As more people visit the town to see the Da Vinci Bridge, Kongsvinger has gained recognition as a destination for those interested in art, history, and innovative design.

Legacy

The Da Vinci Bridge stands as a lasting tribute to the genius of Leonardo da Vinci and the creative vision of architect Vebjørn Sand. It embodies the timeless relevance of da Vinci's ideas, showing how his work continues to inspire and shape the world today. The bridge serves as a powerful reminder of the fusion between art and engineering, illustrating how both disciplines can work together to create something greater than the sum of its parts.

Future Plans and Developments

Looking ahead, the Da Vinci Bridge is expected to remain a key part of Kongsvinger's infrastructure and cultural landscape. Future plans include enhancing the surrounding area to create a more immersive experience for visitors. Potential developments include adding walking trails, seating areas, and informational displays that will educate the public about the history and significance of the bridge.

NEW HIGH LINE BRIDGE (NEW YORK CITY, USA)

The New High Line Bridge in New York City exemplifies modern engineering combined with urban charm and historical preservation. As part of the High Line Linear Park, this bridge serves as a vital link in the city's transit system, merging sustainability, architectural innovation, and history into a single striking structure. It stands as a testament to how infrastructure can be repurposed and celebrated, transforming industrial relics into vibrant, multi-functional landmarks that resonate with the city's dynamic spirit.

History

The story of the New High Line Bridge begins in the 1930s, during an era when elevated rail lines were introduced to lift freight trains above Manhattan's congested streets. This innovation was intended to improve safety and efficiency, with the original High Line serving as a lifeline for industries in the Meatpacking District, Chelsea, and Hell's Kitchen. However, as the mid-20th century saw a decline in freight rail usage, the line fell into disrepair, and by the 1980s, it was on the verge of demolition.

What followed was a remarkable grassroots movement to save the structure. In the late 1990s, urbanists, architects, and community leaders formed the nonprofit group Friends of the High Line to advocate for its preservation and transformation. By the early 2000s, their efforts bore fruit: the rail line was reimagined as an elevated public park, blending natural landscapes with urban design. The New High Line Bridge, added as a crucial component of this redevelopment, preserved the industrial roots of the original structure while catering to the needs of a modern city.

Design

The design of the New High Line Bridge strikes a balance between functionality and artistry. Its minimalist aesthetic, characterized by clean lines and a harmonious interplay of steel and wood, pays homage to the High Line's industrial past while embracing modern architectural sensibilities. Steel, chosen for its durability and historical relevance, forms the structural backbone of the bridge, while wooden accents soften its appearance, providing warmth and inviting textures that contrast with the surrounding urban environment.

The integration of greenery throughout the bridge design is another defining feature. Planters filled with native vegetation line the bridge's edges, creating a seamless connection to the park's lush landscaping. These elements reflect a commitment to sustainability, ensuring that the bridge complements its environment rather than competing with it. Furthermore, the materials used are eco-friendly and low-maintenance, capable of withstanding the heavy foot traffic and harsh weather conditions that come with being a public landmark in the heart of Manhattan.

Cultural Significance

Beyond its structural and functional aspects, the New High Line Bridge has become a cultural icon in its own right. As part of the larger High Line Park, it embodies New York City's ability to adapt and thrive, turning an industrial relic into a celebrated space for recreation, art, and community engagement. The bridge stands as a symbol of urban renewal, where history and modernity coexist, creating a dynamic environment that resonates with locals and tourists alike.

The bridge's cultural impact extends to its role as a platform for creative expression. It serves as a stage for public art installations, performances, and interactive exhibits, fostering a sense of connection and creativity within the city. By preserving its industrial roots while opening up new possibilities for public engagement, the New High Line Bridge has become a microcosm of New York City's resilience and ingenuity.

Functionality

Functionality is at the core of the New High Line Bridge's design. It was built to accommodate a diverse range of users, from pedestrians to cyclists, while maintaining accessibility for individuals of all abilities. The wide pathways allow for smooth navigation, and carefully planned access points ensure that the bridge connects seamlessly to the surrounding neighborhoods.

Perhaps one of the bridge's most striking features is its elevated position, which offers unparalleled views of the Hudson River, Manhattan's skyline, and the High Line's greenery. This multi-dimensional experience transforms a simple transit route into a scenic journey, encouraging people to slow down and take in their surroundings. Whether used for a leisurely stroll, a brisk bike ride, or simply as a vantage point to admire the city, the bridge enhances the quality of urban life.

Renovations and Maintenance

Constructing the New High Line Bridge was no small feat, requiring a careful balance between preservation and modernization. Engineers faced the challenge of integrating the new structure into the existing High Line while maintaining the integrity of its historic framework. This meticulous process involved using advanced construction techniques to ensure the bridge met contemporary safety standards without compromising its character.

Maintenance remains a key priority to keep the bridge in pristine condition. The use of durable materials, such as weather-resistant steel and treated wood, minimizes wear and tear. Regular inspections and upkeep ensure that the bridge remains safe and visually appealing, preserving its iconic status for future generations. The ongoing care also reflects the city's commitment to sustainable urban infrastructure, ensuring that the bridge remains a model of resilience and longevity.

Notable Events

Since its completion, the New High Line Bridge has hosted a wide array of events that highlight its role as a cultural and community hub. From art installations to live performances, the bridge has become a canvas for creative expression. Its integration with the High Line's broader programming means that visitors can encounter everything from large-scale sculptures to experimental theater performances as they traverse the bridge.

These events have helped solidify the bridge's reputation as more than just a transit link—it is a destination in itself. By providing a platform for artists and performers, the bridge contributes to the cultural fabric of New York City, drawing people together in celebration of creativity and community.

Tourism

As part of the High Line, the New High Line Bridge is a magnet for tourists from around the world. Its unique combination of industrial history, natural beauty, and architectural innovation makes it a must-visit destination for anyone exploring Manhattan. Visitors are drawn to the bridge not only for its functional role but also for its breathtaking views, which offer a fresh perspective on the city's iconic landmarks.

The bridge's location within the High Line Park further enhances its appeal. Tourists can enjoy a leisurely walk through the park, marveling at its carefully curated gardens and art installations, before reaching the bridge and taking in the panoramic views. This blend of experiences makes the New High Line Bridge an essential stop on any itinerary.

Legacy
The New High Line Bridge is more than a piece of infrastructure—it is a symbol of transformation and progress. Its creation has revitalized neighborhoods such as the Meatpacking District, Chelsea, and Hudson Yards, spurring economic growth and fostering a sense of community. By turning a neglected rail line into a celebrated public space, the bridge has reshaped perceptions of what urban infrastructure can achieve.

The bridge's legacy also lies in its ability to inspire similar projects around the world. Cities from Paris to Seoul have looked to the High Line as a model for reimagining unused structures, demonstrating the power of innovative design to breathe new life into urban environments.

Future Plans and Developments
As New York City continues to evolve, the future of the High Line and its components, including the New High Line Bridge, looks bright. Plans are underway to expand the park's reach, integrating it more seamlessly with nearby transit systems and neighborhoods. Proposed developments include new access points, additional green spaces, and enhanced programming to keep the bridge relevant and accessible.

Efforts are also being made to introduce cutting-edge technologies, such as interactive exhibits and sustainable energy solutions, ensuring that the bridge remains a leader in urban innovation. These initiatives reflect the city's commitment to maintaining the bridge as a vital and evolving part of its landscape.

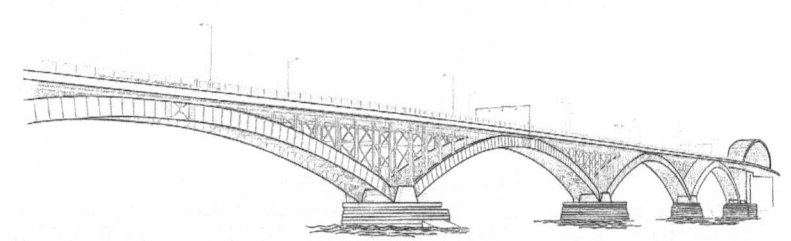

PEACE BRIDGE (BUFFALO, USA/ CANADA)

The Peace Bridge, spanning the Niagara River, connects Buffalo, New York, in the United States with Fort Erie, Ontario, in Canada. This iconic structure symbolizes cross-border unity and facilitates trade, tourism, and cultural exchange between the two nations. Its striking architecture and historical significance make it a landmark of engineering and diplomacy.

History

Completed in 1927, the Peace Bridge was designed by the engineering firm Robinson & Steinman. At its opening, it was celebrated as a marvel of modern engineering and became the first bridge in North America to feature a continuous steel arch. The bridge's construction was overseen by the Buffalo and Fort Erie Public Bridge Authority, an entity established to manage the growing demand for cross-border travel and trade.

The Peace Bridge commemorates over a century of peaceful relations between the United States and Canada, marking a time of flourishing bilateral ties. During World War II, it served as a critical transport route for goods and troops, further solidifying its importance in North American history.

Design
From an engineering perspective, the Peace Bridge showcases a continuous steel arch spanning 1,200 feet across the Niagara River. With a total length of approximately 1,500 feet, the bridge incorporates five spans, including a central arch rising 120 feet above the water. Its double-deck structure was innovative for its time, with the upper deck catering to vehicles and the lower deck to pedestrians.

The use of durable steel ensured the bridge's resilience against Buffalo and Fort Erie's harsh weather conditions, including heavy snow and freezing temperatures. The pedestrian walkway offers breathtaking views of the Niagara River, allowing users to appreciate both the bridge's structural beauty and its surroundings.

Cultural Significance
More than a functional structure, the Peace Bridge stands as a symbol of the friendship between the United States and Canada. Its name embodies the spirit of cooperation and mutual respect shared by the two nations. At the time of its construction, the bridge was envisioned as a physical manifestation of these peaceful relations, reflecting shared values of democracy and

freedom.

Its significance is not merely historical. The Peace Bridge has played a vital role in fostering cultural exchange, trade, and tourism, reinforcing the sense of interconnectedness between the neighboring countries.

Functionality

The Peace Bridge handles millions of vehicles and pedestrians annually, making it one of the busiest border crossings between the United States and Canada. Its role in facilitating economic exchange is particularly evident in industries such as automotive, manufacturing, and agriculture.

For tourists, the bridge serves as an essential connection, linking Buffalo's attractions with Fort Erie's historical sites and natural landscapes. Beyond transport, it has become a gathering point for community events and celebrations, further emphasizing its role as a unifying landmark.

Renovations and Maintenance

To accommodate increasing traffic demands and ensure safety, the Peace Bridge has undergone multiple renovations and upgrades over the decades. These efforts include resurfacing roadways, updating traffic management systems, and expanding border-crossing facilities.

While maintaining its original architectural features, the bridge has been modernized to meet contemporary transportation needs. Its ongoing maintenance ensures its longevity, preserving both its functionality and historical significance.

Notable Events

Throughout its history, the Peace Bridge has hosted numerous important events. During World War II, it was a crucial route for military logistics. In peacetime, it has facilitated economic growth by supporting the flourishing trade between the United States and Canada.

The bridge also serves as a venue for cultural and public events, such as festivals and cross-border celebrations. These gatherings highlight its role in fostering community and promoting cross-border friendship.

Tourism
The Peace Bridge is a popular destination for tourists seeking a unique experience of the U.S.-Canada border. Pedestrians can enjoy panoramic views of the Niagara River from its walkway, while the bridge's illuminated nighttime display adds to its appeal.

Buffalo and Fort Erie benefit significantly from the bridge's tourism, drawing visitors to explore the region's attractions. From Buffalo's vibrant cultural scene to Fort Erie's historical landmarks, the bridge serves as a gateway to discovery on both sides of the border.

Legacy
The Peace Bridge stands as a lasting testament to early 20th-century engineering and the enduring relationship between the United States and Canada. Its graceful steel arch symbolizes resilience and cooperation, qualities that have defined the bridge's history.

Architecturally, the Peace Bridge is a masterpiece of its time, offering a harmonious blend of industrial strength and aesthetic elegance. Its legacy continues to inspire, reminding us of the importance of collaboration and shared values in building lasting connections.

Future Plans and Developments
To meet the demands of modern transportation and enhance its role as a cross-border hub, plans are underway to further upgrade the Peace Bridge. Proposed developments include additional traffic lanes, advanced customs facilities, and improved pedestrian access.

These updates aim to preserve the bridge's historical significance while ensuring it remains a functional and efficient crossing for years to come. As the bridge evolves, it will continue to reflect the spirit of progress and unity that has defined its history.

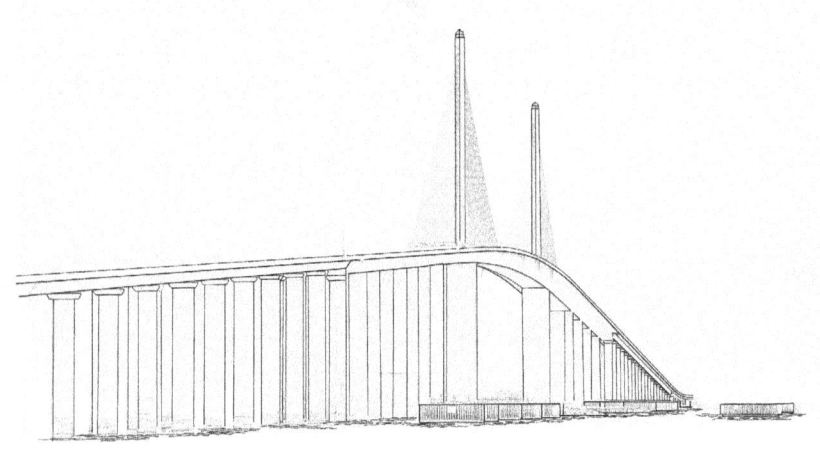

SUNSHINE SKYWAY BRIDGE (FLORIDA, USA)

The Sunshine Skyway Bridge, officially named the Bob Graham Sunshine Skyway Bridge, is a striking cable-stayed bridge that spans Tampa Bay in Florida. Connecting St. Petersburg to Terra Ceia, this 4.14-mile structure is not only a vital transportation link but also an iconic landmark of engineering and design. Its history, cultural significance, and breathtaking aesthetics make it a symbol of resilience and progress for the region.

History

The history of the Sunshine Skyway Bridge is deeply intertwined with both triumph and tragedy. The original bridge, built in 1954, consisted of two cantilever spans designed to connect Tampa and southern Florida. It served as a critical transportation link until May 9, 1980, when a freighter, Summit Venture, collided with the southbound span's support pier during a violent storm. The collision caused a 1,200-foot section to collapse, leading to the tragic deaths of 35 people.

The disaster underscored the need for a safer and more robust structure, paving the way for the construction of the current bridge. Completed in 1987, the modern Sunshine Skyway replaced its predecessor with a design that prioritized safety and resilience. The tragedy of 1980 remains a solemn part of the bridge's history, with memorial markers honoring the lives lost.

Design
The Sunshine Skyway Bridge is a masterpiece of modern engineering and aesthetics. Its cable-stayed design features two pylons that rise 430 feet above the bay, supporting a central span that soars 180 feet high to accommodate large ships passing beneath.

The cables, arranged in a fan-like pattern, are painted a vibrant yellow, symbolizing Florida's sunny skies and adding a cheerful visual touch to the structure. The sleek lines and bright color scheme make the bridge an unmistakable feature of the Tampa Bay skyline. Massive concrete "dolphins" encircle the bridge's piers, designed to deflect ships and absorb potential impacts, ensuring safety and stability.

Cultural Significance
The Sunshine Skyway Bridge has transcended its functional purpose to become a cultural icon. It is celebrated in art, photography, and media, often featured in films and commercials that highlight Florida's Gulf Coast beauty. The bridge's dynamic LED lighting system enhances its cultural relevance, with displays commemorating holidays, events, and causes.

For Floridians, the bridge symbolizes resilience and renewal. It represents the state's ability to rebuild and innovate following the tragedy of 1980. Memorials near the bridge ensure that the lives lost are remembered, fostering a sense of collective reflection and pride.

Functionality
The Sunshine Skyway Bridge is a vital transportation corridor, connecting communities across Tampa Bay and facilitating commerce, tourism, and daily commutes. It carries four lanes of traffic and is designed for a smooth, safe drive, with robust railings and barriers ensuring security for motorists.

The bridge provides an unforgettable experience for those who traverse it. Travelers are treated to panoramic views of Tampa Bay, with its azure waters, distant skylines, and the Gulf of Mexico visible on clear days. Sunrise and sunset crossings are particularly breathtaking, showcasing the bridge's harmonious blend of functionality and beauty.

Renovations and Maintenance
Maintaining the Sunshine Skyway Bridge is an ongoing challenge due to Florida's harsh coastal climate. Salt air, high humidity, and intense sunlight contribute to wear and tear, necessitating regular inspections and repairs. Advanced materials and techniques are employed to address these challenges, ensuring the bridge's structural integrity and longevity.

Efforts include repainting the cables to maintain their iconic yellow color and applying protective coatings to prevent corrosion. These measures reflect the commitment to preserving the bridge as both a functional asset and a visual landmark.

Notable Events
The Sunshine Skyway Bridge has been the site of significant events that have shaped its legacy. The 1980 collapse remains the most notable incident, prompting widespread changes in bridge design and safety standards.

In modern times, the bridge's LED lighting system has been used to mark important occasions, such as national holidays and local celebrations. These displays create a sense of community and add to the bridge's role as a cultural centerpiece.

Tourism

The Sunshine Skyway Bridge is a popular destination for tourists and locals alike. Its scenic location and iconic design attract photographers, artists, and visitors seeking to experience Tampa Bay's natural beauty.

Nearby parks, such as the Sunshine Skyway Fishing Pier State Park, provide opportunities for recreation and stunning views of the bridge. Anglers, nature enthusiasts, and families frequent these areas, drawn by the combination of engineering marvels and vibrant marine life below the bridge.

Legacy

The legacy of the Sunshine Skyway Bridge extends beyond Tampa Bay. It stands as a testament to the resilience of Floridians and the importance of safety and innovation in infrastructure.

The bridge has inspired similar structures worldwide, particularly in its integration of aesthetics and functionality. Engineers and architects study its design as a model for modern bridge construction, emphasizing safety features, visual appeal, and environmental harmony.

Future Plans and Developments

Looking forward, plans for the Sunshine Skyway Bridge focus on enhancing its functionality and preserving its iconic status. Upgrades to the lighting system and traffic management technology aim to improve the bridge's efficiency and safety.

Long-term maintenance projects will address the challenges posed by climate change, such as rising sea levels and increased storm activity. These efforts ensure that the Sunshine Skyway Bridge will continue to serve as a vital link and cultural icon for generations to come.

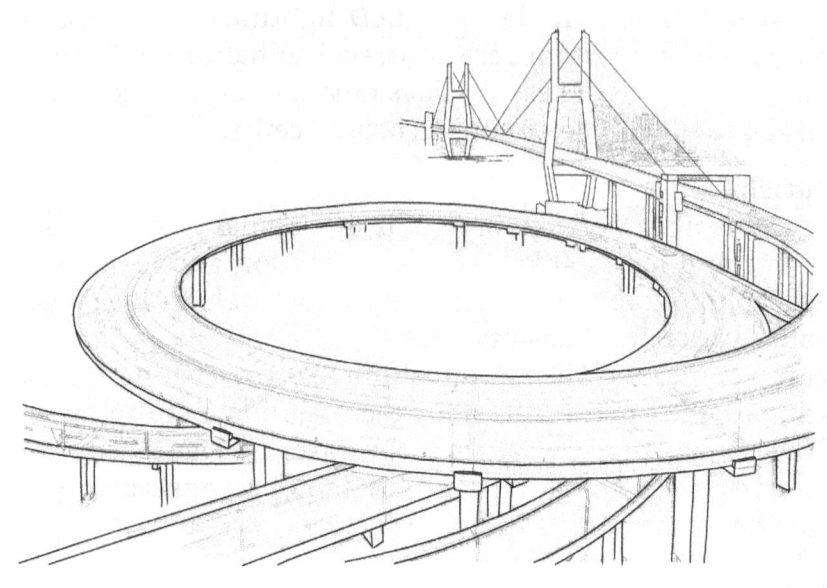

NANPU BRIDGE (SHANGHAI, CHINA)

The Nanpu Bridge in Shanghai, China, stands as an engineering marvel and a symbol of modern urban design, linking the city's bustling districts of Puxi and Pudong over the Huangpu River. Completed in 1991, this bridge is not just a functional infrastructure but also a testament to Shanghai's transformation into one of the most dynamic metropolises in the world. Its construction was pivotal in boosting connectivity and promoting the rapid development of the Pudong area, which was then emerging as a global financial and business center.

History

The construction of the Nanpu Bridge marked a significant milestone in China's engineering history. Completed in 1991, it was the first cable-stayed bridge in the country and among the most ambitious infrastructure projects of its time. Prior to its construction, ferries served as the primary means of crossing the Huangpu River, which had become inadequate due to the city's booming population and economy.

The project brought together Chinese and international expertise, incorporating cutting-edge bridge-building techniques from around the world. Engineers employed advanced materials, such as high-strength steel cables, and utilized precision surveying tools to align the bridge's components perfectly. By facilitating quicker and more reliable transportation across the river, the Nanpu Bridge laid the foundation for Pudong's transformation into a global economic hub.

Design

Spanning a total length of 8,346 meters (27,395 feet), the Nanpu Bridge is among the longest cable-stayed bridges in the world. Its main span, measuring 846 meters (2,776 feet), is supported by 22 pairs of steel cables extending from two towering H-shaped pylons that rise 150 meters (492 feet) above the river. This design ensures the bridge's strength and stability while preserving the waterway for navigation by minimizing the need for piers in the river.

One of the most distinctive features of the bridge is its spiral approach on the Puxi side. Resembling a coiled dragon, this circular ramp efficiently integrates the bridge into Shanghai's dense urban landscape, reducing the gradient for vehicles while minimizing land usage. This innovative and visually striking solution has become an architectural icon frequently photographed for its dramatic curves.

Cultural Significance

The Nanpu Bridge is more than a functional structure—

it symbolizes Shanghai's evolution into a global metropolis. Connecting Puxi, the city's historic heart, with Pudong, its futuristic skyline of skyscrapers, the bridge represents the blend of tradition and modernity that defines Shanghai.

Its construction catalyzed the transformation of Pudong, encouraging investment and development. For residents, the bridge is a source of civic pride, embodying Shanghai's innovative spirit and rapid progress. At night, its illuminated form becomes a glowing ribbon over the river, a beacon of the city's vitality and ambition.

Functionality
As a vital artery in Shanghai's transportation network, the Nanpu Bridge handles an average of 120,000 vehicles daily. It provides a critical connection between Puxi and Pudong, significantly reducing travel times and alleviating congestion. The bridge's strategic importance extends beyond urban mobility, as it supports the flow of goods and services, essential to the city's economy.

For pedestrians, the bridge offers a unique vantage point to view Shanghai's skyline, enhancing its role as both a practical infrastructure and a memorable experience for locals and tourists alike.

Renovations and Maintenance
To maintain its structural integrity and meet the demands of increasing traffic, the Nanpu Bridge has undergone regular maintenance and upgrades. These efforts include reinforcing the steel cables, resurfacing the road deck, and modernizing lighting and monitoring systems. Such measures ensure that the bridge remains a safe, reliable, and visually stunning component of Shanghai's infrastructure.

Notable Events
The Nanpu Bridge has been featured prominently in numerous films, documentaries, and public celebrations, cementing its status as a Shanghai icon. It often serves as the backdrop for major city events, from New Year's Eve fireworks displays to

marathons and cultural festivals. These occasions highlight the bridge's role as both a functional and symbolic centerpiece of the city.

Tourism

The Nanpu Bridge is a popular attraction for visitors to Shanghai, offering unparalleled views of the Huangpu River and the city's skyline. Many tourists make it a point to capture photographs of the bridge from nearby vantage points or while crossing it, particularly at night when its lights create a dazzling display.

For those seeking a closer look, walking or cycling across the bridge offers an unforgettable experience, blending modern engineering with the city's dynamic urban atmosphere.

Legacy

The Nanpu Bridge's legacy extends far beyond its immediate functionality. As the first cable-stayed bridge in China, it set a benchmark for subsequent infrastructure projects nationwide. Its innovative design and urban integration have inspired engineers and architects globally, showcasing how large-scale projects can balance functionality, efficiency, and aesthetics.

Moreover, the bridge's role in transforming Pudong into an economic powerhouse has solidified its place in Shanghai's history, symbolizing the city's rise to global prominence.

Future Plans and Developments

As Shanghai continues to grow, the Nanpu Bridge will likely play an ongoing role in the city's development. Plans for enhanced traffic management systems, additional maintenance, and potential expansions reflect the city's commitment to preserving the bridge's functionality and cultural significance.

Future initiatives may also focus on integrating the bridge more seamlessly with Shanghai's expanding public transport network, ensuring that it remains a vital link in the city's infrastructure for decades to come.

HARBOUR BRIDGE (SYDNEY, AUSTRALIA)

The Sydney Harbour Bridge, one of Australia's most celebrated landmarks, stands as a monumental achievement in engineering and a cultural icon. Situated in Sydney, New South Wales, the bridge spans Sydney Harbour, connecting the central business district (CBD) to the city's northern suburbs. Completed in 1932, this steel arch bridge remains one of the most recognizable structures globally, symbolizing not only Sydney but also the industrious spirit of the people who built it during a challenging economic era. Its sheer size, aesthetic design, and functionality have made it a beloved architectural marvel, drawing millions of visitors annually.

History

The construction of the Sydney Harbour Bridge arose from the necessity of improving transportation across Sydney Harbour. Before its completion, connecting the northern and southern regions of the city required a time-consuming journey by ferry or a 20-kilometer route through five smaller bridges. British engineering firm Dorman Long & Co. Ltd led the project, and Australian engineer John Bradfield, often referred to as the "father" of the Harbour Bridge, oversaw its design.

The bridge was completed in 1932 during the Great Depression, providing employment for over 1,400 workers. Built with 52,800 tons of steel, including 39,000 tons for the arch, and secured by more than six million rivets, the structure was groundbreaking at the time. Upon its completion, it held the title of the world's longest single-span steel arch bridge, stretching 1,149 meters with its arch towering 134 meters above sea level.

Design

The Sydney Harbour Bridge's design is both functional and elegant. Its parabolic steel arch evenly distributes weight, ensuring stability despite its vast scale. The granite pylons on either end, built with locally sourced materials, add symmetry and grandeur to the structure while housing lookout points and exhibitions.

The use of riveted steel, a state-of-the-art technique at the time, contributed to the bridge's remarkable durability. The bridge harmonizes seamlessly with its surroundings, offering stunning views of Sydney Harbour, the Opera House, and the city skyline. Its dual purpose as a functional asset and a visual centerpiece demonstrates the balance of practicality and aesthetic appeal.

Cultural Significance

The Sydney Harbour Bridge holds a special place in Australia's cultural fabric. It has served as a backdrop for countless films, television shows, and travel campaigns, symbolizing Sydney and Australia worldwide. The bridge plays a central role in major celebrations, particularly during New Year's Eve, when it becomes the focal point of internationally broadcast fireworks displays.

Significant events in Australia's history, from royal visits to large-scale public protests, have taken place on or around the bridge, further solidifying its role as a stage for national and civic life.

Functionality

Designed for versatility, the bridge accommodates eight lanes of vehicular traffic, two railway tracks, a pedestrian walkway, and a dedicated bicycle path. This multipurpose usage has ensured the bridge remains vital to Sydney's infrastructure, facilitating tens of thousands of commuters daily.

Over the years, modifications such as expanding traffic lanes and implementing advanced tolling systems have kept the bridge relevant to modern transportation needs. Its wide pathways promote walking and cycling, aligning with Sydney's vision for sustainable urban development.

Renovations and Maintenance

Preserving a structure of this magnitude requires ongoing maintenance. The bridge has undergone multiple repainting efforts to protect it from corrosion, involving the removal and replacement of 485,000 square meters of paint. This meticulous work ensures the longevity of the bridge's structural integrity and its iconic appearance.

Despite its age, the Sydney Harbour Bridge remains robust, a testament to the high-quality materials and craftsmanship of its original construction. Maintenance teams continue to uphold the bridge's safety and functionality while respecting its heritage value.

Notable Events

Throughout its history, the Sydney Harbour Bridge has hosted numerous significant events. Its opening in 1932 was marked by grand celebrations, including a ceremonial ribbon-cutting by then-New South Wales Premier Jack Lang.

The bridge also served as a focal point for the Sydney 2000 Olympic Games, with its arches illuminated to showcase the city's spirit of unity and achievement. In addition, royal visits and large-scale demonstrations have utilized the bridge as a gathering place, emphasizing its importance in both celebratory and political contexts.

Tourism
The Sydney Harbour Bridge is a major draw for visitors worldwide. BridgeClimb, launched in 1998, allows participants to ascend its towering arches, offering breathtaking views of Sydney Harbour and its surroundings. This guided activity has become a bucket-list experience for tourists and locals alike, highlighting the bridge's engineering and scenic significance.

The granite pylons house exhibitions detailing the bridge's history and construction, enriching the experience for history enthusiasts. Additionally, the pedestrian walkway and cycle paths offer free, accessible ways to enjoy the bridge while taking in the beauty of Sydney's landscape.

Legacy
As a symbol of Australian resilience, innovation, and community spirit, the Sydney Harbour Bridge's legacy extends far beyond its physical structure. Built during the Great Depression, it provided employment and hope to thousands of workers. Its completion marked a turning point in Sydney's development, improving connectivity and fostering urban growth.

The bridge's influence on Australian culture and identity remains profound. It represents the ingenuity and determination of its creators and continues to inspire admiration and pride among Australians and international visitors.

Future Plans and Developments
While the Sydney Harbour Bridge has stood the test of time, future plans aim to enhance its functionality and accessibility

further. Proposals include upgrading its pedestrian and cycling infrastructure to accommodate increasing usage, as well as introducing advanced technology to streamline traffic flow.

Efforts to reduce the environmental impact of maintenance activities are also underway, ensuring the bridge remains sustainable in the face of modern challenges. These developments will reinforce the bridge's role as both a vital transportation link and a cultural icon, securing its place in Sydney's evolving urban landscape.

The Sydney Harbour Bridge is more than just an architectural marvel; it is a living, breathing part of Sydney's identity. Whether admired during a fireworks display, traversed on a daily commute, or climbed for its panoramic views, the bridge continues to inspire awe and connection, embodying the very essence of Australia's ingenuity and resilience.

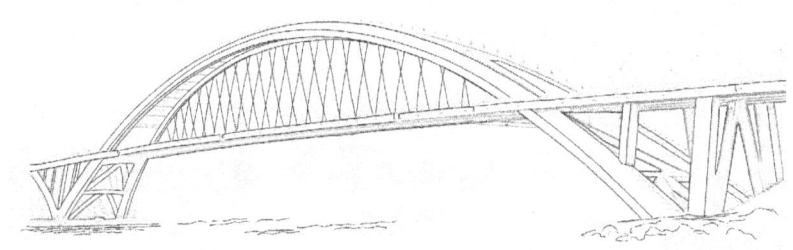

LUPU BRIDGE (SHANGHAI, CHINA)

The Lupu Bridge in Shanghai, China, is a remarkable example of modern engineering and design, symbolizing the city's rapid growth and ambition to establish itself as a global hub. Stretching over the Huangpu River, the bridge connects the districts of Huangpu and Pudong, both critical to Shanghai's economic and cultural vibrancy. Opened in 2003, the bridge earned international acclaim as the world's longest steel arch bridge, boasting a main span of 550 meters. This feat of engineering not only showcases advanced construction techniques but also reinforces Shanghai's reputation as a city of innovation.

History

The Lupu Bridge's name derives from the first syllables of the districts it unites: Luwan (now part of Huangpu) and Pudong. This naming underscores the bridge's role as a vital connection between these bustling areas. Built to address growing urban transportation needs, the bridge was completed during a period of rapid infrastructure development in China. By linking Shanghai's older, historic areas with its modern, rapidly developing zones, the Lupu Bridge became a symbol of the city's transformation. Its construction also marked a significant milestone in China's ability to execute world-class engineering projects, earning widespread admiration and recognition upon its opening.

Design

The Lupu Bridge is defined by its sweeping steel arch, a structural and aesthetic centerpiece that rises 100 meters above the Huangpu River. This arch not only ensures clearance for large ships but also contributes to the bridge's striking visual appeal. Spanning a total length of 3.9 kilometers, including its approaches, the bridge is a dominant feature of Shanghai's skyline. Over 35,000 metric tons of steel were used in its construction, emphasizing its scale and durability.

The incremental launching method, used to assemble and position sections of the arch, required precision and advanced modeling tools. This approach ensured the stability of the massive structure while showcasing the innovative techniques of Chinese engineering. The bridge deck accommodates six lanes of traffic, facilitating efficient movement between districts. A unique feature is the observation deck atop the arch, accessible via a staircase, providing panoramic views of Shanghai's diverse skyline and bustling river below.

Cultural Significance

Beyond its functional role, the Lupu Bridge holds cultural and symbolic value. Its elegant design has made it a popular subject for photographers, artists, and filmmakers, capturing its essence as an icon of modern Shanghai. Its proximity to landmarks like the Mercedes-Benz Arena and the China Art Museum further cements its place in the city's cultural narrative.

The bridge's lighting system transforms it into a radiant spectacle at night. Dynamic lights illuminate its curves, creating a stunning visual display that often changes during festivals and special events. These lights celebrate Shanghai's lively spirit and highlight the bridge's role as a centerpiece of urban pride.

Functionality
The Lupu Bridge is a critical transportation link, easing congestion between Huangpu and Pudong, especially during peak hours. Its six-lane design accommodates a steady flow of vehicles, significantly enhancing connectivity and efficiency in one of China's busiest cities. For pedestrians, the bridge offers an experiential attraction. The observation deck, perched atop the arch, provides unparalleled views of Shanghai, allowing locals and tourists to appreciate the city's architectural evolution and vibrant urban landscape.

Strategically located near the 2010 World Expo site, the bridge played a pivotal role in managing the surge of visitors during the event. Its capacity and design ensured smooth transit, making it a key component of Shanghai's infrastructure for hosting international gatherings.

Renovations and Maintenance
Maintaining a structure of this magnitude is a complex task, particularly given the challenges posed by Shanghai's urban environment. Regular inspections and maintenance ensure the bridge's safety and longevity. Engineers employ advanced monitoring systems to track structural integrity, addressing wear and tear from heavy traffic and environmental factors. Periodic repainting and reinforcement of the steel components protect against corrosion, preserving the bridge's functionality and aesthetic appeal.

Notable Events
The Lupu Bridge has witnessed many significant moments in

Shanghai's history. During the 2010 World Expo, the bridge became a vital artery for transportation, seamlessly connecting key venues and showcasing its importance in urban planning. It has also served as the backdrop for various cultural events, including citywide celebrations and light shows during national holidays. These events highlight the bridge's dual role as both a functional infrastructure piece and a symbol of Shanghai's progress.

Tourism
Tourists are drawn to the Lupu Bridge for its architectural splendor and the unique experience it offers. The observation deck is a major attraction, providing visitors with panoramic views of Shanghai's historic Bund, modern skyscrapers in Pudong, and the winding Huangpu River. This vantage point offers a perspective of Shanghai's harmonious blend of tradition and modernity, making it a favorite among photographers and sightseers.

The bridge's illuminated nighttime display further enhances its appeal. Visitors flock to witness its dynamic lighting, which reflects the festive atmosphere of Shanghai's many cultural and celebratory events.

Legacy
Although relatively young, the Lupu Bridge has firmly established itself as an iconic part of Shanghai's skyline and cultural identity. It represents China's engineering prowess and Shanghai's rapid urban development, symbolizing the city's transformation into a global metropolis. For locals, the bridge is an essential part of daily life, while for visitors, it serves as an introduction to Shanghai's energy, sophistication, and architectural beauty. Its legacy lies not only in its functionality but also in its ability to inspire awe and admiration.

Future Plans and Developments
As Shanghai continues to grow, the Lupu Bridge will likely undergo further upgrades to meet increasing transportation demands. Future plans may include enhancements to its lighting systems, improved pedestrian access, or even

integration with emerging transportation technologies. These developments aim to preserve the bridge's relevance while maintaining its status as a symbol of innovation and progress.

The Lupu Bridge's future reflects Shanghai's broader vision of sustainable urban development, ensuring that it remains a vital and cherished landmark for generations to come.

FUTURE AND EXPERIMENTAL BRIDGES

As we look to the future, the next generation of bridges promises to be even more innovative, incorporating new materials, smarter technologies, and more sustainable practices. Engineers are experimenting with new forms, such as floating bridges, self-healing concrete, and even 3D-printed structures. The future of bridge-building is also being shaped by environmental concerns and the increasing need for sustainability. Bridges of the future will not just be designed to last—they will be designed to minimize environmental impact and adapt to the changing climate. These bridges represent the next frontier in the union of technology, ecology, and human progress, ensuring that future generations will continue to benefit from these vital connections.

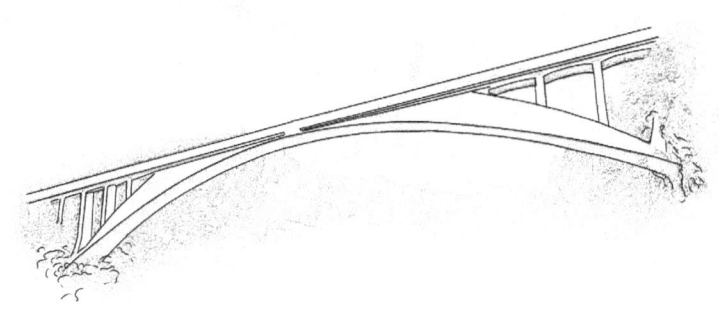

SALGINATOBEL BRIDGE (SWITZERLAND)

The Salginatobel Bridge, located in the picturesque Graubünden region of Switzerland, is a stunning example of engineering ingenuity. Designed by Swiss engineer Robert Maillart and completed in 1930, it spans the Salgina Valley and has become a significant landmark in the history of bridge construction. The bridge's design and materials have inspired generations of engineers and architects, making it a celebrated achievement in civil engineering.

History

The Salginatobel Bridge was completed in 1930 and is one of the finest works by Swiss engineer Robert Maillart. Maillart, known for his innovative approach to concrete construction, was already recognized for his work on other bridges such as the Schwandbach and Tavanasa. The Salginatobel Bridge marked a turning point in bridge design by using reinforced concrete in a way that had never been done before. The success of this bridge cemented Maillart's reputation as a pioneer of modern bridge engineering.

When the bridge was constructed, the use of reinforced concrete was still in its early stages. Maillart took the risk of utilizing this relatively new material to build a bridge that could span the deep and narrow Salgina Valley. The project was not without challenges, particularly due to the difficult access to the site, the terrain, and the harsh alpine weather. However, the bridge's successful completion demonstrated the potential of reinforced concrete for large-scale engineering projects.

Design

The design of the Salginatobel Bridge is characterized by its three-hinged arch structure, which was revolutionary for its time. Unlike traditional stone or metal arches, the reinforced concrete arch provided a much lighter and more efficient solution for spanning the valley. The arch's sleek, graceful lines make the bridge an aesthetic marvel, while its engineering ensures stability and durability in a challenging environment.

The bridge stretches 90 meters across the Salgina Valley, crossing over a river below. The narrow valley, coupled with fluctuating weather conditions, posed significant challenges during the design and construction phases. Maillart's use of the three-hinged arch allowed the structure to adapt to temperature and weather changes, ensuring that the bridge could flex slightly without compromising its integrity. The design maximized the use of materials, ensuring both efficiency and strength.

Cultural Significance

Beyond its technical prowess, the Salginatobel Bridge has become an important cultural and architectural symbol. The bridge's design, combining elegance with functionality, has earned it widespread admiration and recognition. In 1991, the Salginatobel Bridge was named an International Historic Civil Engineering Landmark by the American Society of Civil Engineers, acknowledging its historical significance in the development of modern engineering.

The bridge has been featured in various publications and is often cited as one of the most beautiful examples of early 20th-century concrete arch design. It is celebrated not only for its structural innovation but also for its seamless integration into the natural landscape, which has made it a beloved subject for photographers and artists. The Salginatobel Bridge continues to inspire engineers, architects, and artists alike, representing the harmony between human creativity and the natural environment.

Functionality

While the Salginatobel Bridge is admired for its aesthetics, its primary function is to serve as a means of crossing the Salgina Valley. The bridge has been integral to transportation in the region, enabling movement across a previously impassable area. Maillart's design has proven to be highly durable and functional, enduring through decades of use and the challenges posed by the alpine environment.

The use of reinforced concrete and the three-hinged arch design has ensured that the bridge remains stable despite the fluctuations in temperature and weather that affect the region. The bridge has withstood the tests of time, proving that a well-designed structure can meet the demands of both function and form.

Renovations and Maintenance

Over the years, the Salginatobel Bridge has been maintained and preserved through regular restoration efforts. Its longevity can be attributed not only to its innovative design but also to the care it has received throughout its lifetime. Despite being nearly a century old, the bridge remains in excellent condition, thanks to the ongoing efforts to preserve its structural integrity. These maintenance efforts ensure that the Salginatobel Bridge continues to stand strong, serving as a functional and aesthetic asset to the region.

Notable Events

The Salginatobel Bridge has witnessed several notable events throughout its history. In 1991, it was officially recognized as an International Historic Civil Engineering Landmark by the American Society of Civil Engineers. This prestigious recognition further cemented its place in engineering history and highlighted its influence on modern bridge construction. The bridge has also been featured in numerous engineering and architecture publications, gaining international attention for its unique design.

While the bridge is not commonly used for major events, its status as a landmark means it is frequently visited by tourists, architects, and engineers from around the world. The surrounding area of Graubünden, known for its beautiful landscapes, has made the bridge a key part of the region's cultural heritage.

Tourism

The Salginatobel Bridge is a popular tourist attraction, drawing visitors from around the world to witness its architectural beauty and learn about its historical significance. The bridge's location in the scenic Graubünden region, with its lush valleys and towering mountains, makes it a highlight for travelers to the area. Visitors often come to photograph the bridge, marvel at its design, and enjoy the picturesque views of the surrounding landscape.

The bridge's elegance and harmony with the natural environment have made it a subject of admiration for photographers, filmmakers, and artists. Its combination of engineering brilliance and aesthetic grace continues to captivate visitors, ensuring its place as a cultural icon.

Legacy
The legacy of the Salginatobel Bridge extends beyond its function as a transportation route. As one of the most iconic examples of early 20th-century concrete arch design, the bridge has inspired countless engineers and architects. It serves as a model of how modern materials and design techniques can be used to create structures that are both functional and beautiful. The Salginatobel Bridge's enduring beauty and technical achievements have ensured that it remains an important landmark in the history of civil engineering.

The bridge has also played a significant role in raising awareness of the possibilities of reinforced concrete. Its success demonstrated the material's strength and versatility, leading to its widespread use in bridge construction around the world.

Future Plans and Developments
The Salginatobel Bridge is expected to remain a vital part of the region's infrastructure for the foreseeable future. Continued maintenance and preservation efforts will ensure its structural integrity, allowing it to stand as a symbol of engineering excellence for generations to come. There are no major plans for development or reconstruction at this time, as the bridge continues to serve its original function effectively.

However, with the increasing popularity of the bridge as a tourist destination, efforts to manage visitor traffic and ensure the preservation of the site will likely become a focus for local authorities. The Salginatobel Bridge's combination of engineering innovation and natural beauty makes it a timeless structure, one that will continue to inspire and captivate for many years to come.

GATESHEAD MILLENNIUM BRIDGE (UK)

The Gateshead Millennium Bridge, also known as the "Winking Eye Bridge," is a striking feat of modern engineering that spans the River Tyne in the United Kingdom. Situated between the city of Newcastle and Gateshead, this pedestrian and cyclist bridge is celebrated for its innovative design and its contribution to the region's urban renewal.

History

The idea of creating the Gateshead Millennium Bridge was born out of the UK's national Millennium celebrations, which inspired numerous projects aimed at revitalizing the country's public spaces. The bridge was conceived as part of a broader urban regeneration project along the River Tyne, intended to foster connectivity between the cities of Newcastle and Gateshead while promoting pedestrian access. The project was realized with the collaborative efforts of the Gateshead Council and various local stakeholders. The bridge's design was selected through an international competition held in 1996, where London-based architects Wilkinson Eyre emerged as the winners. The bridge was officially opened to the public in 2001, making it one of the standout landmarks of the early 21st century.

The bridge quickly became an icon of modern engineering, and its construction marked the start of a series of rejuvenation efforts along the River Tyne. The nearby Sage Gateshead, BALTIC Centre for Contemporary Art, and the iconic Tyne Bridge all contributed to a cultural shift in the region, strengthening the relationship between the people of Newcastle and Gateshead.

Design
The Gateshead Millennium Bridge stands out for its innovative design and its ability to blend form and function in a way few structures do. The bridge's most remarkable feature is its tilting mechanism, which allows the bridge deck to rotate, enabling ships to pass underneath. It is the world's first tilting pedestrian and cyclist bridge, making it a groundbreaking example of modern civil engineering. The bridge's design is inspired by the principles of simplicity, elegance, and efficiency. The curved, sleek steel frame allows the bridge to maintain both a visually appealing and highly functional form, balancing aesthetic beauty with practicality.

Cultural Significance
The Gateshead Millennium Bridge is a powerful symbol of

regeneration and the aspirations of the people of Newcastle and Gateshead. Situated in a region with a rich industrial heritage, the bridge represents a shift toward a modern, creative, and forward-looking future. The structure is a visual representation of the positive changes taking place along the River Tyne and has become an emblem of the revitalization of the area. The bridge has played an important role in reshaping the identity of Gateshead and Newcastle, strengthening their position as key cultural hubs in the UK.

Functionality
While the Gateshead Millennium Bridge is celebrated for its aesthetic value, it also serves an essential role in the city's infrastructure. The bridge facilitates pedestrian and cyclist movement between Gateshead and Newcastle, reducing the reliance on cars and contributing to a more sustainable city. The bridge is part of a broader effort to encourage walking and cycling within urban environments, and it connects two key cultural districts: the Quayside in Newcastle and the Gateshead Quays area, home to the BALTIC Centre for Contemporary Art and the Sage Gateshead.

The bridge's ability to tilt allows large vessels to pass through the River Tyne, ensuring that the transportation of goods and services remains unaffected. This combination of aesthetic appeal and practicality has made the Millennium Bridge a highly effective means of connecting two of the region's most important urban areas while preserving the vitality of the River Tyne as a shipping route.

Renovations and Maintenance
Since its completion in 2001, the Gateshead Millennium Bridge has undergone minimal renovations, thanks to its robust construction and durable materials. The bridge was designed to withstand the harsh conditions of the River Tyne, including exposure to saltwater, wind, and heavy traffic. Regular maintenance is carried out to ensure the continued

safe operation of the bridge's hydraulic systems and structural integrity. The rotating mechanism is periodically tested, and minor repairs are conducted as needed to keep the bridge functioning smoothly.

The bridge's design also makes it relatively easy to maintain. With its minimalist structure and straightforward mechanical systems, repairs are less frequent compared to more complex designs. The materials used in construction, including steel and reinforced concrete, are specifically chosen for their durability, further reducing the need for extensive upkeep.

Notable Events

The opening of the Millennium Bridge in 2001 was a highly anticipated event that drew crowds from across the UK and beyond. Since then, the bridge has been the focal point of numerous cultural events, celebrations, and public performances. One of the most notable moments in the bridge's history was during the NewcastleGateshead 2008 bid for European Capital of Culture. The bridge became a symbol of the region's cultural ambitions and was featured prominently in promotional materials.

Throughout the years, the bridge has hosted a variety of public art installations, performances, and celebrations, further cementing its role as a cultural and artistic landmark. The bridge is also a popular site for photographers, artists, and film crews, capturing its striking design against the backdrop of the River Tyne.

Tourism

The Gateshead Millennium Bridge is a major tourist attraction, drawing visitors from all over the world. Its unique design and position along the river make it a must-see landmark for anyone interested in modern architecture and engineering. Visitors often take advantage of the nearby cultural venues, including the BALTIC Centre for Contemporary Art and the Sage Gateshead, to create a full cultural experience.

Legacy
The Gateshead Millennium Bridge is widely regarded as one of the finest examples of contemporary bridge design. Its innovative use of technology and artistic design has left a lasting impact on the field of architecture and engineering. The bridge is a testament to the power of creative thinking and the ability to blend function and form in a way that enhances the urban landscape. It has set a precedent for future bridge designs, demonstrating that engineering can be both functional and beautiful.

Future Plans and Developments
Looking ahead, the Gateshead Millennium Bridge will continue to play a vital role in the region's development. Plans are in place to further integrate the bridge into the surrounding urban environment, with improvements to the accessibility and connectivity of the area. These include the potential for better pedestrian and cyclist pathways, as well as additional public art initiatives that will complement the bridge's aesthetic appeal.

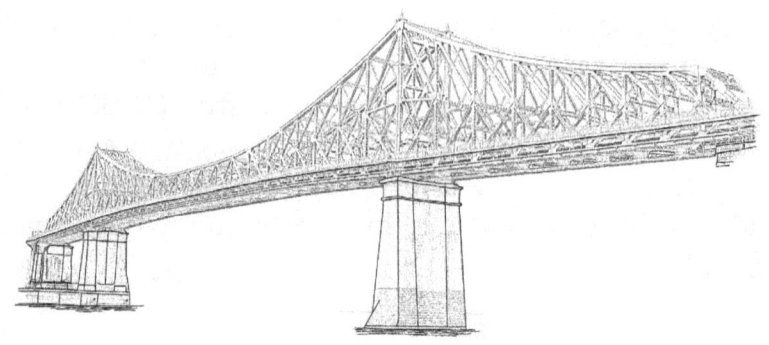

JACQUES CARTIER BRIDGE (CANADA)

The Jacques Cartier Bridge, a renowned landmark spanning the Saint Lawrence River in Montreal, Canada, stands as a testament to both engineering prowess and the evolving spirit of the city. Completed in 1930, the bridge connects Montreal to the South Shore, facilitating traffic between the island of Montreal and the city's suburban areas.

History
The history of the Jacques Cartier Bridge begins in the late 19th century when the city of Montreal recognized the need for better connectivity between the island and the South Shore. The

desire for a more efficient transport route led to the conception of the bridge, named after the French explorer Jacques Cartier, who was the first European to map the area. Construction began in 1925, and the bridge was officially opened to the public in 1930. At the time, the Jacques Cartier Bridge was considered a marvel of engineering, incorporating state-of-the-art materials and technology to ensure its longevity and reliability.

Design
The Jacques Cartier Bridge is an outstanding example of early 20th-century bridge design. Its cantilevered steel structure spans 2.3 kilometers (1.4 miles) across the Saint Lawrence River, making it one of the longest and most striking bridges in Canada. The bridge's design is characterized by its graceful arches and symmetrical layout, with four lanes for vehicular traffic and a dedicated walkway for pedestrians and cyclists. Its striking turquoise color adds a vibrant touch to the Montreal skyline, and the bridge's distinctive art-deco elements contribute to its historical and aesthetic significance.

One of the most notable features of the Jacques Cartier Bridge is its two main spans, which are supported by massive steel towers at each end. These towers, along with the bridge's bold, sweeping curves, create a visually impressive silhouette against the backdrop of the city. The bridge was initially constructed using riveted steel, a common technique of the time, but over the decades, it has been upgraded with modern materials and technologies to ensure its structural integrity.

Cultural Significance
Over the decades, the Jacques Cartier Bridge has become a beloved symbol of Montreal, featured prominently in the city's visual identity. It holds cultural significance for residents and visitors alike, as it represents both the city's historical growth and its connection to the wider world. The bridge has been central to numerous cultural events, from festivals to public celebrations, and it plays a pivotal role in the city's national identity.

One of the most remarkable ways the Jacques Cartier Bridge

is celebrated is through its role in Montreal's famous "Bridge Lighting" event. In this spectacle, the bridge is illuminated with a colorful array of lights, creating a stunning visual display that has become a part of the city's seasonal celebrations, especially during major festivals and the holidays. This event not only showcases the bridge's architectural beauty but also highlights the city's creative spirit and pride in its infrastructure.

Functionality

The primary function of the Jacques Cartier Bridge is to facilitate the flow of traffic between Montreal and its neighboring South Shore. As one of the busiest bridges in the country, it plays a critical role in supporting the daily commute of thousands of Montrealers, as well as the transportation of goods and services. The bridge's four lanes of traffic accommodate cars, trucks, and buses, making it a crucial part of the city's public transportation network.

Renovations and Maintenance

As a major transport route, the Jacques Cartier Bridge has undergone extensive renovations to maintain its structural integrity and functionality. One of the most significant upgrades occurred in the 1990s when the bridge's aging steel structure was replaced with new materials to ensure its continued safety. Regular maintenance is also conducted to prevent rust and corrosion, particularly due to the proximity to the river and the harsh winters of Montreal.

In 2017, a major refurbishment project was launched to improve the bridge's infrastructure and extend its lifespan. The renovation included the replacement of steel components, repaving of roadways, and modernization of lighting and electrical systems. The project also included upgrades to the pedestrian and cyclist paths to ensure better safety and accessibility. The bridge continues to receive ongoing investments, ensuring that it remains a reliable transportation route for future generations.

Notable Events

The Jacques Cartier Bridge has witnessed many notable events throughout its history. Perhaps one of the most famous moments in the bridge's history was its role in the celebrations marking Montreal's 350th anniversary in 1992, when it was illuminated in honor of the occasion. The bridge has also been an integral part of several international events, including the 1967 Expo, which brought global attention to Montreal.

The Jacques Cartier Bridge has also become a prominent location for Montreal's New Year's Eve celebrations, with the bridge often being illuminated for the festivities. In recent years, the bridge has become a central part of Montreal's dynamic cultural scene, serving as a backdrop for large-scale public events such as festivals and parades.

Tourism
The Jacques Cartier Bridge has become a key attraction for both locals and tourists visiting Montreal. Its stunning architecture and panoramic views of the Saint Lawrence River, Old Montreal, and the city skyline make it a popular spot for sightseeing. Tourists often walk or cycle across the bridge, taking in the breathtaking views of the city, especially at sunset or during the evening when the bridge is beautifully lit.

Legacy
The Jacques Cartier Bridge has a lasting legacy in Montreal's history and urban development. It symbolizes the city's growth and its expanding role as a cultural and economic hub in Canada. As a piece of infrastructure, the bridge continues to serve the needs of the city, connecting communities and facilitating the flow of people and goods. Its design and engineering have influenced the development of other bridges, both in Canada and internationally.

Future Plans and Developments
Looking ahead, there are plans for continued modernization of the Jacques Cartier Bridge to ensure it remains an integral part of Montreal's infrastructure. The bridge's ongoing renovation projects are aimed at improving the flow of traffic, enhancing safety measures, and ensuring the bridge's environmental sustainability. Additionally, efforts are underway to incorporate

more green initiatives, such as energy-efficient lighting and improved pedestrian access, in order to align with the city's long-term vision for sustainability.

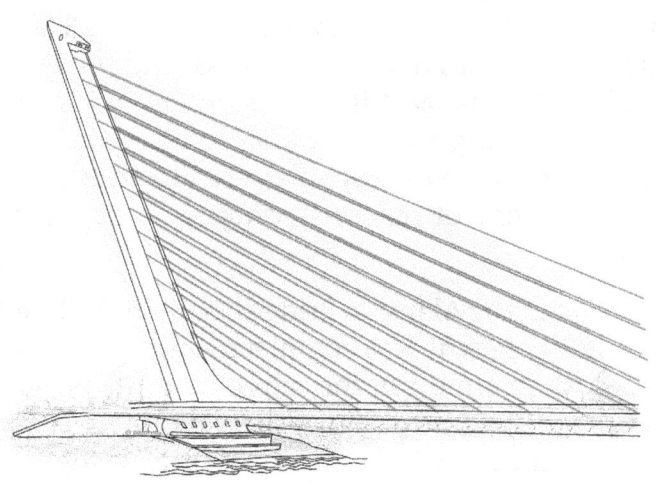

ALAMILLO BRIDGE (SEVILLE, SPAIN)

The Alamillo Bridge in Seville, Spain, is a striking example of modern engineering and design, known for its elegant form and the dramatic way it spans the Guadalquivir River. Located in the southwestern part of the city, it provides a vital connection between the district of La Cartuja and the western areas of Seville, while also acting as an architectural and cultural landmark.

History
The Alamillo Bridge was designed as a key infrastructure project for the city's Expo '92, an event that aimed to showcase Spain's

role in global cultural and technological advancements. The World's Fair, held in Seville, spurred a number of architectural and engineering projects throughout the city. The bridge was commissioned to provide direct access to the Expo site on the island of La Cartuja, and its construction was seen as a vital element in ensuring smooth transportation during the event. Designed by the renowned Spanish architect Santiago Calatrava, the bridge was one of the most ambitious projects undertaken for Expo '92.

Construction of the Alamillo Bridge began in the late 1980s, and despite a few delays, it was completed and opened to the public in 1992, just in time for the exposition. It stands as one of Calatrava's most iconic designs, showcasing his signature style that blends sculptural aesthetics with cutting-edge engineering. Since its completion, the Alamillo Bridge has not only been a key transportation link but also a symbol of Seville's modernity and its ambition to embrace the future.

Design

The Alamillo Bridge is known for its striking and minimalist design. Unlike traditional cable-stayed bridges that feature multiple support towers, the Alamillo Bridge is characterized by a single, slanted pylon that supports a series of cables, creating a visual impact that seems almost sculptural. The pylon itself rises at a 58-degree angle and towers over the river, resembling a giant harp or an abstract form of a sail, which adds a dynamic, organic quality to the structure.

The bridge spans 200 meters across the Guadalquivir River, and its slender profile makes it seem almost delicate, despite its impressive size. The design is a departure from conventional bridge structures, utilizing a unique approach to balance aesthetics with functionality. The cables are arranged in a fan-like pattern, stemming from the central pylon, which not only enhances the visual effect of the bridge but also optimizes the distribution of forces, providing an efficient and sturdy support structure.

Cultural Significance

The Alamillo Bridge holds significant cultural importance for Seville and Spain as a whole. It represents a break from the traditional forms of bridge design, reflecting the country's desire to embrace modernity during the early 1990s. Its association with Expo '92 further solidified its place in the city's history, as it was one of the primary architectural landmarks of the exposition. For Seville, the bridge symbolizes the city's growing international presence and its integration of cutting-edge technology and design into its historic urban fabric.

Culturally, the bridge also represents the spirit of innovation that defined Expo '92. It was a time when the city was embracing contemporary architecture and rethinking its public spaces. The Alamillo Bridge, with its bold and futuristic form, became a symbol of this transformation, helping to position Seville as a city that not only respected its history but also looked toward the future with ambition and creativity.

Functionality
Despite its artistic and aesthetic qualities, the Alamillo Bridge was designed with functionality in mind. It serves as a major transportation route connecting the district of La Cartuja to the western parts of Seville, facilitating both vehicular and pedestrian traffic. The bridge provides an important connection to the Expo '92 site and continues to play a crucial role in the city's transportation network.

Renovations and Maintenance
The Alamillo Bridge has required relatively few renovations since its opening in 1992, a testament to its durable construction and the thoughtful selection of materials. Like any major infrastructure, the bridge undergoes regular maintenance to ensure the safety and integrity of the structure. The cables, pylon, and deck are carefully inspected to check for wear and tear, and necessary repairs are made to address any issues related to corrosion, especially given the bridge's exposure to the elements.

Notable Events
While the Alamillo Bridge is best known for its role in Expo

'92, it has since become an enduring symbol of Seville's modern architectural landscape. The bridge has been part of several significant events in the city, including celebrations of Spain's national holidays and cultural festivals. Its prominence in Seville's skyline has made it a natural location for various media appearances, from films to television shows, where its sleek, modern aesthetic serves as a dramatic backdrop.

The bridge's association with Expo '92 has also meant that it continues to be a reminder of that transformative year in the city's history, when Seville was placed on the international stage as a center of innovation and cultural exchange.

Tourism

As one of Seville's most iconic landmarks, the Alamillo Bridge draws a significant number of tourists each year. Visitors to the city often make a point to see the bridge, whether from the riverbanks or from a nearby vantage point that allows them to appreciate its sweeping form. The surrounding area, particularly the Isla de la Cartuja where the Expo site was located, is a popular destination for both locals and tourists, and the Alamillo Bridge serves as a key entry point to this district.

Legacy

The Alamillo Bridge has left a lasting legacy in the world of architecture and engineering. Its innovative design has influenced other bridge projects globally, and its combination of form and function has become a model for modern infrastructure projects. The bridge's role in Expo '92 also helped to shift global perceptions of Seville, marking the city as a place of architectural experimentation and cultural growth.

Future Plans and Developments

Looking to the future, the Alamillo Bridge will continue to serve as an essential part of Seville's infrastructure. Plans to improve pedestrian access and integrate the bridge further into the city's urban development are under discussion, with a focus on enhancing the overall accessibility of the area. Future projects may involve improving connections between the bridge and surrounding parks, as well as expanding the pedestrian and cycling routes.

The Alamillo Bridge will remain a symbol of Seville's commitment to modernity and innovation, ensuring that it remains an integral part of the city's identity for years to come.

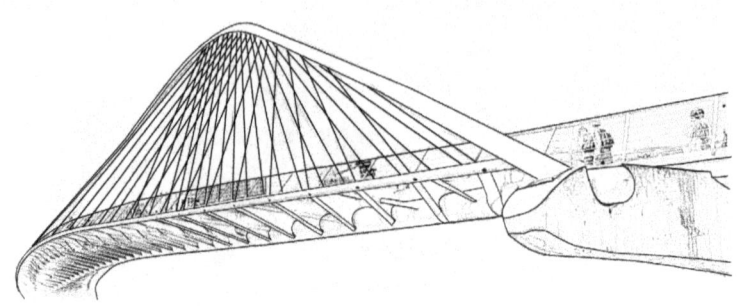

ZUBIZURI (BILBAO, SPAIN)

The Zubizuri, or "White Bridge," is a striking pedestrian bridge located in the heart of Bilbao, Spain. It spans the Nervión River, connecting the districts of Uribitarte and Campo de Volantín. Known for its unique design and location, the bridge is not only an essential part of Bilbao's transportation network but also a prominent piece of modern architecture that blends functionality with artistic expression.

History
The idea of constructing the Zubizuri bridge emerged during the urban revitalization efforts of Bilbao in the 1990s. At the

time, the city was undergoing a transformation that aimed to modernize its infrastructure and elevate its status as a cultural and economic hub. Bilbao had traditionally been an industrial city, but as the 20th century progressed, there was a concerted effort to rejuvenate its downtown area, particularly around the Nervión River.

As part of this revitalization, the city sought to improve pedestrian access across the river, which was a vital element in connecting different districts and enhancing mobility within the urban landscape. In 1994, the city of Bilbao invited renowned architect Santiago Calatrava to design a pedestrian bridge that would seamlessly integrate with the city's evolving architectural landscape. The bridge was constructed between 1995 and 1997, becoming one of the city's most distinctive landmarks upon its completion.

Design
The Zubizuri bridge stands out for its innovative design, characterized by an elegant, curved white steel structure that arches above the Nervión River. The bridge is designed to resemble a sail, with its central arch gracefully bending upward, evoking a sense of movement and lightness. This dynamic form gives the bridge a sculptural quality, making it not just a means of crossing but also an art installation in the public space.

The bridge is 75 meters (246 feet) long and 20 meters (66 feet) wide, with a pedestrian walkway supported by a series of thin steel cables that radiate from the central arch. The deck of the bridge is covered with a glass and steel grid, which allows for a clear view of the river below. This transparent design adds a modern, minimalist touch while providing a sense of openness. The structural integrity of the bridge is achieved through the use of steel, which contrasts with the glass, giving it both strength and elegance.

Cultural Significance
Zubizuri is not just a bridge; it is a symbol of Bilbao's rebirth as a modern and cosmopolitan city. Its design reflects the spirit of innovation that marked the city's transformation in the late

20th century, from an industrial hub to a cultural and artistic center. The bridge is part of a larger urban regeneration plan that included the construction of other iconic structures, such as the Guggenheim Museum Bilbao, which helped reposition the city on the international stage.

Functionality

While Zubizuri is undoubtedly an architectural masterpiece, it also serves a practical function. The bridge is designed primarily for pedestrians and cyclists, providing a safe and efficient crossing over the Nervión River. It plays an important role in connecting various parts of the city, linking the districts of Uribitarte and Campo de Volantín, which are both popular areas for locals and tourists alike.

Renovations and Maintenance

Despite its innovative design, Zubizuri has faced some challenges over the years, particularly with regard to its maintenance and safety. The bridge's glass surface, which was initially chosen for its aesthetic appeal, became slippery during rainy conditions, leading to concerns about pedestrian safety. In response, the city implemented several renovations to improve the functionality of the bridge.

In 2007, the glass tiles on the bridge were replaced with a more durable, anti-slip material to reduce the risk of accidents. This was part of an ongoing effort to address the bridge's safety concerns while preserving its iconic design. In addition to these safety improvements, regular maintenance is carried out to ensure that the structure remains in good condition. This includes inspecting the steel cables and supporting elements, as well as ensuring that the white paint on the bridge is kept pristine.

Notable Events

Zubizuri has played host to several notable events over the years, further cementing its status as a cultural landmark. As part of Bilbao's urban rejuvenation, the bridge has been included in various citywide festivals and celebrations. Its striking design makes it an ideal backdrop for public art displays, performances, and cultural exhibitions.

Tourism

Zubizuri has become a popular tourist attraction due to its remarkable design and central location. The bridge's status as one of Bilbao's architectural icons makes it a must-see for visitors exploring the city. Tourists often stroll across the bridge, enjoying the panoramic views of the Nervión River and the surrounding cityscape. Zubizuri is also close to several other major attractions, including the Guggenheim Museum, making it an integral part of Bilbao's cultural tourism circuit.

Legacy

Zubizuri is widely regarded as a landmark that helped define the modern architectural identity of Bilbao. It represents a shift in the city's architectural language, blending functionality with artistic expression. As part of the city's larger urban renewal project, the bridge helped transform Bilbao from an industrial town into a city known for its contemporary art, design, and cultural landmarks.

Future Plans and Developments

City planners have considered integrating green initiatives into the bridge's design, such as incorporating energy-efficient lighting and green spaces along the pedestrian paths. These developments would further align with Bilbao's commitment to sustainable urban planning and environmental stewardship.

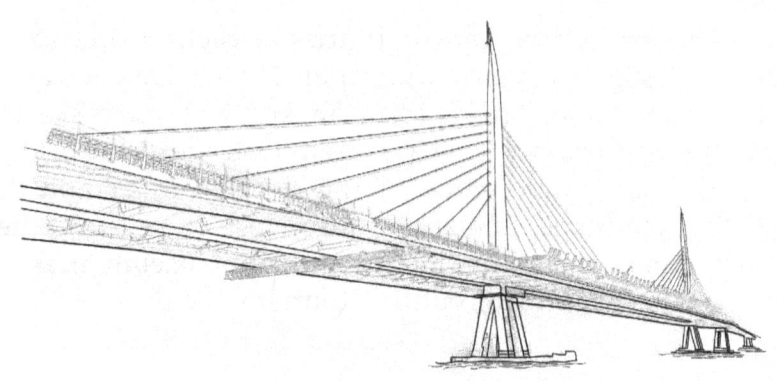

GOLDEN HORN METRO BRIDGE (ISTANBUL, TURKEY)

The Golden Horn Metro Bridge, located in Istanbul, Turkey, is a vital piece of infrastructure that connects the districts of Beyoğlu and Fatih, crossing the Golden Horn, an inlet of the Bosphorus. This cable-stayed bridge, completed in 2014, is an essential part of the Istanbul Metro, serving as a crucial link in the city's public transportation network.

History
The Golden Horn Metro Bridge is part of a larger transportation

project designed to improve Istanbul's metro system. The bridge was built to meet the growing demands of the city's rapidly expanding population and to reduce traffic congestion in the historic heart of Istanbul. The need for the bridge arose from the city's efforts to modernize its public transportation infrastructure, particularly in the busy Golden Horn area.

Construction of the bridge began in 2013, with the goal of easing traffic on Istanbul's main roads and providing a faster, more efficient means of transportation for residents and tourists. The bridge was completed and opened in 2014 as part of the extension of the M2 metro line, which connects the city's northern and southern districts. Its completion was seen as a significant milestone in Istanbul's ongoing modernization, contributing to the overall vision of transforming the city into a global hub of commerce and tourism.

Design

The Golden Horn Metro Bridge is a visually striking example of modern bridge architecture, with its sleek design making it an immediate landmark in Istanbul. The bridge spans 1,200 meters across the Golden Horn, providing both pedestrian and metro traffic access. The most prominent feature of the bridge is its cable-stayed design, with two central towers supporting a series of steel cables that hold up the deck. The bridge's design is minimalistic yet elegant, using clean lines and a streamlined profile that allows it to blend into the urban landscape without overwhelming it.

The two towers, which rise 45 meters above the water, support the bridge's deck and give it its distinctive appearance. The cables extend from the towers in a fan-like formation, adding a sense of dynamism and fluidity to the structure. The deck of the bridge is made from steel and reinforced concrete, providing a durable and sturdy platform for the metro trains that cross it daily. The overall aesthetic of the bridge reflects Istanbul's blend of ancient history and modern progress, with its sleek, contemporary lines standing in stark contrast to the city's older architecture.

Cultural Significance

The Golden Horn Metro Bridge holds significant cultural importance for Istanbul and Turkey as a whole. It is emblematic of the country's commitment to modernizing its infrastructure while respecting its rich cultural and historical heritage. The bridge serves as a physical representation of Istanbul's status as a city that bridges the gap between East and West, both geographically and culturally.

Istanbul, historically a crossroads of civilizations, has long been a city of contrasts, where ancient traditions coexist with modern development. The Golden Horn Metro Bridge symbolizes this duality, as it combines advanced engineering with the city's storied past. Its location, spanning the Golden Horn, one of the most iconic waterways in the city, further highlights its cultural relevance. The bridge also stands as a testament to Istanbul's ongoing transformation, helping to shape its future while acknowledging its past.

Functionality

The Golden Horn Metro Bridge is a key component of Istanbul's metro system, specifically the M2 line, which connects the northern and southern parts of the city. The bridge serves as a vital link between the districts of Beyoğlu and Fatih, two of the most important areas of Istanbul. The metro line that runs across the bridge is heavily used by both locals and tourists, providing an efficient and reliable means of transportation across the Golden Horn.

Renovations and Maintenance

Since its completion in 2014, the Golden Horn Metro Bridge has required regular maintenance to ensure its structural integrity and functionality. Like all major infrastructure projects, the bridge undergoes periodic inspections to monitor for any signs of wear and tear. The most important aspect of maintenance is ensuring that the cables, deck, and towers remain in optimal condition to support the traffic that crosses the bridge daily.

Notable Events

Although the Golden Horn Metro Bridge is primarily used for transportation, it has also been the site of notable events in Istanbul. Its completion was celebrated as a major achievement in the city's efforts to modernize its infrastructure, and the opening of the bridge was attended by local officials and residents alike. The bridge has since become a significant part of the daily commute for thousands of people, contributing to the city's ongoing growth and development.

Tourism

The bridge offers stunning views of the Golden Horn, the Bosphorus Strait, and the city of Istanbul, making it a popular spot for both locals and tourists to visit. The pedestrian walkway allows people to experience the beauty of the city from a unique vantage point, providing an opportunity to take photographs or simply enjoy the view.

Legacy

The bridge is not just a functional piece of infrastructure but also a visual and cultural symbol of Istanbul's forward-looking approach to development. It has become an enduring icon of the city's modern architecture, and its presence has helped shape the identity of the Golden Horn area.

Future Plans and Developments

The future of the Golden Horn Metro Bridge is tied to the continued development of Istanbul's transportation network. Plans for expanding the metro system and improving connectivity across the city will likely include further enhancements to the bridge and its surrounding infrastructure. Future developments may focus on increasing the capacity of the metro line to accommodate the growing population of Istanbul and expanding pedestrian access to encourage sustainable transport options.

PONTE RIO-NITERÓI (RIO DE JANEIRO, BRAZIL)

The Ponte Rio-Niterói, or Rio-Niterói Bridge, is an iconic structure connecting the cities of Rio de Janeiro and Niterói, two key urban areas in southeastern Brazil. Spanning Guanabara Bay, this remarkable bridge has become an essential part of the region's transportation infrastructure, serving as a vital link between the two cities.

History
The history of the Ponte Rio-Niterói dates back to the mid-20th

century when the need for a more efficient way to connect Rio de Janeiro and Niterói became apparent. Prior to the bridge, the only practical means of crossing the Guanabara Bay was by ferry, which was often overcrowded and time-consuming, particularly during rush hours. The increasing population and economic activity in the region created pressure on the existing transportation infrastructure, leading to a demand for a more direct and reliable crossing.

In the 1950s, the idea of building a bridge over the bay was proposed, but it took nearly two decades of planning, negotiations, and technical studies before construction could begin. Brazilian engineers and architects had to consider various challenges, including the difficult geography of the bay, strong currents, and seismic activity, all of which complicated the project.

The construction of the bridge began in 1968 under the leadership of the federal government, which saw the project as a necessary step in boosting regional development. The bridge was designed by the Brazilian engineer Eugenio Lind, who was responsible for overseeing the project, along with a team of specialists. After six years of construction, the Ponte Rio-Niterói was officially opened to the public on March 4, 1974, with a ceremony attended by high-ranking government officials. The completion of the bridge marked a significant achievement in Brazilian engineering and provided a crucial solution to the region's transportation challenges.

Design

The Ponte Rio-Niterói is a cable-stayed bridge, characterized by its distinctive design and impressive dimensions. Stretching 13.29 kilometers (8.26 miles) from end to end, it is one of the longest bridges in Brazil and among the longest in Latin America. The bridge connects the city of Rio de Janeiro to the municipality of Niterói, crossing the Guanabara Bay, with the bridge's main span measuring 1,200 meters (3,937 feet).

The design features a series of cables that support the bridge's deck, which is elevated high above the water, providing both functionality and aesthetic appeal. The cables fan out from central support pylons, creating a visually striking structure. The steel and concrete combination ensures the stability and durability of the bridge while allowing for the required strength to withstand the challenges posed by the bay's turbulent waters.

Cultural Significance
The Ponte Rio-Niterói is an integral part of the cultural and economic landscape of Rio de Janeiro and Niterói. It is more than just a physical link between two cities; it has become a symbol of the growth and modernization of Brazil. The bridge's construction represents the country's aspirations for progress and development, showcasing its ability to undertake large-scale infrastructure projects.

Functionality
The primary function of the Ponte Rio-Niterói is to facilitate the movement of people and goods between Rio de Janeiro and Niterói, significantly improving the efficiency of travel between the two cities. Before the bridge, the only alternative was the ferry system, which was often overcrowded and unreliable. The bridge has revolutionized transportation in the region, offering a faster, more direct route for commuters, tourists, and businesses alike.

Today, the bridge handles a significant amount of traffic, with an average of over 100,000 vehicles crossing it daily. It is a vital part of the region's transportation network, allowing for smoother connections to Rio de Janeiro's bustling port, international airport, and commercial districts. The bridge also serves as an important route for the transportation of goods, facilitating trade between the two cities and beyond.

Renovations and Maintenance
In recent years, the bridge has received significant improvements, including resurfacing of the roadways and the addition of new safety measures. The installation of modern lighting and surveillance systems has enhanced security, while technological advancements have made traffic management more efficient. These efforts have helped extend the life of the

bridge and ensure that it remains a safe and reliable route for travelers.

Notable Events

The Ponte Rio-Niterói has witnessed several notable events throughout its history. One of the most significant was its opening in 1974, which was celebrated as a triumph of Brazilian engineering. Over the years, the bridge has also played a role in various cultural and political events, including demonstrations, parades, and public gatherings.

Tourism

Tourists visiting Rio de Janeiro and Niterói often take the time to cross the Ponte Rio-Niterói, either by car or public transport, to experience the breathtaking views of the bay and the surrounding scenery. The bridge is an essential part of the tourism experience in the region, providing visitors with a unique perspective of the cities and the natural beauty of the area.

Legacy

As one of the largest bridges in Latin America, the Ponte Rio-Niterói stands as a testament to Brazil's engineering prowess and ambition. It remains an essential part of the region's transportation network, offering a critical link for residents, businesses, and tourists alike.

Future Plans and Developments

Looking to the future, there are ongoing discussions regarding the bridge's continued maintenance and potential upgrades. As traffic volumes increase, there are plans to improve traffic flow, reduce congestion, and enhance the bridge's capacity to handle modern demands. These developments may include expanding lanes, improving public transportation access, and incorporating more sustainable and environmentally friendly practices into the bridge's operations.

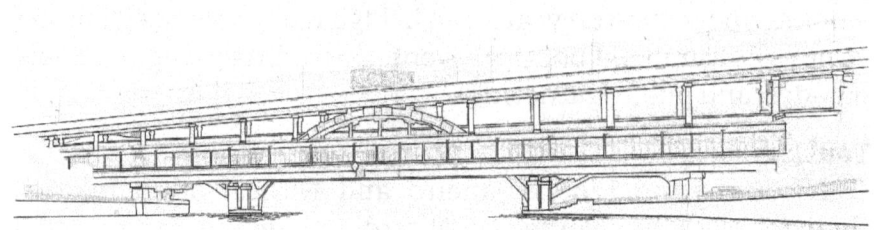

LUZHNIKI METRO BRIDGE (MOSCOW, RUSSIA)

The Luzhniki Metro Bridge, located in Moscow, Russia, is a vital structure that serves as a key transportation link between the Luzhniki Stadium area and the city's metro network. This bridge is integral not only for its transportation function but also for its aesthetic contribution to the Moscow skyline.

History
The Luzhniki Metro Bridge was constructed to meet the increasing demand for transportation access to the Luzhniki

area, particularly in connection with the Luzhniki Stadium. The bridge's construction was driven by the need to improve connectivity to this significant sports and cultural hub in Moscow. Its development coincided with the overall expansion and modernization of the city's transportation infrastructure in preparation for large-scale events, such as the 2018 FIFA World Cup, which saw Luzhniki Stadium become one of the tournament's main venues.

Planning for the bridge began in the early 2000s as part of a broader initiative to expand Moscow's metro network and improve access to key areas of the city. Construction officially began in 2007, and the bridge opened in 2009, as part of the Luzhniki Metro Station's expansion. The bridge became a crucial piece of the city's transportation network, facilitating faster, more efficient travel for the thousands of people who visit the area every day.

Design
The Luzhniki Metro Bridge features a sleek, modern design that integrates seamlessly with its surroundings. The bridge is a cable-stayed structure, characterized by its central towers and the network of cables that extend outward to support the bridge deck. The towers rise above the Moskva River, with the bridge's central span connecting the two banks of the river and allowing for metro trains to cross without obstruction.

Cultural Significance
The Luzhniki Metro Bridge is deeply intertwined with the cultural identity of Moscow, particularly in relation to the Luzhniki Stadium. Luzhniki Stadium has long been one of Moscow's most important sports venues, hosting international sporting events, concerts, and other cultural activities. The bridge is essential in facilitating access to this iconic location, which has hosted high-profile events such as the 1980 Summer Olympics and the 2018 FIFA World Cup.

The bridge's significance extends beyond its practical role; it symbolizes the ongoing modernization of Moscow's infrastructure and the city's efforts to position itself as a global city on the world stage. It is a physical manifestation of Russia's ambitions to modernize its capital and enhance its international appeal, particularly in light of global events such as the World Cup.

Functionality
The primary function of the Luzhniki Metro Bridge is to serve as a transportation link for the Moscow Metro system. The bridge facilitates the smooth transit of metro trains across the Moskva River, connecting the Luzhniki area with other parts of the city. This is particularly important for easing congestion in the area, especially during peak times when events are being held at Luzhniki Stadium or the adjacent Luzhniki Sports Complex.

Renovations and Maintenance
As with any major infrastructure project, the Luzhniki Metro Bridge requires regular maintenance to ensure its structural integrity and continued functionality. The bridge is inspected regularly to monitor for any signs of wear and tear, particularly the cables and towers that support the bridge's deck. Maintenance is performed by specialized teams that ensure the bridge remains safe for use by both metro passengers and pedestrians.

Given the harsh winters in Moscow, the bridge's materials are regularly maintained to prevent damage from ice, snow, and salt used to de-ice roads. The steel and concrete components of the bridge are regularly cleaned and reinforced to ensure they remain durable and weather-resistant. The cable-stayed design also requires occasional adjustments to ensure the cables maintain proper tension and that the bridge remains stable.

Notable Events
The Luzhniki Metro Bridge has been associated with several significant events, particularly those held at Luzhniki Stadium. One of the most notable events in recent history was the 2018 FIFA World Cup, where the bridge played an important role in facilitating the flow of fans and participants to and from the stadium. During the tournament, the bridge was crucial in handling the large influx of visitors, providing an efficient

link to the surrounding metro system and helping manage the crowding that typically accompanies such large-scale events.

Tourism

Tourists visiting Moscow often cross the Luzhniki Metro Bridge as part of their journey to Luzhniki Stadium and other nearby attractions. The bridge offers stunning views of the Moskva River and the city skyline, making it a popular location for photographs. Additionally, the bridge provides a direct route to the Luzhniki area, which is home to several important landmarks, including the Moscow State University, the Moscow City business district, and Gorky Park.

Legacy

The Luzhniki Metro Bridge has become an integral part of Moscow's transportation infrastructure and urban landscape. It has facilitated the city's continued development and modernization, enabling better connectivity across the Moskva River and providing a vital link to one of the city's most important cultural and sporting hubs. The bridge's role in Moscow's growth has cemented its place as a key piece of the city's architectural legacy.

Future Plans and Developments

As Moscow continues to grow, the Luzhniki Metro Bridge will likely play an even greater role in the city's transportation system. Future plans for the bridge may involve expanding its capacity to accommodate more metro trains and enhancing pedestrian access. Given Moscow's ambition to improve its public transportation system, the bridge will remain a critical part of the city's infrastructure.

DRAGON BRIDGE (DA NANG, VIETNAM)

The Dragon Bridge (Cầu Rồng) in Da Nang, Vietnam, is an iconic architectural marvel that spans the Han River, linking the city center to the western districts. Known for its unique design and cultural significance, the bridge has become one of the most important landmarks in Da Nang.

History
The Dragon Bridge was conceived as part of Da Nang's efforts to modernize and improve infrastructure to accommodate the growing population and boost tourism. The project was initiated by the city's local government in the early 2000s, with

construction starting in 2009. Da Nang, known as a coastal hub and one of Vietnam's major cities, was experiencing rapid economic growth, and improving transportation was seen as a key to further development.

The bridge's construction was aimed at easing traffic flow and connecting the two sides of the Han River more efficiently, as previous bridges were unable to handle the increasing traffic volumes. After four years of work, the Dragon Bridge was completed and opened to the public on March 29, 2013, in time for the city's annual festival.

Design
The Dragon Bridge is a striking example of modern engineering fused with traditional cultural symbolism. The most notable feature of the bridge is its dragon-shaped design, which was inspired by the image of the dragon in Vietnamese mythology. The dragon, a symbol of power and strength, is a revered figure in many Asian cultures, and its presence on the bridge signifies the city's prosperity and auspicious future.

The bridge spans 666 meters in length, and its design incorporates sleek, flowing curves to mimic the shape of a dragon. The head of the dragon sits at the western end of the bridge, with its body curving gracefully over the Han River. The bridge is constructed from steel, reinforced concrete, and glass, making it both durable and visually striking. The dragon's body is illuminated by LED lights, which create a spectacular visual display at night, adding to its appeal as a tourist attraction.

Cultural Significance
The Dragon Bridge holds deep cultural significance for the people of Da Nang and Vietnam as a whole. The dragon is a highly revered figure in Vietnamese folklore, often associated with good fortune, protection, and the prosperity of the land. In traditional Vietnamese culture, dragons were believed to bring rain to the fields, which were essential for rice cultivation. As such, the dragon represents not only power and strength but also the blessings of nature and agriculture.

The bridge has become a focal point for local festivals and celebrations, especially during the Lunar New Year (Tết) and Da Nang's annual International Fireworks Festival. It serves as a physical manifestation of the city's modernity, while also celebrating its traditional roots.

Functionality
The primary function of the Dragon Bridge is to serve as a vital transportation route connecting the eastern and western parts of Da Nang. Before its construction, the traffic flow across the Han River was limited by older bridges, causing congestion, particularly during peak hours. The Dragon Bridge, with its six lanes, helps alleviate this issue by providing a more direct and efficient route for vehicles and pedestrians.

Renovations and Maintenance
Since its opening in 2013, the Dragon Bridge has been subject to periodic renovations and maintenance to ensure its safety, functionality, and aesthetic appeal. As a major piece of infrastructure, the bridge requires ongoing upkeep to maintain its structural integrity, especially considering the environmental conditions of Da Nang, such as the salty air from the nearby sea.

Maintenance work has primarily focused on the bridge's lighting system, which undergoes regular upgrades to incorporate new technologies and improve energy efficiency. The bridge's structural components are also routinely inspected to prevent wear and tear from the heavy traffic it accommodates. Regular cleaning and repainting help preserve the dragon's distinctive appearance, ensuring that the bridge continues to serve as a striking symbol of the city.

Notable Events
The Dragon Bridge has become a venue for several notable events since its inauguration. One of the most famous occurrences is the "Dragon Breathing Fire" spectacle, which takes place on weekends and during special events. Every Saturday and Sunday evening, the dragon's head "breathes" fire

and water in a dramatic display that has become one of Da Nang's most popular tourist attractions.

Tourism

Tourism plays a significant role in Da Nang's economy, and the Dragon Bridge has become one of the city's most iconic landmarks, attracting visitors from around the world. The bridge's dragon design and stunning lighting displays at night make it a must-see destination for tourists visiting Da Nang. It has become a favorite spot for photography, with many visitors capturing the bridge's majestic appearance against the backdrop of the Han River and the city's skyline.

The Dragon Bridge also plays a role in boosting local businesses, as tourists often flock to nearby areas for dining, shopping, and sightseeing. Its proximity to other attractions in Da Nang, such as My Khe Beach and the Marble Mountains, makes it a popular starting point for exploring the city.

Legacy

The Dragon Bridge is a symbol of Da Nang's transformation into a modern, thriving city. It stands as a testament to the city's ability to blend traditional cultural elements with contemporary engineering. The bridge has become a focal point of civic pride and a symbol of the city's aspirations for progress and prosperity.

Future Plans and Developments

As Da Nang continues to grow and develop, future plans for the Dragon Bridge focus on maintaining its role as a key piece of infrastructure. There are ongoing efforts to enhance the bridge's sustainability, improve traffic management, and ensure that it remains a modern and efficient route for the city's residents and visitors.

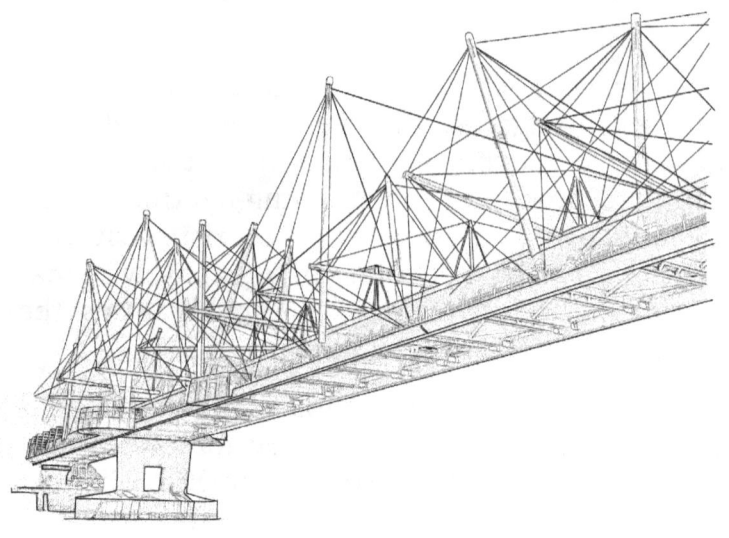

KURILPA BRIDGE (BRISBANE, AUSTRALIA)

The Kurilpa Bridge is one of Brisbane's most innovative and visually striking landmarks, connecting the cultural heart of the city with its expanding urban landscape. Completed in 2009, the bridge spans the Brisbane River, linking the Brisbane central business district (CBD) to the South Bank. It is a pedestrian and cyclist bridge, known for its unique design and its role in enhancing the city's public transport and recreational spaces.

History

The concept for the Kurilpa Bridge was born from a need to improve the infrastructure in Brisbane, particularly in connecting key areas like the South Bank and the Brisbane CBD. South Bank, known for its cultural venues and parklands, had become one of the city's busiest destinations. However, it was only accessible via a few bridges, and pedestrian access across the river was becoming increasingly limited.

Planning for the Kurilpa Bridge began in the early 2000s, as part of a broader project to improve Brisbane's public transport and pedestrian networks. A design competition was held in 2005, and the winning proposal, developed by the architectural firm Arup, focused on creating an iconic bridge that would not only serve as a functional transportation route but also as a visual and cultural landmark for the city.

Construction of the bridge began in 2007, with the intention of completing it before the 2010 World Expo, which would bring thousands of visitors to Brisbane. The Kurilpa Bridge was officially opened in 2009, after more than two years of construction. Since then, it has been an essential part of Brisbane's urban transport system, helping to ease traffic congestion and increase connectivity between the CBD and South Bank.

Design
The Kurilpa Bridge is an architectural marvel, designed to be both functional and aesthetically striking. Its most notable feature is its unique, twisting shape. The bridge's structure is made of steel and concrete, and it is supported by a series of large, sweeping cables that create a dynamic, curved form. The design incorporates elements of both a suspension bridge and a cable-stayed bridge, with the cables not only providing structural support but also contributing to the bridge's distinctive visual appeal.

At its center, the Kurilpa Bridge rises high above the river, allowing boats to pass underneath, while the sides slope gently to accommodate pedestrians and cyclists. The bridge's dynamic shape is a nod to the organic forms found in nature, and its fluid lines have been compared to the curves of a sailing ship or the folds of a wave. The curves of the bridge are not only an aesthetic choice but also a functional one, providing more space for pedestrian and cyclist traffic.

The bridge's surface is made of a smooth, anti-slip material, ensuring the safety of pedestrians and cyclists, even in wet conditions. The sides of the bridge are also equipped with stainless-steel handrails, which provide a sense of security while offering uninterrupted views of the river and the surrounding cityscape. At night, the bridge's design comes to life, with a series of integrated LED lights illuminating the structure, adding a glowing effect to the riverfront.

Cultural Significance
The Kurilpa Bridge has become a symbol of Brisbane's transformation into a modern, vibrant city. Its innovative design and construction have helped to position the city as a hub of design and culture in Australia. The bridge is located within proximity to several of Brisbane's cultural institutions, including the Queensland Performing Arts Centre (QPAC), the Queensland Art Gallery, and the State Library of Queensland, making it a vital link between the city's cultural and recreational areas.

Functionality
The Kurilpa Bridge was designed primarily as a pedestrian and cyclist crossing, but it also serves a broader role in the city's transport network. By providing an alternative route for pedestrians and cyclists to cross the Brisbane River, the bridge helps reduce traffic congestion on other major crossings, such as the Victoria Bridge and the William Jolly Bridge. It has become particularly useful for those traveling between the bustling South Bank precinct and the Brisbane CBD, allowing pedestrians and cyclists to bypass the city's busy roadways.

Renovations and Maintenance
Since its completion, the Kurilpa Bridge has been regularly maintained to ensure its safety and longevity. The bridge's steel structure requires periodic inspections to assess its integrity

and address any potential issues related to wear and tear. Additionally, the LED lighting system is maintained to ensure the bridge remains illuminated at night, contributing to both its safety and its aesthetic appeal.

Notable Events

The Kurilpa Bridge has been the site of several significant events and celebrations since its opening. These include major cultural festivals, New Year's Eve fireworks displays, and public gatherings that celebrate Brisbane's artistic and cultural life. The bridge's unique design and location make it an ideal venue for such events, offering a striking backdrop for performances, fireworks, and other public celebrations.

Tourism

Tourists visiting Brisbane often find themselves crossing the Kurilpa Bridge as part of their exploration of the city. The bridge is located in an area rich with attractions, including the South Bank Parklands, the Wheel of Brisbane, and the Queensland Cultural Centre. Visitors can enjoy a leisurely walk across the bridge, taking in the views of the Brisbane River, the city's skyline, and the lush parklands on either side.

Legacy

The Kurilpa Bridge has cemented its place as one of Brisbane's most iconic structures. Its striking design and emphasis on sustainability have helped to define the city's commitment to modern, environmentally conscious infrastructure. The bridge is a reminder of Brisbane's ongoing efforts to blend functionality with aesthetic appeal, contributing to the city's growing reputation as a center for design and innovation.

Future Plans and Developments

As Brisbane continues to grow, the Kurilpa Bridge is likely to remain an integral part of the city's transportation network. Future developments may include expanding pedestrian and cyclist access to accommodate the city's increasing population and demand for sustainable transport options. Additionally, the continued integration of green technologies and energy-efficient systems could further enhance the bridge's sustainability and reduce its environmental impact.

www.ingramcontent.com/pod-product-compliance
Lightning Source LLC
Chambersburg PA
CBHW050855160426
43194CB00011B/2160